The Eclipse of the Utopias of Labor

forms of living

Stefanos Geroulanos and Todd Meyers, *series editors*

The Eclipse of the Utopias of Labor

Anson Rabinbach

FORDHAM UNIVERSITY PRESS

NEW YORK   2018

Fordham University Press has no responsibility for the persistence
or accuracy of URLs for external or third-party Internet
websites referred to in this publication and does not guarantee
that any content on such websites is, or will remain, accurate or
appropriate.

Fordham University Press also publishes its books in a variety of
electronic formats. Some content that appears in print may not
be available in electronic books.

Visit us online at www.fordhampress.com.

Library of Congress Cataloging-in-Publication Data

Names: Rabinbach, Anson, author.
Title: The eclipse of the utopias of labor / Anson Rabinbach.
Description: First edition. | New York, NY : Fordham University
    Press, 2018. | Series: Forms of living | Includes bibliographical
    references and index.
Identifiers: LCCN 2017041246 | ISBN 9780823278565
    (cloth : alk. paper) | ISBN 9780823278572 (pbk : alk. paper)
Subjects: LCSH: Labor supply. | Human–computer interaction. |
    Human mechanics. | Robots.
Classification: LCC HD5706 .R27 2018 | DDC 331.01—dc23
LC record available at https://lccn.loc.gov/2017041246

Printed in the United States of America

20 19 18   5 4 3 2 1

First edition

CONTENTS

My 1990 book, *The Human Motor: Energy, Fatigue, and the Origins of Modernity* (New York: Basic Books), revolves around the distinction between machines and motors as metaphors of the body at work. Modern productivism, I argue, presupposes that human society and nature are linked by the primacy and ultimate interchangeability of productive activity of the body, technology, or nature. The social imaginary of productivism is characterized by an understanding of the conversion of force or energy, an idea which first appeared in the second half of the nineteenth century. In the premodern Newtonian universe, diverse forces (gravity, wind, water, or horses, for example) push, pull, or turn machines, generating motion. In the Helmholtzian universe, which had matured by the 1850s, force or *Kraft* is converted into work by motors—whether human or human-made. Unlike the metaphor of the machine, the metaphor of the motor is productivist because it rests on an industrial model of a calculable channeling of energy, converted from nature to society. Comparing the human body to a motor rather than a machine meant making it something altogether other than a conduit of force: it was a converter of energy identical to the action performed by technology or nature.

My investigation of the human motor as a figure of nineteenth-century transcendental materialism was also an attempt to elaborate on the distinction between the image of the motor and earlier representations of the working body. In that book's conclusion, I anticipated a further study of the ways in which the metaphor of the motor lost much of its compelling power in the second half of the twentieth century, in large part because of the emergence of a different set of metaphors designed to articulate the experience of the digital workplace and its concomitant impact on the figure of working bodies. This book takes up that challenge, but it does so indirectly because it looks at a more complex theater of operations. In essence, I now divide the history of the relationship between bodies and machines into three eras: mimetic, transcendental, and digital. At the same time, I attempt to map the metaphors of the body proper to each era onto the social utopias of labor developed in the second and undermined in the third of each of these eras. I argue that these utopias of labor were the fundamental representations that mediated between the *perception and rationalization* of the working body and the goals of the welfare state.

The first, mimetic relationship, is characteristic of the eighteenth century and is exemplified by the wondrous clockwork automata (androids in today's parlance) that were capable of imitating human movements and functions with extraordinary verisimilitude. From the mid-nineteenth century to the late twentieth century, a second relationship developed: the metaphor of the motor exercised enormous explanatory and social power, regarding the body as productive in the sense that it is capable of converting energy into work. Energy became a transcendental principle, equally omnipresent in nature and society, the driving force of labor power and all other manifestations of work. Central to this development was "social energeticism," the doctrine that saw human beings and workers in particular as creatures that are driven by energy, that drive the economy and production through energy, and that threaten the social order through fatigue. This conception was linked to a variety of utopian projects for rationalizing the worker's body, engineering both a more perfect workplace and, through it, a more perfect society. For example, the leading Marxists of the Russian Revolution, Lenin and Trotsky, were ardent admirers of American industrial capitalism's program of scientific management—of Taylorism and its European offshoots. Europeans were preoccupied with psychotechnics and industrial psychology as methods of reducing fatigue, not only to raise efficiency but also to reduce industrial accidents. During the interwar period, the dominant Taylorist, Soviet, and National Socialist models for the workplace became the foundations of social models linking work to both the human body and society. Convinced of the crisis in industrial productivity, the Nazis blended modernism and the cult of productivity and efficiency together with an aestheticized workplace in their Beauty of Labor program.

The metaphor of the motor reached its zenith after World War II and by the 1980s began a steep decline as the digital relationship of man to machine developed with the advent of the post-Fordist era. The growing pace of computerization after the 1960s led to a third era. In it, the metaphor of the machine ceased to be transcendental and became allegorical in Walter Benjamin's sense that the primacy of bodily functions was now replaced by the manipulation of signs. Computerization began, as we shall see, with the attempt to effect Alan Turing's thesis that any mathematical operation can be reproduced mechanically by algorithmic, symbolic encoding—a principle that led not only to the Taylorization of mental activity but also to the principle of simulation, since such machines could mimic the operation of any other machine, and vice versa. Debates on work and leisure became more central but by the 1980s, it had become commonplace to anticipate that computer-driven technologies would dramatically change *how* we work, *where* we work and *what* we really produce. Moreover, if the long nineteenth century was at bottom an era of disciplinarity, it was precisely this rigid, uniform, and authoritarian dimension of the workplace that by the year 2000 was most often accused of inhibiting productivity and lacking the necessary qualities—flexibility, autonomy, and judgment—that workers supposedly needed to succeed in the digital workplace governed by computers rather than industrial manufacturing.

The book weaves the history of representations of the body to intellectual history, the history of labor, and the history of the welfare state. It reprises and elaborates on themes addressed in *The Human Motor* by extending the time frame backward to the eighteenth century while focusing on the twentieth century up to the present. It investigates some of the most important signposts in the emergence and decline of the great utopias of labor, including Marx's productivism, Taylorism, Communism, the Nazi Beauty of Labor program, and the discourses of the digital workplace in the later twentieth century. It asks in far greater detail how the worker was placed into a context leading from automata to digitization and was seen at once as exemplary of the human being and central to any understanding of man's mechanized behavior and quality. Last, the book's attention to labor itself as a figure for creating human hopes is at the core of my argument: the eclipse of work-centered utopias.

Chapter 1 offers an overview of the three ages of machine metaphors—mimetic, transcendental, and digital. One focus of this chapter is Marx's adoption of the notion of labor-power and the accompanying change in his understanding of freedom as existing outside of and through the reduction of energy expenditure. I argue that Marx became a productivist when he imagined the utopia of labor in terms of an ever-decreasing labor-time. A similar preoccupation with determining the optimal, quantifiable, and ultimately practicable output of energy characterized the European physiologists and ergonomists who brought their innovative methods and technologies into the industrial workplace.

Chapter 2 centers on how progressive European scientists and entrepreneurs—most prominently the wealthy chemist and industrialist Ernest Solvay, the sociologist Émile Waxweiler, and two German scientists, the chemist Wilhelm Ostwald and the physiologist Max Rubner—developed the principles of "social energeticism." They insisted that a social policy grounded in the irrefutable advances of science could stand above the interests of social classes and political imperatives. The mediating role played by social energeticism and productivism in the social imaginary of the late nineteenth and early twentieth centuries remains underappreciated throughout the history of communism and the social history of labor in the West. Indeed, social energeticism—built as it was on productivism—offered ways of directing the metaphor of the body into a transcendental representation.

Chapter 3 focuses on the battleground of the new energeticism: the industrial accident. Industrial accidents were in the forefront of state social policies that sought to compensate for the "modernity of risk." Given the belief that responsibility for the dangers of industrial labor fell to the state, these risks could be ascertained by a proliferation of social knowledge—statistical surveys, parliamentary investigations, medical records—giving rise to new professions (such as social medicine and social hygiene) and new specializations (such as labor law, insurance law) that emerged in tandem with social reform legislation in the earliest phase of European state social policy.

Chapter 4 turns to the fragility of the human motor, most evident in the intense debates about neurasthenia which was not only identified as the chief disability of the industrial age but also charted the limits of the energy expenditure of the working body. As pathological fatigue, neurasthenia became at once a disorder and a diagnosis, and ultimately an incentive to strengthen the resistance of the will against the vicissitudes of modernity.

Chapter 5 investigates some of the professional, intellectual, and political controversies that surrounded the establishment of industrial psychology as a discipline in the Weimar Republic. The arrival of the American system of Frederick Winslow Taylor's "scientific management" challenged European methods of production by promising higher wages and greater profits through more effective deployment of labor power. The result split the European sciences of work between those who regarded the new psychophysics as an adjunct to Taylorist disciplinary methods and those who, like Otto Lipmann, tried to mitigate the profit-driven system with a more rational and humane industrial psychology. Lipmann's sad fate, discussed in this chapter, underscored the consequences of the Nazification of industrial policy and psychology in the 1930s.

Chapter 6 details the Beauty of Labor program developed by Hitler's architect Albert Speer to provide Nazi productivism with an industry-centered utopianism. Increasing output would be based on aesthetics and an appeal to joy in work, without forgoing discipline or obedience. Specifically, aesthetic motifs would be woven into work in an effort to outdo a simple all-too-mechanical technocracy and the limitations of recent industrial ideas and compromises. Beauty of Labor represented the utopian side of Nazi industrial policy, choreographing the destruction of trade unions and intensification of work discipline with the ideological patina of beautified workplaces.

Chapter 7 offers some thoughts on the eclipse of the great utopias of labor and the crisis in the metaphor of the human motor brought about by widespread automation and the emergence of the digital workplace. The so-called Fordist system, introduced after World War I, guaranteed higher income, relatively secure employment, and expanding consumption levels in exchange for enduring hierarchical, rule-bound, and routinized labor. By the 1960s, however, the affluent society that was being promised to what Herbert Marcuse called the "one-dimensional man" began to develop serious liabilities. Especially in the United States, it became evident during the 1980s that the Fordist system had become dysfunctional, lacking in precisely the flexibility, judgment, and communicative skills demanded by the new digital workplace. Discipline did not disappear, but disciplinarity no longer made sense as both blue- and white-collar workers inhabited fast and furious workstations governed by computer-driven imperatives. Parallel to the problematization of disciplinarity came the discourse of computerization, which completed the digitization and allegorization of the "body as machine" metaphor. With the eclipse of the great utopias of labor, both totalitarian and liberal democratic, the work-centered society is undergoing a major transvaluation.

This book evolved over a long period of time and was thoroughly revised in 2016. Chapter 6, "The Aesthetics of Production in the Third Reich," was the earliest and in many respects the prelude to my understanding of productivism as having a history long before its adoption by the Nazis. During the 1970s I conducted a series of interviews with Albert Speer, who, perhaps inadvertently, provided me with a number of clues to trace that prehistory into the nineteenth century. I first outlined chapters 2 and 3 around the time that I was writing *The Human Motor*; chapters 4 and 5 were written somewhat later. Chapters 1 and 6 profited greatly from a considerable body of recent literature. An earlier version of chapter 1 was published in *A Cultural History of the Human Body in the Age of Empire*, ed. Michael Sappol and Stephen R. Rice, 237–260 (London: Bloomsbury Publishing 2012). Chapter 3 was previously published in *States, Social Knowledge, and the Origins of Modern Social Policies*, ed. Dietrich Rueschemeyer and Theda Skocpol (Princeton, NJ: Princeton University Press, 1996) 48–89. Chapter 4 was first published in *Incorporations*, ed. Jonathan Crary and Sanford Kwinter, 178–189 (Cambridge, MA: Zone Books, 1992). Chapter 6 was originally published in *The Journal of Contemporary History* 11, no. 4 (1976): 43–74. Chapters are reproduced by permission of the respective publishers.

This book owes its existence to the indefatigable Stefanos Geroulanos, always up for new ideas and for testing the limits of the old ones. And special thanks to Kenny Chumbley for his meticulous work on the manuscript and permissions.

The Eclipse of the Utopias of Labor

From Mimetic Machines to Digital Organisms: The Transformation of the Human Motor

Along with major shifts in the nature of industrial and postindustrial work at the beginning of the twenty-first century, there has also been a deep crisis of the metaphors mobilized to frame and embody the nature of what we call work. A new image of the symbiosis of body and machine has emerged which the historian Bruce Mazlish aptly called the "fourth discontinuity"— an allusion to Freud's three great illusory "divides" or discontinuities of man and the cosmos (Galileo), man and animals (Darwin), and man and nature (Freud)—since today the dominion over machines can no longer be taken for granted.[1] One can even go one step further, and argue that the metaphor of the human machine or human motor has as much to do with the transformation of work throughout modern history as do machines and industrial processes themselves. The metaphor of the body as machine/motor can plausibly be compartmentalized into three simple and distinct historical types: mimetic, transcendental, and digital. Each of these, in turn, can be represented by a different technology.

The mimetic technology of the eighteenth century is exemplified by a clockwork whose mechanical precision is capable of replicating certain biological processes with remarkable verisimilitude. This form of human or animal machine is exemplified by the artisanal automata of the great eighteenth-century clockmakers, such as the "flute player" of Jacques Vaucanson or the "writing boy" of Jacquet Droz. The transcendental materialism of the industrial revolution is in turn illustrated by motors that convert energy to produce motion: the steam engine, the automobile, and the Taylorist worker. Today's digital metaphor derives its inspiration from computers as the new "human machines" and is best understood in terms of artificial intelligence, "microworlds," or "digital organisms." In what sense can digital technology be considered according to the machine or motor metaphor? Is artificial intelligence, for example, a variant of energeticism? Do we need a different vocabulary to describe the interface between humans and their cyber creations than motors or machines? What interests me is not simply these changes in the operative metaphor per se, but in how and whether these shifts in the metaphor serve as vehicles through which we negotiate the divide between the artificial and the natural and conjure up very different notions of the biopolitics of work.[2]

The heyday of the automata was the eighteenth century, when craftsmen of extraordinary skill endowed their intricate mechanisms with movements of such delicacy that they seemed to mock the boundary between life and technology. Most celebrated among them was Vaucanson, who became an overnight sensation at the age of twenty-eight. In 1738, he astonished Paris with a life-sized faun capable of playing the flute with such precision that incredulous audiences accused him of concealing a tiny musician inside its body. Vaucanson followed with his most celebrated creation, a mechanical duck that flapped its wings, pecked at its food, drank water, and evacuated a fetid pellet apparently after passing it through a digestive system. Vaucanson's remarkable defecating fowl (along with his flutist and mechanical drummer), became a popular (and commercially successful) attraction, drawing "amazed spectators" to the King's Theater in London in 1742, and touring Germany two years later.[3] Vaucanson combined his performing simulacra with a perceptual and pedagogical aim—the illustration of a physiological principle (that digestion occurs by a chemical process rather than by pulverizing the food). Yet however much he had "endeavored to make it imitate all the actions of the living animal," Vaucanson stopped short of identifying life with the machine. He knew that the duck did not actually convert food to poop, but as Jessica Riskin observes: "Even when he cheated, his dishonesty was in the service of verisimilitude, not virtuosity; making the machine seem *lifelike* in the earthiest sense."[4] His reticence demonstrates that he understood that though his duck might simulate physiological function and illustrate a natural principle, it could never attain the "self-moving power" that was life.

These simulacra were not merely models; they strove "not only to mimic the outward manifestations of life, but to follow as closely as possible the mechanism that produced these manifestations."[5] The automata were both epistemological machines, functioning illustrations of a biomechanical mode of explanation, and performative simulacra that seemed to embody the self-moving power and capacity for generation which inevitably eluded them.[6] Locating the automata between the performative and the pedagogical is a sign of their author's own ambivalence vis-à-vis these wondrous machines.

The automata were also a combination of inscription and simulation, technologies that could "write" or "inscribe" actual writing (as in the writing boy) or sound (as in the flute player) in a machine that reproduced the effects of our sensory apparatus while assuming its external form. Mimesis, as Walter Benjamin reminds us, is not merely the imitation of nature by artifice, but a faculty that is the "weak remnant of a powerful compulsion to be and act similarly."[7] The unmistakable presence of the occult in Benjamin's theory of technical mimesis points to why two central aspects of the eighteenth-century automata were so often combined: as scientific creations and performance pieces, their powerful attraction rested on their unfulfilled ontological promise—the reproduction of nature and ultimately of life. They were designed to appear to embody the capacity to generate their own motion.

During the nineteenth century, the automata divided into two distinct types, those that were life-like representations of specific physiological processes and those that just replicated their mechanical effects. The latter were no longer replicas but prostheses, extensions of human sense organs.[8] In his excellent book on sound technologies, James Lastra has drawn the consequences of this distinction. If the "classical automata" mimetically replicated or duplicated organic or corporal movement, nineteenth-century devices such as the phonograph and the telephone abandoned the quest for imitation but were capable of more effectively copying nature—perhaps even more perfectly than nature itself.[9] This process, which might be called the demystification of the automata, greatly diminished the phantasmagoric character of simulation, while perfecting inscriptions of sound or more precisely, the material form of sound. As simulacra, they no longer had any need to imitate the attributes of living beings, and, ontologically speaking, such simulacra are indifferent to the question of what constituted the "life" of the beings that were being created in the laboratory.

The problem—classically posed by Descartes, for whom, no matter how superbly produced, the automata were lacking in self-moving power (a soul, emotions, language, spontaneity) and thus remained merely *mimetic* beings, mere *correspondences to life*—was rendered moot. Even earlier, during the eighteenth century, we can already observe certain gestures toward the demystification of the automata even in staunch materialists. Julien Offray de la Mettrie, the famous author of *L'homme machine* (1748) admitted that living machines exceeded mere machines. In the end, the "classical" automata of Vaucanson, Droz, and Menzel could do no more than illustrate the principle of self-moving power which they so patently failed to embody.

The eighteenth-century automata were not working machines in the strict sense, though from a scientific point of view they did perform "work." Their energy (or force) was provided by their creators while they simultaneously served as entertainment and illustrations of the principles of physiology. To be sure, their authors saw their productive potential and in the case of Vaucanson, led to his invention of the world's first mechanical loom in 1745.[10]

By contrast, the productivism of the industrial revolution was governed by a very different conception of force, one that entirely rejected "self-moving power" as a phantasm and by the realization that human society and nature are linked by the primacy and ultimate interchangeability (convertibility) of all productive activity. As the principles of thermodynamics came to be understood, a new social imaginary emerged that presupposed an entirely different metaphor of the motor.[11] Hermann von Helmholtz, its most passionate popularizer, liked to point out that the discovery of the laws of thermodynamics proved that the authors of the automata were hopelessly implicated in what he called their "mimetic error"—the belief that beasts and human bodies corresponded to apparatuses that "moved themselves energetically and incessantly . . . and were never wound up."[12] Self-moving power was a chimera; all beings and machines are moved by energy converted into motion.

The Discovery of Labor Power

The metaphor of the motor appeared during the first quarter of the nineteenth century. After Sadi Carnot's discovery of "the motive power of heat" in 1824, it became clear that all the forces of nature are essentially different varieties of a single, universal energy or *Kraft*. The discovery of thermodynamics revealed the mimetic machine to be an epistemological dead-end, since energy is always universally present in all nature and technology.

The machines of the preindustrial age differed from mid-nineteenth-century productivism in their lack of a unifying, transcendental metaphor. In the Newtonian universe, diverse forces (gravity, wind, water, horse) pushed, pulled, or turned machines, generating motion. In the Helmholtzian universe, energy is converted into work by motors (natural, human, and technological). Unlike the metaphor of the machine, the metaphor of the motor is productivist: it refers not simply to the mechanical generation of movement but to the industrial model of a calculable and natural channeling of energy *converted* from nature to society and back again. To borrow a line from Henry Adams, the nineteenth-century energeticist metaphor of production was framed by "incessant transference and conversion" while the eighteenth-century concept of labor operated in the framework of "creation."[13] The productivism of the industrial revolution was governed by the realization that human society and nature are linked by the primacy and ultimate interchangeability (convertibility) of all productive activity, whether of the body, technology, or nature.

If the eighteenth-century machine was a refraction of the Newtonian universe with its multiplicity of forces, disparate sources of motion, and reversible mechanisms, the nineteenth-century metaphor of the machine was drawn from the thermodynamic engine, the servant of a powerful nature conceived as a reservoir of undiminished motivating power. The machine is capable of work only when powered by some discrete external source; the motor, by contrast, is regulated by internal, dynamic principles, converting calories into heat and heat into mechanical work.[14] The body, the steam engine, and the cosmos were thus connected by a single and unbroken chain, by an indestructible energy, omnipresent in the universe and capable of infinite mutation, yet immutable and invariant.

The law of energy conservation endowed the concept of force undisputed primacy in the explanation of the natural world.[15] Physics became the supreme science: the discovery of the laws of energy elevated the concept of work to the dignity of a universal principle of nature, irrespective of the "moral perfection" of servants or any other workers. Helmholtz frequently mentions the implications of his new understanding of nature for the meaning of work. The shift from mechanical forces to the language of a universal energy eliminated the need for a spiritual understanding of labor; the work ethic was eclipsed by the quantitative economy of energy. "Hence, in a mechanical sense," he noted, the idea of work has become "identical with that of the expenditure of force."[16] The new technology of the industrial age thus produced a new image of the body whose origins lie in labor power, and which is not simply analogous to but essentially identical with a thermodynamic machine: "the animal body therefore does not differ from the steam-engine as regards the manner in which it obtains heat and force, but does differ from it in the purpose for, and manner in which the force gained is employed."[17] Helmholtz did not simply equate the living creature with a machine, he transposed the character of an energy-converting machine— an automata—to the body, the industrial dynamo, and indeed, to the universe itself.

Helmholtz saw the social vision implicit in the idea of self-moving power: redemption from painful labor, a society of perpetual idleness, and of course, money for nothing: "To the builders of the automata of the last century, men and animals appeared as a clockwork which was never wound up, and created the force which they exerted out of nothing. They did not know how to establish a connection between the nutriment consumed and the work generated. Since, however, we have learned to discern in the steam-engine this origin of mechanical force, we must inquire whether something similar does not hold good with regard to men."[18] The inventors of the automata envisaged a body without fatigue, without discontent, and without aversion to work. But they also revealed their ignorance of the how motors convert the supply of nourishment into heat, and heat into force. Perpetual motion could never be discovered, since no novel source of energy was ever produced in nature. Conversion of force did not merely solve the problem of mimesis, it superseded it by reducing the mimetic machine to the illusion of a body that "creates energy out of itself."[19] The "transcendental materialism" of the nineteenth century produced a powerful metaphor of how nature, technology, and the human body all operate under the same dynamic laws of force—a homogeneity that is much more than the reduction of the life process to the model of industrial technology. As Helmholtz observed: "When we consider the work done by animals, we find the operation comparable in every respect with that of the steam-engine. Animals, like machines, can only move and accomplish work by being continuously supplied with fuel (that is to say, food) and air containing oxygen."[20] For those, like Helmholtz, who grasped the secrets of the cosmos in terms of the industrial dynamo, life was equivalent to force, and force was the physio-chemical principle that governed the universe. "Life" was redefined to mean not mechanical motion, nor anything having to do with living being, but rather the particular form taken by the universal force of motion that propels all of nature. There is no essential distinction between the work of the industrial dynamo, the hefty blows of the preindustrial blacksmith, the delicate movements of the lacemaker, or the precise fingering of the concert violinist. Nature became a vast cistern of protean energy awaiting its conversion to work.

Before the motor came into its own, the metaphor that defined labor was that of a generative activity derived from the classical theorists of labor: John Locke, Adam Smith, the Abbe Siéyés, and of course, Karl Marx. In his 1844 *Economic and Philosophical Manuscripts*, Marx famously saw labor as the anthropological universal that is both a meaning-bestowing and historically constituting activity, a "metabolic exchange" between history and nature. The emancipation of labor is the emancipation of society and the individual, of free production and expression. After 1859, however, Marx increasingly reframed the distinction between concrete and abstract labor in the language of labor power, as an act of *conversion* rather than *generation*.[21] According to Engels, Marx considered the discovery of labor power his most important achievement.[22] His use of the term credits early nineteenth-century French engineers who analyzed steam engines and the discoveries of William Thomson and Helmholtz, who first used the concept of *Arbeitskraft* (labor power) to describe how energy is converted into work, whether in the cosmos, in nature, in the body, or in technology.[23] As a result, labor power became quantifiable and equivalent to all other forms of labor power (in nature or in machines).[13] Marx readily adopted the language of labor power which, for him, became the engine of historical development. He thus shifted his focus from the emancipation of mankind *through* labor to the emancipation *from* productive labor by an even greater productivity. Marx became a productivist when he no longer considered labor to be an anthropologically paradigmatic mode of activity, and when, in harmony with the new physics, he saw labor power as an abstract magnitude (a measure of labor time) and a natural force (a specific set of energy equivalents located in the body). For his previous generative view of labor, emancipation occurs within labor itself, whereas from the point of view of *conversion*, it occurs only *apart* from the act of labor, in the form of shorter hours or reduced physical and mental exertion.

In *Capital*, the concept of labor power is also a quantitative measure of the expenditure of human energy in production: "Tailoring and weaving, although they are qualitatively different productive activities, are both a productive expenditure of human brains, muscles, nerves, hands, etc. . . . merely two different forms of the expenditure of human labor power."[24] Or even more strikingly: "On the one hand, all labor is, speaking physiologically, an expenditure of human labor power, and in its character of identical abstract human labor, it creates and forms the value of commodities. On the other hand, all labor is the expenditure of human labor power in a special form and with a definite aim."[25]

By the time he wrote *Capital*, Marx had reframed the distinction between concrete and abstract labor in the language of labor power, as an act of *conversion* rather than of *generation*. His acknowledged source was William Robert Grove (1811–1896), whose accessible summary of thermodynamics, *On the Correlation of Physical Forces*, published in 1846, was reprinted at least six times in England. Marx saw Grove's lucid discussion as confirmation of the notion of labor power: "The amount of labor which a man had undergone in the course of 24 hours might be approximately arrived at by an examination of the chemical changes which had taken place in his body, changed forms in matter indicating the anterior exercise of dynamic force."[26]

Engels too registered the importance of Grove's contribution: "Grove— not a natural scientist by profession but an English lawyer—proved that all so-called physical energy, mechanical energy, heat, light, electricity, magnetism, indeed even so-called chemical energy, became transformed into one another under definite conditions without any loss of energy occurring."[27] Of course, adopting Grove's theorem, did not mean that Marx reduced value to the product of muscular labor or human beings to the status of energy-producing machines. But the substitution of labor power for vaguer terms such as "laboring capacity" permitted him a more sophisticated analysis of the relationship of the laborer to machines and more importantly (as is evident from Marx's *Grundrisse*) to an understanding of how, from the standpoint of capital, what is actually exchanged between capital and labor is the commodity labor power: "What the free worker sells is always nothing more than a specific, particular measure of force-expenditure [*Kraftäusserung*]; labor capacity as a totality is greater than every particular expenditure."[28] As Marx explains: "The capitalistic mode of production (essentially the production of surplus-value, the absorption of surplus labor), produces thus, with the extension of the working day, not only the deterioration of human labor power by robbing it of its normal, moral and physical, conditions of development and function. It produces also the premature exhaustion and death of this labor power itself."[29]

Labor power is the motor of history, the natural force that makes possible its own supersession by the machine. Insofar as the physical aspect of labor becomes first naturalized and ultimately mechanized, the distinction between the emancipation of labor as a creative and organic reality and the metamorphosis of the material process of production is blurred.[30] The realm of necessity is characterized by the regulation of the expenditure of energy and the realm of freedom by the liberation of human energy from external constraint. According to Marx:

> Freedom in this field can only consist in socialized man, the associated
> producers, rationally regulating their interchange with Nature, bringing it
> under their common control, instead of being ruled by it as by the blind forces
> of Nature; and achieving this with the least expenditure of energy and under
> conditions most favorable to, and worthy of, their human nature. But it
> nonetheless still remains a realm of necessity. Beyond it begins that development

of human energy which is an end in itself, the true realm of freedom, which, however, can blossom forth only with this realm of necessity as its basis. The shortening of the working day is its basic prerequisite.[31]

If the eighteenth-century automata were mimetic machines capable of simulating motion, the sciences of work inscribed labor in a process of conversion. Conversion of force was always accompanied by some degree of loss, depletion, or diminution of energy. In other words, the conversion of energy was always accompanied by entropy, by a loss in all energy exchanges.

Clausius's second law of thermodynamics seemed to point to a far more negative and potentially catastrophic theory of production. The notorious "heat death of the universe" hypothesis follows from the entropy law, according to which the energy in the universe will eventually reach a state of equilibrium; as work is converted into heat there will be a dissipation or loss of energy eventually resulting in what Helmholtz called the "cessation of all natural processes."[32] Indeed, as Elizabeth Neswald has shown, Clausius himself—like Helmholtz and William Thomson, among others—posited the possibility of an end state in which energy is converted into heat leaving the universe in a state of "eternal death."[33] The powerful and protean world of work, production, and performance is set against the disintegrating order of fatigue, exhaustion, and ultimately the ecological catastrophe— global freezing—frequently depicted in nineteenth-century imagery as the apocalyptic figure of cosmological exhaustion and state of eternal rest.

Why neither Marx nor Engels registered this phenomenon preoccupied critics, especially the philosopher Leszek Kolakowski, who argued that although Engels enthusiastically adopted the first principle of conservation of energy, he rejected the second law because he regarded such a "thermic death sentence on the universe" as "ideologically dangerous," thereby evading the destructive ecological consequences of socialism.[34] To be sure, Engels was hardly alone in his skepticism of the "heat death" hypothesis.[35] Contemporary critics contend that by failing to adopt the second law, Marx and Engels severed any possible connection between classical Marxism and the destructive ecological consequences of productivism.[36] It is clear, however, that if they considered the heat death of the universe theory implausible, neither Marx nor Engels entirely rejected the second law of thermodynamics. In fact, there is considerable evidence to the contrary, that both tried to understand the implications of the "exhaustion," "loss of motion," and destructibility theorem.

Marx and Engels may not have fully explored the implications of the second law for the labor theory of value, but they did devote some attention to this line of thought as developed by the Ukrainian physician and socialist Sergei Podolinsky (1850–1891).[37] Beginning in 1880, Podolinsky persistently tried to persuade Marx and Engels of the relevance of his as yet unpublished book "Human Labor and the Conservation of Energy," which claimed that Marx's theory of labor and production could be expressed in the language of thermodynamics. Engels read and commented on an Italian version published in English as "Socialism and the Unity of Physical Forces," and it is likely that Marx read it as well.[38] Among other themes, Podolinsky focused on entropy, arguing that human labor has the power to augment the amount of solar energy on earth, thereby potentially mitigating the negative effects of capitalist productive relations. He also observed that the ultimate limits to economic growth lay not solely in the shackles of the relations of production, but directly in the cosmos, in physical and ecological laws of entropy. Although Marx made extensive notes on Podolinsky's article and Engels acknowledged it as "a valuable discovery," he ultimately concluded that Podolinsky's effort to see the laborer as "an energy-consuming animal" went too far and that his attempt to find direct calorie equivalents for labor expenditure was misguided. Above all, he was skeptical of Podolinsky's claim that the human laborer constitutes the most perfect thermodynamic machine.[39] Engels wrote to Marx in 1882: "What Podolinsky has completely forgotten is that the working man is not only a fixer of present solar energy, but more than that, a squanderer of past solar heat. The degree of wastage of energy reserves, coal, minerals, forests, etc., you know only too well, more than I do."[40] By that time, Marx was too ill to pursue the issue. But there is little doubt he understood that unprecedented advances in labor productivity, the enormous increases in matter and energy drawn from the natural environment, and capitalism's enormous appetite for raw materials and energy sources had to be understood in both thermodynamic and political economic terms.

Following the later Marx, the "Pope" of German socialism, Karl Kautsky, rejected the Prometheanism and authoritarianism of Bolshevism and adopted Marx's vision of a future brought into being by the energy unleashed by the machine. Truly productive labor in art, science, and human well-being could be achieved only as a consequence of a reduction of the working day. More than any other Marxist intellectual, Kautsky painted the socialist future in vivid terms: "It is not the freedom of labor but the freedom from labor, which in a socialist society the use of machinery makes increasingly possible, that will bring to mankind freedom of life, freedom for artistic and intellectual activity, freedom for the noblest enjoyment."[41] It is no coincidence that the eight-hour day was the most lasting contribution of the Socialist International. As Kautsky wrote in 1892: "Labor is the condition of life. But their efforts will necessarily be directed toward reducing their hours of labor far enough to leave them time to live."[42]

The Science of Work

In the capitalist West, it was not Marxism but the American system of Frederick Winslow Taylor—scientific management—that put the Helmholtzian revolution in sync with the industrial workplace, inaugurating what Charles Maier has called "the heralded utopian change from power of men to the administration of things."[43] Taylorism was but one among many scientific approaches to labor that shared a fetishism of corporal rationalization, and promised the end of class conflict through the greater productivity achieved by conserving the workers' energy. On the continent, a variety of approaches claimed to be capable of producing a more rational and scientifically governed laboring process—*science du travail, Arbeitswissenschaft*, human science of work, ergonomics, and so on.

The Turin physiologist Angelo Mosso—the Galileo of modern fatigue research whose *La Fatica* (1891) became the standard work for generations of scientists, and who developed the technology of fatigue measurement—identified the chief obstacle to work not in the weakness of moral character, but in the depletion of physical and mental force.[44] Fatigue, which could be inscribed and measured by newly invented devices (such as the Ergograph), was—unlike purely "subjective" tiredness—measurable and quantifiable and always represented the objective limit or "optimal" point of exertion, the outermost boundary of the human motor. The new physics and the physiological theories that emanated from it dissolved the old moral categories by absorbing them into the fragile scaffolding of a universe built out of labor power. Fatigue thus emerged at the threshold of the body's economy of energies; it was the corporal horizon of a mechanical universe, with its own internal laws of energy and motion.

The pioneering ergonomist and fatigue expert Jules Amar argued in his *Le moteur humain* (1913) that a worker's movements could be carefully observed and charted "with a view towards eliminating all that is unnecessary."[45] Amar was firmly convinced that all tasks utilizing the same tool required a similar output of energy, and that when a muscular action was exercised in the same fashion, it always resulted in the same tracing. Any variation could be explained "principally because the worker is lacking in skill."[46] Comparing the results obtained by a "good workman, skillful and well trained" with those of a less practiced apprentice, he found that the accomplished journeymen normally adopted an efficient economy of motion that starkly contrasted with those of an apprentice, whose "chief defects are irregular and spasmodic action leading to unduly rapid fatigue."[47] Amar called his most important insight—that "a muscle returns more speedily to its condition of repose in proportion to its rapid performance of the work"—Amar's law.[48] This discovery, he claimed, had practical consequences: by correcting the trifling defects of position "the worker's fatigue is diminished without injury to his daily output."[49]

Amar studied the mechanics of the human body in microscopic detail, under experimental conditions, and with strict mathematical and scientific rigor. He was the first to apply the different techniques of measurement that had been developed since Étienne-Jules Marey's pioneering tracings of the body in motion to different types of work, which he reproduced in his laboratory. He made tracings of the work of the hands, the legs, and of workers' using different tools.[50] Amar also investigated the transformation of chemical and caloric energy into work, as well as the nature of respiration, diet, clothing, and hygiene. He took measurements in the field, conducting experiments sanctioned by the colonial authorities in Algerian prisons and in small industrial workshops. He developed techniques of measurement to a high degree of technical sophistication, inventing almost all of the basic techniques of modern ergonometric measurement—including the first exercise bike (ergocycle). He pioneered the training of apprentices and the study of their aptitudes for different types of work—which were in part based on "morphological" comparisons of different body types.[51] With Amar's systematic research, the search for the dynamic laws of fatigue were superseded by the search for the dynamic regularities of work. Amar was motivated by a single principle: for the performance of a maximum amount of work with a minimum amount of fatigue, there was an optimal speed and position which could be scientifically predetermined. He applied this research to different national and ethnic groups, creating a comparative anthropology of labor power. Indefatigable in his pursuit of the laws of economic expenditure of energy, Amar applied his theory to a wide variety of activities from writing to musical instruments "to those of the athlete, the sportsman and the soldier."[52]

In 1919, Amar reviewed his first decade of experimentation: "[I] tried [it] first, and many times upon myself; this method has for ten years given proof of its simplicity and reliability. During that time, it has been applied to about a thousand persons—Parisian working-men, soldiers, and natives of North Africa. it is therefore of universal applicability, and for that reason eminently scientific."[53]Amar was convinced of the intimate connection between social efficiency and social harmony. "On the average one third of the available energy of man is wasted," he argued, whereas "methodical organization could increase the industrial output in the same proportion."[54]

Before World War I, the hope that the state would perform the task of ensuring a thorough rationalization of the workplace in the interests of capital and labor remained utopian. However, the arrival of the American Taylor system—as scientific management—in Europe brought a competing model of rationalizing labor power into sharp conflict with proponents of the science of labor. Both the European science of work and Taylorism claimed validity as a scientific approach: each claimed that precise analysis of the worker's minute movements could produce efficiency through the elimination of wasteful expenditure of energy; each was preoccupied with economizing motion; each adapted the body to technology; and each claimed to stand above class interests and ideology. Yet in contrast to the science of work, which relied on laboratory research far from the workplace, the Taylor system relied on engineers who, in close cooperation with plant management, worked at the level of the individual firm to reduce costs and maximize profits.

The state played no role in Taylor's initial conception of the workplace. Scientific management was directed at owners of industry offering them a method of rationalizing production while inhibiting socially disruptive activities. French proponents of the Taylor system, such as Henri Louis Le Châtelier, by contrast, argued that the American system was socially neutral and promised greater production and higher wages. Its staunch opponents, such as Amar and the labor physiologist Jean-Marie Lahy, argued that the Taylor system ignored the physiology and above all the health of the worker. It was, as they saw it, unregulated "super production."[55]

The Great War did not so much further the invention of new techniques of testing aptitude, combating fatigue, diagnosing and treating psychological illness, improving efficiency, and boosting output, as much as it eased the extensive employment of these techniques for the first time. The war provided those trained in psychotechnical methods with a vast laboratory to demonstrate the utility of their knowledge. By 1915, a new generation of unskilled workers, composed largely of women and adolescents, were at work in industrial and munitions plants with little or no training, at lower wages, and with longer hours. The war gave legitimacy to the aptitude test, the neurasthenia (and shock) diagnosis, and the industrial reeducation and rehabilitation of the maimed and wounded—especially through the science of prosthetics.[56] In Germany, as early as 1915, aptitude tests developed by the "psychotechnicians" Walther Moede and Curt Piorkowski were used to select, for example, aviators, drivers, and radio operators.[57] The war also furthered the scientific study of what was termed "human economy"—the point of intersection between production techniques, mobilization of national resources, and the politics of demography. As Fritz Giese, a leading psychotechnical expert in Weimar Germany, remarked of his own wartime service: "the war not only presented psychology with new knowledge, it also created new subject matter, which, without that sad occasion would surely have remained estranged from it."[58]

After the war, professional academic or quasi-academic subdisciplines with applied or practical interests in labor management (such as industrial physiology, industrial medicine, industrial psychology, and industrial sociology) emerged in almost all European countries with the express purpose of forestalling or circumventing a potentially cataclysmic breakdown. In the interwar era, not merely the social relations of the workplace but the working body became the arena of the psychosocial contestation over labor power. By extension, the pervasive fear of the body's total breakdown represented a threat to industrial civilization. The preoccupation with corporeal fatigue as the universal form of resistance to work, represented both the limits of the excessive demands of industry and, somewhat paradoxically, the last line of defense against the super exploitation of the industrial Moloch.

This was especially true in Germany where industrial psychology first achieved professional legitimacy. The chair in applied industrial psychotechnics—established at the Berlin Institut für Industrielle Psychotechnik at the Technische Hochschule Charlottenburg shortly after the war and occupied by Georg Schlesinger—championed government-sponsored efforts to improve the efficiency of industrial labor during the early 1920s. By mid-decade, engineering students at German universities were required to complete a course in scientific management and scientific factory organization, including the latest developments in applied psychology.[59]

During the 1920s, numerous forward-looking physiologists employed several strategies of "psychotechnics," a term invented in 1903 by the psychologist William Stern to describe the uses of applied psychology for investigating "the diverse external conditions affecting human work in the school and in the occupations." Popularized by Hugo Münsterberg in his 1914 book *Psychotechnik*, psychotechnics sought to combine quasi-Taylorist methods to improve "psycho-physical capacity for performance" with reduction of fatigue and its concomitant accidents. The movement embraced the vision of the body as a thermodynamic system, traversed by flows of energy and fatigue, while at the same time, expressing fears that a new urban order—what Andreas Killen has called an "Electropolis," a highly rational, yet crisis-ridden product of industrial civilization—could threaten the integrity of the human motor. If the body conjured up an image of order, the possibility of disruption, confusion, social chaos, and systemic breakdown was so omnipresent that by 1926 traumatic neurosis was no longer compensated as an illness by the German welfare state.[60]

German psychotechnicians were a heterogeneous community made up of academic psychologists, engineers, and physiologists who shared a commitment to rationalization and a belief that their approach to optimizing labor efficiency was superior to the allegedly purely economic rationality of Taylorism. Beyond that, their approaches diverged, sometimes significantly. During the early Weimar era, at least three distinct strands of psychotechnics emerged. Professionally, the movement was composed of both engineers and academics. In reality, the two were hard to distinguish, as evident in the case of Schlesinger, who was called the "German Taylor" for his enthusiasm for scientific management, as he envisioned workers as "working machines, perpetually exhausting and regenerating themselves."[61] The academics regarded the Taylor system with profound suspicion and in 1927, in an effort to refute Taylorist assumptions, Edgar Atzler and one of his collaborators, Günther Lehmann, attempted to calculate the expenditure of energy and the food required by Taylor's famous human "ox," the Dutchman Schmidt, whose legendary brute strength and dumb obsequiousness were recounted in the most famous passage of Taylor's *Principles of Scientific Management*. Schmidt, despite his supposed super human productivity, they discovered, ate more than he produced. Their calculation was that Schmidt expended the equivalent of more than 5,515 calories in ten hours, making him less than cost efficient. They concluded that "the process of work had to be adapted to the special nature of the human motor," extracting optimal not maximal output.[62]

A second direction was represented by the tragic figure of Otto Lipmann, who was an academic psychologist and a socialist. Lipmann sought to fashion a version of industrial psychology more consistent with a politically sensitive, rational, and humane worldview (see chapter 5). By siding with the needs of industry to "sort out" the most unproductive workers and maintain those who were both reliable and effective, Lipmann rightly saw that psychotechnics had simply become one tool among other, harsher management practices. By contrast, he argued, the purpose of industrial psychotechnics was not to intervene in class conflict but can only remain neutral. Labor power was in his eyes not reducible to mere calculations of energy expenditure; it was a larger, cultural problem, one that engaged workers' entire being, including their satisfaction, health, mental well-being, and general moral sensibility, as well as their relations to the larger social body.

A third direction was represented by the nationalists, most prominently, Fritz Giese and Karl Arnhold—technocrats and "reactionary modernists"— who embraced the Nazi cause in the 1930s. In post–World War I Germany, psychotechnics, Giese claimed, held the key to national regeneration and to maximizing labor power. As Killen points out, though indebted to Münsterberg's work, Giese sought to go beyond what he perceived as the limitations of the "human-motor" model favored by his American counterpart. Labor power was in his eyes not reducible to mere calculations of energy expenditure; "it was a cultural problem that engaged the workers' entire being."[63]

Under the auspices of the Ministry of Labor, testing stations had been created across Germany. A veritable psychotechnical craze was born and Giese—using the mechanical devices he improved upon—was contracted to provide measurements on the employees, mostly women, at the telephone exchanges of the Imperial Post Office. Between 1925 and 1933, Giese's political views underwent a significant shift. In his pro-American study, *Girlkultur*, he expressly favored the more sporting American body culture over Prussian militarism.[64] In his writings of the early 1930s, however, with the American model tarnished by the world economic crisis, Giese embraced the new body culture valorized by the Nazis and after 1933, he exempted attributes such as courage and nobility—the masculine virtues—from psychotechnical analysis, placing them beyond experimental determination.[65] Although already committed to such a view, the implications of this gendering of the psychotechnical subject would only become clear with Giese's embrace of the National Socialist body ideal of the "sovereign" male warrior in a hypergendered social order.[66]

Arnhold founded the Deutsche Institut für technische Arbeitsschulung (DINTA) in fall 1925, with the financial help of considerable support from Ruhr Industrialists and from the conservative Deutsche Nationale Volks Partei (DNVP). Arnhold conceived of his mission to put psychotechnics on an anti-Socialist and a nationalist course, to create "a new industrial species, [the] carrier of a German ethos from the old Germanic epoch."[67] Aggressively anti-American and anti-republican, the DINTA was absorbed into the German Labor Front and became the representative organization of industrial psychology in Nazi Germany.

In February 1933, the editors of the *Psychotechnische Zeitschrift* announced their allegiance to National Socialism. Tragically, Lipmann, who had never held a university post, was hounded from his library and institute and committed suicide in October 1933.

Helmholtz's vision of the universe as *Arbeitskraft*, Marx's theory of the transfiguration of labor power into capital, and Taylor's method of subordinating the worker's body to the rational intelligence of the engineer were all variations on the theme of the metaphor of the human motor, of the working body as a medium for converting energy into work. In the totalitarian models of the work-society (in both Soviet Russia and Nazi Germany), Fordist modernism was fused with regimentation and indoctrination. Disciplinarity reigned supreme.

Totalitarian Taylorism

The Bolshevik founding fathers, Lenin and Trotsky, readily grasped the significance of the Taylorist revolution, differing only in the intensity of their utopian impulses and the locales of their respective "hypermodernist" models. Lenin's utopia in *State and Revolution* drew on the German organized *Finanzkapital* described by Rudolf Hilferding, whereas Trotsky's vision was of the "Americanized Bolshevism [that will] crush and conquer imperialist Americanism." Already in 1914, Lenin enthused at the prospect of applying Taylorism to the regulation of all social labor, dramatically reducing labor time and raising productivity.[68] Trotsky gave Soviet productivism an even more Faustian demeanor, culminating in his grand design for the "militarization of labor" to which "the positive creative forces of Taylorism should be used and applied."[69] Both Lenin and Trotsky were Americanists, but, as Peter Beilharz points out, only Trotsky had a "futuristic conception of Americanism."[70]

Stalin's five-year plans required a massive militarization of Soviet society in peacetime. As Sheila Fitzpatrick points out, the Soviet campaigns to mobilize society for rapid heavy industrial growth during the 1930s were accompanied by a military rhetoric couched almost entirely in the vocabulary of "battles," "fronts," "shock-brigades," and "sabotage."[71] Stalinist productivism criminalized resistance to work with his famous dictum: "People who talk about the necessity of *reducing* the rate of development of our industry are enemies of Socialism, class enemies."[72] Still, the "showpieces" of Stalin's industrialization program—Magnitogorsk and the Stalingrad Tractor Plant—could not overcome pervasive chaos, worker resistance, absenteeism, and low productivity.[73]

Under Nazism, some of the key precepts of the Fordist system of the 1920s were reinvigorated through organizations such as Arnhold's DINTA, which combined economic and firm rationalization with authoritarian social poli-cies. While the factory or firm "community" was promoted—along with efficiency, planning, beauty, and joy in work—obedience and hierarchy were required, and "all influences that were foreign to or hostile to the firm" were eliminated, especially trade unions.[74] Unlike Stalinism which glori-fied the heroic super-worker but not the architecture and aesthetics of the model factory, Nazi productivism went beyond specific policies aimed at increasing production and guaranteeing workers' discipline. At the level of ideology, the redemptive ideal of German national renewal was embodied in a metaphysical conception of work that combined theological, onto-logical, and morphological elements. As Werner Hamacher points out, Hitler regarded German "creative work" as a means of "resurrection" of a people whose essence *is* work, and which redeems itself *through* labor—as opposed to those parasitic races, for example, Jews, whose work is de-structive. In its ontological variant, Heidegger's notion of "spiritual" work regarded work and knowledge as identical modes of *techne*, as world-constituting and world-creating modes of Being. Ernst Jünger's image of *The Worker* gave full expression to the totalitarian ideal of a world trans-formed by the convergence of power and nature, a world that increasingly assumes the character of a "work-world."[75] As Jünger, who described mod-ern warfare as a gigantic *Arbeitsprozess* (labor process) recognized, both fascism and communism required the disciplined society to be run "with the strict regularity of a mechanized enterprise."[76]

As Hannah Arendt recognized in the 1950s, the aim of totalitarian pro-ductivism was to make production obsolete. As is well known, she saw a link between the "unpolitical" character of totalitarian society and crimes that broke with "the continuity of Occidental history." "Marx's socialized mankind, [which] unlike Plato's republic whose ideocracy was meant to conceal and justify the rule of the philosopher, would be a real ideocracy in which some idea of the nature of man would rule mercilessly over all men."[77] For that reason the regimes of labor characteristic of the 1930s and 1940s did not, as Jünger thought, mean that the "worker" or "fabricator" would become the new "form" of socialized humanity. Rather, the result was terror—"the fabrication of mankind"—which sacrifices the individual to its social project.[78]

Post-Fordist Productivism

Although the Fordist model of disciplinarity dominated the post–World War II era of prosperity (1945–1973), in the last decades of the twentieth century, a broad consensus gained ground among many observers of the global economy that the classical Fordist constellation of growth, prosperity, and social equity had reached its limit, forcing capital to adapt new and more flexible consumer-oriented strategies of production and distribution. Instead of standardized mass production, innovative firms stressed flexible batch production, smaller inventories, short-term labor contracts and niche markets. Instead of highly centralized labor systems, decentralization is highly preferable; even in the public sector, the only growth sector for trade unionism in the USA, outsourcing became the watchword of the new economy. In Europe and the United States, rigidly time-bound factory labor began to suffer an irreversible decline, and even in that sector, flexible work schedules and remote work from home rapidly became the norm. Instead of top-down control over un- or de-skilled routinized industrial labor, management experts, corporate "intellectuals," and neoliberal politicians proclaimed the bright future of more desirable skilled, educated workers, capable of working in tandem with superiors and subordinates. "Democracy" and "communication," not hierarchy and authority, were the watchwords of the new workplace. Does this presage the end of "disciplinarity"? The new workplace has introduced a new form of "discipline": the discipline of permanent, unrelenting, insecurity and fear.

The disappearance of the older Fordist disciplinary ideal may be one of the most prominent features of the new post-Fordist productivism. Even a cursory glance at the industrial management textbooks provide a glimpse of what the new culture of work looks like. Instead of top-down industrial discipline, democratic and "communicative" communities of fewer but more elite workers capable of "intersubjectivity" and "synergy" are in greater demand. Post-Taylorist/Fordist industrial relations specialists reject the obsolete model of a homogenous workforce composed of an uneducated worker subjected to hierarchical control and prescribed tasks. In the early 1990s, it became a mantra for economists such as Lester Thurow, Robert Reich, and Charles Heckscher to reinforce the notion that the chief liability of the

American workplace was its double Taylorist legacy: intense labor capital conflict, as well as strict rule-bound production, both of which are dysfunctional in a digital environment. The new economy favors a flexible strategy toward work and work time; union norms and adversarialism must be sacrificed to "knowledge-based" cooperation, profit sharing, work sharing, flexible work schedules, incentive pay for innovation, and so on.[79] If the managerial manuals are any indication, the disciplined rule-bound worker has given way to the ideal of "flexible, internally motivated, continuously learning work force," obsolete bureaucratic structures are replaced by "a strong internal culture to support information sharing and participation in problem solving," commands will give way to "balancing dialogue and discussion," hierarchy will be redefined as the "delegation or shared responsibility in recognition that dispersed activity requires local action and flexibility."[80]

The "work-centered society" of the nineteenth and early twentieth centuries was to a large degree a phenomenon that relied heavily on the metaphor of the human motor. To the extent that this metaphor has begun to wane, the emphasis on disciplinarity has also begun to disappear. But this does not mean that we are any less a work-centered society; in fact, today's workers may be more disciplined and overworked than their predecessors.[81] None of this suggests that control of the workforce will diminish; on the contrary, discipline may be far more intense and internalized, coerced by the threat of total insecurity, as the dot-com collapse made abundantly evident just one decade later. What has changed is that the body no longer occupies the same space in the metaphoric economy of work. With the gradual eclipse of the metaphor of the human motor, the "work-centered model of society" was emptied of its most compelling metaphor.

What metaphors occupy the space of the "mimetic" machine or the "transcendental" motor now? If labor power is no longer the site of the central metaphor of productivism, what does this mean for the new configuration of labor and the model of labor based on information processing rather than the generation of things or the conversion of force? It has sometimes been suggested that computers are in fact a new kind of automata, presaging a "workless" world in which human beings do not so much control the robot as become syntactically merged with it. As one might have predicted, the phantasm of a body without fatigue and labor—the ghost of the classical automata—has also reemerged. Historian Bruce Mazlish, for example, envisioned a new "species"—computers implanted in robots (he calls them "combots") that will do far more than perform mundane household tasks. The potential for humans to evolve into a new species in tandem with the post-Cartesian robot, a kind of "thinking machine" which he calls "homocomboticus," is "open and realizable."[82]

Whether this prophecy will be fulfilled remains to be seen, but there are some readily observable consequences of how digital machines are already altering the way we think about work. The most dramatic is the computerized simulacra of the work process itself. Shoshanna Zuboff has studied how paper production follows a digitally simulated computer pattern that occurs virtually just moments before it occurs in a human free factory environment. This allows the overseer of the digital process to preemptively shut down the actual process, anticipating problems. As she explains, "when the textualizing consequences of an informating technology become more comprehensive, the body's traditional role in the production process (as a source of effort and/or skill in the service of *acting-on*) is already transformed."[83] With the eclipse of the great utopias of labor, the body reduced to an element in the *conversion* of force is being replaced by the digital model of work as the computer-driven *simulacra* of combined technological, physical, and mental labor.[84] Like Taylor's system, information technology continues to remove skill and knowledge from the "sentient" body, but, it now also demands an interactive relationship to its object, a precise interaction with digital "events" that occur before, and hence anticipate, real-time events. These technologies require a profound "reskilling" and an adaptive change in the relations of authority in the workplace. Instead of reducing the "realm of necessity" (labor time) to a few dull hours a week, the new work demands its own realm of freedom in cohabitation with the machine. Consequently, work loses its materiality, its corporeality, and spatiality. The manipulation of vast quantities of data also demands not discipline and the subordination of the body to external norms, but flexibility, judgment, engagement, and commitment. This sort of work, as the commercials for Wi-Fi connectivity on the beach tell us, occurs not merely in the workplace but in any place that the worker may be.

These developments are not merely a consequence of the technology itself but of how the computer has provided management experts with a new image of organization that apparently does away with cumbersome top-down authoritarian forms of management. As I suggested, an intellectually vigorous new discourse of "antidisciplinarity" has found a niche in the boardrooms of corporations and on the editorial pages of influential newspapers and periodicals. Take the *Wall Street Journal*, for example, which in the 1990s campaigned against the lingering consequences of the Taylorist/Fordist workplace: firms sticking to an outdated model in which management distrusts the autonomy of workers, prescribes dull routinized tasks, curbs creativity, and creates a workplace ill-suited to "literate, independent-minded workers."[85] The most elaborate vision of neoromantic anarcho-capitalism can be found in an influential manifesto by Kevin Kelly, founder and executive editor of the influential periodical *Wired*, under the apt title, *Out of Control: The New Biology of Machines*. According to Kelly, digital machines offer a different biophysical metaphor for the operations of nature than did thermodynamics.[86] Like beehives, computer "swarms" are adaptable, resilient, evolving, and constantly generating novelty. Socialism, deep ecology, and the early experiments in artificial intelligence were all flawed by an obsolete, top-down, engineering approach.[87] Unlike the old "clock ware" that required intricate, and inefficient central planning, he argues, bottom-up, evolutionary, swarm logic allows computers to map "the morphology of the amorphous." In other words, the new logic allows new forms of life and society to *emerge* spontaneously. Kelly's "swarm consciousness" might have only appealed to the T-shirt and rollerblade capitalists of the dotcom bubble, but it is ultimately indebted to far more serious thinkers who for several decades have contended with the forms of "artificial life" produced by digital machines.

According to the theorists of artificial life, aliveness is a property of form and logic, not of carbon molecules. In the words of its foremost spokesman, Christopher Langton, artificial life is "the attempt to abstract the logic of life in different material forms."[88] Cellular automata (and here I rely on Langton's own description) do not merely directly code the "organism" (as in creating a pattern or a blueprint), but allow for an open-ended set of local rules to emerge. From the perspective of artificial life, biology is only one variety of a much larger conception of life that reaches beyond our own carbon-based world, perhaps even beyond electronic digital life, to what

Kelly calls "hyperlife," a kind of quantum biology that maps the space of all possible life. "Deep evolution" as some of its adherents call it, is an amalgam of environmentalism, computer simulations, sociobiology, and old-fashioned market economics. Like most organicist thinking it betrays a deeply conservative impulse, the desire to project back onto a benign nature the *summum bonum* of all experience. There is a new ontology at work, here, one that interestingly recalls the way in which thermodynamics regarded the classical automata as a kind of error based on a misunderstanding of what constitutes life. This time, however, the error lies in the reductionist idea of life as simply the law-bound conversion of energy. Computers can simulate the flocking behavior of birds, grow vast botanical gardens of flora and fauna, and evolve insect-like creatures that behave in ways remarkably like those in the natural world. Many of the properties that biologists would consider as intrinsic to life: evolution, self-organization, emergence, parallel processing, occur in these computer simulations. Such computer-generated algorithms are symptomatic of the belief that new organizational systems, like this redefined "life" itself, are emergent rather than structured by management. At bottom, the image of a world that is out of control promises not chaos, but hyper control without central authority. Like Mandeville's 1714 *Fable of the Bees*, the lesson of the swarm is that private vices bring public benefits.

Critics of artificial life point out that the idea of life as emergence is itself a phantasm: life eludes computation because "it stands in a permanent non-deterministic and pragmatic relation to its environment." This "slimy" quality, argues the biologist Claus Emmeche, rather than "carbon chauvinism," has to do with the question of whether biological processes can be grasped *entirely* in syntactical, computational terms. In short, as Emmeche puts it, despite the ontological claim that computers have already produced an alternative life form, they have not demonstrated that "we are in fact speaking of a *realization* of new forms of life (in another medium) and not simply a *simulation* of life."[89] Despite the claims of the artificial life theorists, the capacity of computers to simulate life has not transcended the bounds of eighteenth-century automata—they have not become "life." Like the old automata, they are merely simulacra conceived as proofs, not only that life can be created "in silica," but as Emmeche put it, as "a broad analogy, a class of models of complex calculated systems that share ecological and evolutionary conditions with many of the real organisms found in nature."[90]

Emmeche's sober conclusion points to the weaknesses of Kelly's overarching hypersynthesis of biology and technology. But, the readiness with which such computer-driven visions of a nonauthoritarian, bottom-up, open-ended, flexible, and "emerging" workplace have been accepted are significant on their own terms. The discourse of emergence and the fact that work is now imagined in digital rather than disciplinary terms, does not do away with exploitation, overwork, or "sweating" in vast computer barns. Just as Taylorism and Fordism relegated the worker to a function, so the workstation is just an interactive site in the internet universe. At the same time, the replacement of *organization* by *emergence* signifies a fallacy similar to the one that governed assumptions about Fordism, namely that such processes are automatic, autonomous, and independent of the vicissitudes of the market. In the United States, and even more strongly in Europe, from the end of World War II to the late 1960s, the Fordist social contract guaranteed high wages, high purchasing power, a comfortable old age, and above all, the relative security that each generation can expect to achieve a higher standard of living than the previous one. Today, none of these assumptions can be taken for granted. Insecurity, short-term work contracts, a stagnant economy, and rising income disparity are the more likely outcomes. Indeed, the discussion of what constitutes artificial intelligence has shifted away from "ontological" questions about whether artificial intelligence is comparable to human intelligence to more realistic questions of whether too many jobs are being lost to intelligent machines and whether gains in output are inevitably yoked to immiseration. "Eight years after leading artificial intelligence scientists said their field did not need to be regulated, the question of government oversight has re-emerged as the technology has rapidly progressed."[91]

With this transformation, we may also have reached the "end of the work-centered society," but not the abolition of labor, discipline, or the reduction of work—time to a socially necessary minimum. Reforms that encourage the reduction of work time, more flexible work situations and arrangements, as well as reductions in unemployment demand a far more radical rethinking of the relationship between politics and market forces. But with the eclipse of the great productivist utopias of the twentieth century—Taylorism, the science of work, Fordism, fascism, communism—work has ceased to be the defining activity of modernity and, regrettably, no longer offers the vision of a more just or more dynamic future.

Social Energeticism in Fin-de-Siècle Europe

The transformation of energy is the primary phenomenon [*Urphänomen*] of all occurrence.

—WILHELM OSTWALD

In the second half of the nineteenth century, a series of sensational discoveries in the physical and biological sciences provided progressive reformers with a plethora of normative concepts that offered an apparently neutral and objective basis for promoting the ideal of a society that might ensure social harmony while guaranteeing progress and increasing productivity. The biology of Xavier Bichat and Jean Baptiste de Lamarck redefined human beings as organisms that prospered only in a delicately maintained and optimally structured "milieu."[1] Similarly, Darwin's discoveries were combined with anthropological insights to produce a variety of sciences dedicated to ridding civilization of the discontents of infertility, criminality, and declining intelligence.[2] Among these novel scientific doctrines, the discovery of the laws of thermodynamics and the formulation of conservation of force during the 1840s played a central role in providing a rationale for conserving the health and safety of the worker which, reformers argued, would inevitably lead to greater productivity and profit. Until the last decade of the century, however, there was no general synthesis that reformers could draw upon to have this rather arcane body of scientific knowledge influence legislative proposals for social policy.

After 1890, the translation and adaptation of the doctrine of energy conservation to society was elaborated by the Belgian entrepreneur and chemist Ernest Solvay, the sociologist Émile Waxweiler, the chemist Wilhelm Ostwald, and the physiologist Max Rubner. Grounded in the irrefutable principles of science and based on the laws of nature, they claimed, social policy could stand above the interests of social classes and political imperatives.

Neo-Saint Simonianism: Ernest Solvay and the Institut de Sociologie

Writing in the Belgian socialist journal *Le Peuple* (July 15, 1903), Émile Vandervelde—the secretary of the Second International and one of the leading figures of European Socialism—remarked, "Saint Simonians no longer exist, with the exception of Ernest Solvay, who is an authentic Saint-Simonian, which is to say, a liberal."[3] Vandervelde's characterization of Solvay as a late nineteenth-century Saint-Simonian and a liberal is accurate, even though his Saint-Simonianism was filtered through the ideas of Auguste Comte, Hermann von Helmholtz, and Claude Bernard. Vandervelde's comparison of Solvay to Saint Simon is useful, since much of what can be described as scientific materialism or "social Helmholtzianism" might well be considered a late nineteenth-century variant of Saint Simonian or even Comtean ideology. Solvay certainly shared Count Henri de Saint Simon's confident view that scientists and engineers could decisively alter the organization of industry and that industrial entrepreneurs could be enlisted into the service of a new mode of production organized according to scientific principles. Both men also shared a contempt for religion, wanted to do away with inherited wealth, and, above all, gave science and the state a decisive role to play in the creation of a new and rational industrial social order.

Solvay himself conceded the point a few days later. In a lengthy letter to the editor of *Le Peuple*, he admitted: "I am ready for my part to satisfy the historians, and to be recognized as a composite of a crowd of predecessors, of which one of the most recent would be Saint-Simon."[4] The rest of the letter was characteristically devoted to refuting Vandervelde's arguments on behalf of "nationalization and collectivization."[5]

Unlike Saint Simon, whose career demonstrated a romantic proclivity for failed conspiracies, and whose ideas generally came to little practical end, Ernest Solvay was by all measures an extraordinary success in his own lifetime. He was a successful industrialist, a generous philanthropist, and an amateur social philosopher.[6] Ironically, Solvay's success came about in part because of the unfortunate fate of another eighteenth-century French savant, Nicolas Leblanc. Leblanc was an industrial chemist who, in 1775, developed an innovative method of converting common salt into sodium bicarbonate or washing soda (used in the manufacture of soap). When Leblanc's mentor, Louis Philippe II, Duke of Orléans, ran afoul of the Committee of Public Safety in 1793, the inventor's deserved claim to a patent and a prize offered by the Academy of Sciences was abruptly canceled. His new process, revolutionary as it was, brought him little personal profit and Leblanc ended his own life in desperation and penury. His true heir turned out to be Solvay, son of a small salt merchant in Belgium. Solvay's uncle, who employed the young man at the gas works which he managed, asked if he could find some use for the liquid gas (largely ammonia) which accumulated there as waste. Recalling Leblanc's cumbersome method of converting salt into soda ash, Solvay thus "discovered" the ammonia process, which replaced the less efficient and more costly Leblanc process.[7]

Obtaining a patent for the process in 1861, the "soda king" and his brother Alfred entered into a partnership, establishing a small factory near the town of Charleroi. By 1867, the brothers Solvay, together with the English businessman Ludwig Mond, had established several soda plants in France and Germany and built one of the largest soda plants in the world near Norwich, England. From then on Solvay's soda plants proliferated—there were twenty-three by 1914—as did his enormous personal wealth.[8] Solvay's "ammonia process" not only contributed to the enormous expansion of soda-ash manufacture but also to a decline in its price worldwide—from 140 dollars per ton in 1850 to 22 dollars per ton in 1902.[9] The result was a precipitous decline in the cost of soap, Solvay's contribution to the rising level of personal hygiene in the second half of the nineteenth century.

Solvay's extraordinary achievement was marred by the death of his brother Alfred in 1894. As a result, Ernest succumbed to a "suspicious neurasthenia" sealing himself off from the world for several years in Alpine seclusion. According to the few friends admitted to the retreat, he took on "the pallor of a dying ember." It was during this period of extreme neurasthenic withdrawal in the Austrian Tyrol that Solvay conceived of a plan to realize his most passionate dream of unifying science and social reform under the single rubric of what he called "energeticism."[10]

Emerging from his seclusion a year later, Solvay's wealth allowed him to fulfill his "most fundamental impulses" as a scientific reformer. He dedicated his talents to furthering the advancement of pure science and subsequently to promoting his social ideas, which he acquired without any formal training. Solvay used his fortune to endow separate research institutes for chemistry, physics, physiology, and eventually sociology. A remarkable entrepreneur, autodidact, and philanthropist who once described himself as having a "gift of prophecy," Solvay was considered by colleagues to be a "*philosophe* and perhaps even a bit of a mystic."[11] Sublimating his "torture" at not having himself been a true scientific genius (he once remarked, "Je ne suis pas un savant!") into a passion for social schemes, Solvay conceived of himself as a modern visionary, a "physicist of society."[12]

An avid reader of Helmholtz, Julius von Mayer, Étienne-Jules Marey, Claude Bernard, and Darwin, but also of Hegel, Kant, Jacob Moleschott, and Ludwig Büchner, Solvay wedded the advances he saw in contemporary science to the idea of a rational social order. As early as 1871, he began to formulate his vision of a rational solution to the "social question" which, he argued, had to be provided with a plan for "rejuvenation." This program, he cautioned, "should not be presented to our century as a maxim of charity, but on a firm social basis, appealing to the interests of all." It had to appeal to egoism, but "not the egoism of brutality, but the egoism of rationality."[13] In a revealing remark he characterized the modern individual, and perhaps himself, as "a being stirred by the noble and penetrating discoveries of the Enlightenment and by positive truths," and at the same time, as a being "fatigued" by vague and indeterminate concepts.

In 1879, Solvay published his first nonscientific work, a thirty-six-page brochure entitled *Science contre Religion*, dedicated to replacing the archaic views of Catholicism with a model of science whose "ideal temple is constructed, stone by stone, that is to say, *law by law*, without an architect."[14] Solvay's earliest effort was a proposal to counter religious ideas by creating a scientific "catechism" that condensed the discoveries of modern science in simple formulas easily accessible to a wide, and most importantly young, public.[15] Despite his lifelong antipathy to religion, the parallels between Solvay's conception of science and the Catholicism he rejected is often painfully apparent. His "positive" approach to society challenged the teachings of the church, yet offered simple scientific substitutes for its dogmas. For example, in rejecting the church's doctrine on free will, Solvay absolutely denied all free choice, admitting only to rational submission to the "fatal laws" of nature and society. Echoing the notion of the "average man" (*l'homme moyen*) developed by the great mid-century Belgian statistician Adolphe Quételet, Solvay argued that the fact that "suicides, duels, crimes, marriages, and so forth, acts that are committed *voluntarily*, regularly apportion themselves in the columns of society's account books" was irrefutable evidence of the inefficacy of human interference with natural and social laws.[16] These laws were both irrevocable and progressive, since the society of the future will inevitably be ruled by scientifically trained elites and by an expanded technology.

Above all, Solvay claimed that modern science was dominated by the sovereign concept of energy. "It orients its researches in the realm of the organic, the mineral, it is the movement, the unity, the order, the law."[17] No aspect of the universe was untouched by the basic principle of *energeticism*— it encompassed all aspects of nature. Life, according to Solvay was essentially a system of reactions or exchanges that can be classified under the concept of "exo-energetic" conversions, or exchanges of energy. These conversions constantly aimed at a restoration of the balance or equilibrium between the energy consumed and the energy liberated in the exchange. The success or failure of the conversion is determined above all by the specific "milieu" in which the exchange takes place: either it serves the exchange by restoring the balance or it inhibits it, reducing the optimal energy released in the process.

Solvay called his own doctrine "productivism," which he defined as "the social equivalent of energeticism."[18] Society was nothing but a higher level of "energetic phenomenon." For Solvay, "life can be characterized as *the state of exo-energetic* activity," the organism was a "transformer of energy that is employed as a coefficient of social utility."[19] Productivism could be summed up as a human *and* physiological principle—"the best existence" is nothing but the "physical-chemical law of maximum work."[20]

For Solvay, the individual is an "energetic-productivist being" because of "vital necessity"—social energy is the sum total of individual energies available for social use.[21] Each excessive consumption of energy, Solvay argued, had a double effect on general social efficiency, because "an excessive energeticism" among certain individuals might set into motion an "energetic deprivation" for others. "The antisocial character of abusive and excessive consumption can be clearly illuminated in this manner."[22] Solvay also considered class struggle a wasteful and "colossal illusion" because it distracted individuals from the principle that all organisms and societies must be encouraged to function according to their most integral nature: "maximum efficiency."[23] "To be a productivist," he claimed, "is to recognize the true march of progress to assure the well-being of human beings is the development, by all possible means, of the production of material things in a quantity and a quality appropriate to temperament, general state of health, country inhabited, and the mode of work."[24]

However, Solvay recognized that the efficiency, or what he called "socio-utilisability" of that energy, varied greatly with age, health, and circumstance. For Solvay all human activities, including cerebral work and the consumption of material goods, could be expressed in mathematical terms as "physio-energetic units."[25] The goal of a scientific approach to society, therefore, was to determine the maximum disposable energy available to society and to enhance the economic capacities of individuals for production, both materially and intellectually, present and future. The normal state of all organisms, Solvay claimed, always tends toward maximum energetic efficiency. The law of progress was therefore grounded in the "organic regime" in which the species is embedded. The problem, however, was to translate this natural law into a social mechanism. Solvay's "positive political program" did not challenge the existing order of property relations but conceived of what he called "free-socialization," or scientifically informed policies aimed at increasing general productivity, voluntarily undertaken and encouraged by the state. Solvay also proposed that an elite "governmental class of social scientists [*savants sociaux*]" be established to explore the possible routes to the intellectual advancement of mankind, to discover its laws of development and determine which are most likely to advance society. Solvay proposed this idea to the Belgian Senate on May 24, 1894, when he appealed to the government to create a special agency charged with examining a series of social issues.[26] Initially, Solvay did not offer a concrete program of social reform, although he advocated certain broad principles by which such a program might be established. He believed that there were a small number of laws, according to which society could be regulated by a minimum of effort and a maximum of social justice, above all his supreme principle that the equitable distribution of justice was predicated on "general prosperity." But, after 1886, Solvay experienced a "change of heart" brought on by the events of the "terrible year" in Belgium, when an anarchist demonstration in memory of the Paris Commune ended in rioting which spread to several industrial establishments throughout the country. In contrast to most Belgian industrialists who condemned the strikes as the work of "alien disrupters of the social order" (*l'excitation des étrangers*), Solvay argued that progress could only be guaranteed by the steady expansion of productivity, and that if the interference of the state to prevent social misery served that end, it was justified on universal principles. "The society of the future," he noted, "is condemned to justice under pain of death. It will be the only means of defense against the growing means of destruction."[27]

The 1886 riots provoked Solvay to put forward an increasing number of "positive" and concrete reforms. Drawing on the experience of his own enterprises, where he had introduced shorter hours, accident insurance, pensions, medical attention and housing, Solvay claimed that ultimate responsibility for the reorganization of society fell not to the state, but to the employers who stood to benefit most from the greater productivity accrued from the cooperation and well-being of their employees. Maintaining the health and hygiene of the work force, protecting them against accidents, providing medical and pharmaceutical supplies, offering good housing, and even providing wholesale stores, not only improved productivity but also greatly enhanced the authority and legitimacy of the firm.[28]

According to Solvay, the primary responsibility of the state was to mobilize the resources of science to enhance the capacity of the producers. The state could also further the development of a scientific and technical elite and provide for education of the "productive capacities of individuals" by promoting "the acquisition of social knowledge by the salaried employees."[29] The state also should take responsibility for retraining the "involuntarily unemployed." But, the state should not too greatly expand its social and political role. Rather it should encourage private initiative as opposed to authoritarian control: It combats social parasitism, privilege, and idleness, and provides education in economic and social principles, and for the free association of individuals. All of these measures, Solvay believed, could be funded by an inheritance tax and by a tax on excess profits both of which would contribute to a "social fund."[30] Productivism permitted society to be run like a great industrial enterprise, regulated with a minimum of effort and a maximum of social justice. Elected to the Belgian Senate as a Liberal deputy in 1892, Solvay pleaded the cause of reform among conservative bankers and politicians with little resonance.[31] At that time, the Liberal party in Belgium was championing public education as the most suitable means for the diffusion of the ideals of the enlightenment. Solvay's rational and social liberalism was definitively opposed to the "romantic liberalism" of the French revolution whose greatest illusion, he believed, persisted in the belief that it was sufficient to abolish antiquated institutions and proclaim the right of all individuals to realize their natural talents. The result of this myopic view, he argued, was not less state intervention, but even greater political intervention in what had long since become a permanent social war. Instead, Solvay argued that it was necessary to organize economic and social life according to strictly rational principles without increasing the authority of the state, to balance "productive capacity" with "needs of consumption."[32]

Solvay was not a lonely prophet of the application of scientific advances to social problems. Possessing the means to realize his ends, he founded, in 1895, the Institut des Sciences Sociales at the University of Brussels, the first scientific institute for the study of sociology in the world.[33] In 1900, Solvay met a young researcher at the Ministry of Labor, Émile Waxweiler, whom he designated as director of a sociological institute which he planned to include among his already established institutes of chemistry, physics, and physiology. The following year, under Waxweiler's direction, he established the Institut de Sociologie in Brussels's Parc Léopold. At that time, he noted with apparent pride: "And I, who never even received a classical education, dare to have the ambition to conspire to the edification of modern science. I have had the audacity to create a plan of study, as an architect might embellish the temple of his dreams."[34] A special building was planned with excellent library facilities, separate divisions for anthropology, technology, history, and demography. Located between the already established institutes of anatomy and physiology, their physical proximity to the sociological institute reflected what Solvay saw as a conceptual proximity as well. The physical layout of the Institut de Sociologie, as Waxweiler put it, was "already a kind of program in the largest sense of the word."[35] He continued: "Ernest Solvay wished it thus, despite the astonishment of specialists in physiology and anatomy, at the time of the institute's construction, on seeing the sociologists, who had more literary than scientific renown, installed so near them. He intended, thereby to give bodily expression to the synthesis of his preoccupations, and he associated the buildings in order to affirm the affiliation of his ideas."[36] Solvay's rationale for establishing a new institute remains obscure, but it is clear that his decision to dissolve the Institut des Sciences Sociales and replace it with one under Waxweiler's direction was motivated in part by his concern that some of his most distinguished Belgian socialist collaborators—including Émile Vandervelde, Guillaume de Greef, and Hector Denis—embraced a collectivism far more revolutionary in inspiration than his own convictions could tolerate.[37] If, in fact, the original institute had for some time come under the influence of the Belgian socialists who regarded it as a useful opportunity for advancing their own ideas, Solvay also exerted an influence on them.[38] Denis, for example, who was a deputy in the Belgian lower house, was an advocate of improving workers' health, and Vandervelde penned a brochure favorable to Solvay's banking scheme, *comptabilisme social*.[39]

Solvay's ideas departed from those of the socialists in several other respects. He opposed the use of force and the expropriation of property, and he feared that a general socialization on behalf of the working class would result in a general flight of capital.[40] Whereas traditional liberalism was impeded by its ideological attachment to noninterventionist economics, the socialists, he argued, were equally hampered by their attachment to what he called the "social mirage" of perpetual economic expansion. Instead, Solvay proposed a system that would balance equality and social justice with the guarantee of technical and economic efficiency.[41]

Solvay outlined his "productivism" in a series of works which he published under the auspices of the Institut de Sociologie in rapid succession. The general purpose of the institute was to replace the arbitrary and irrational calculations that governed economic and social existence with positive physiological and social principles. Above all the institute would promote the ideas of the new energeticism in the social domain, encourage research, and create an international committee of authorities who would be the core of a future international party of "positive politics."[42] Solvay's *Plan Social* was dedicated to substituting what he perceived as the anarchy of modern industrial society with a scientifically designed society dedicated to economic order and social justice. Predicated on his maxim that the greatest profit for all would result from the "maximum yield of human energy" he argued that the natural tendency of all modern societies toward greater equality would necessarily result from scientific and technical progress. Since all human existence automatically followed the law of "the tendency to achieve maximum efficiency with minimum effort" the true social imperative was to increase production, since production was the ultimate source of all well-being.[43]

Preparing individuals for future tasks in their capacity as organic parts of the production process was as directly beneficial to productivity as was removing the discontents and disadvantages that prevented them from realizing their social talents. Since all natural phenomena fell under the laws of the conservation and transformation of energy, human intelligence had the capability to accelerate the laws of social development by improving social adaptation or by placing an organism in a milieu most suitable to its existence.

Solvay also developed a series of specific proposals, above all a monetary scheme, *Social Comptabilisme*, which he believed would eliminate exploitation, interest, and profiteering by replacing currency with a system of social accounting and accounting books.[44] He also proposed a state-sponsored adult education program to create a new class of technical professionals. Society would thus raise its own producers to the highest level of technical and scientific expertise while eliminating anarchy within and ultimately, Solvay prophesized, between nations. Eventually, technical development would lead to a higher degree of moral universalism, culminating in what he called the "Société des Sociétés," a kind of League of Nations avant la lettre.

Naive as it may appear today, Solvay's productivism was the first attempt to provide the energy doctrine with a commensurate social and political doctrine, and to make its social imperatives accessible and practicable. His unabashed optimism establishes his place in the pantheon of nineteenth-century thinkers, who, in the tradition of Saint Simon and Auguste Comte attempted to harness the forces of science to society through "positive philosophy."

Émile Waxweiler: Energetic Sociology

An engineer by training, Émile Waxweiler was thirty-three years old when he assumed the directorship of the Institut de Sociologie in 1901. Like his benefactor, Solvay, he was deeply affected by the Belgian riots of 1886. In the mid-1890s, he had already turned his attention to the resolution of the "labor question" quickly establishing a reputation as the leading Belgian expert on methods of remuneration and wages, especially profit-sharing schemes for workers.[45] His travels in the United States, his work for the Belgian Labor Office (for which he studied labor conditions in Germany and Switzerland), and his success as a statistician and organizer of the inquiry into the state of Belgian industry and commerce in 1896, provided Waxweiler with a first-hand understanding of labor policy. His astonishing capacity for work also included a talent for administration.[46] His publications and lectures at the University of Brussels, where he supervised the seminar in political science, left little doubt that Waxweiler was endowed with considerable intellectual gifts.

As director of the Institut de Sociologie, Waxweiler's first task was to develop a program of study in concert with Solvay's ideas. He began work on a theoretical synthesis that he thought could serve as the guide for the institute's studies. The result was his *Esquisse d'une sociologie*, a work explicitly conceived in the spirit of August Comte, a grand and systematic "scientific sociology" that unified the different branches of human knowledge according to their place in the general process of "socialization." Adopting Solvay's credo that the human being is in essence a "physico-chemical reaction," Waxweiler saw sociology as the study of "phenomena of reaction resulting from the mutual excitation of individuals of the same species without regard to sex."[47] Taking as his point of departure the adaptation of all organisms to the biological milieu, Waxweiler traced human development through the emergence of the "social formation," the acquisition of "social aptitudes," and the proliferation of social activities or reactions, culminating in "social synergy" or social coordination. Thus habits, rules, usages and institutions were ever more complex manifestations of the basic biological imperative of individuals to adapt to their given social milieu. In this sense sociology, or better biosociology, replicated, by other means, the investigations of the *milieu intérieur* pioneered by Claude Bernard and other contemporary biologists and physiologists.[48]

Waxweiler's theoretical efforts were not, as might be anticipated, favorably received when his *Esquisse* first appeared in 1906. Pretentious in style, superficial in approach, and dogmatic in its insistence on the biological basis of all social life, the *Esquisse* exhibited all the weaknesses of Solvay's *productivism* without its optimistic verve. Waxweiler soon found himself at loggerheads with Durkheimianism, the dominant school of French sociology in the early twentieth century. The Durkheimians mounted an attack on Waxweiler for his insistence on reducing social phenomena to biological imperatives, and for his explicit rejection of social facts.[49] Unlike Solvay, who was content with general statements on behalf of the social implications of energeticism and his programmatic ideas, Waxweiler's attempt to produce a science of society modeled on biology was deeply indebted to the influential neo-Lamarckian movement in France (which at that time included the biologists Alfred Mathieu Giard and Charles Philippe Robin).[50] According to the Lamarckians the modification of the environment and the reaction of the organism to the environment were always reciprocal, a principle that Waxweiler took as scientific confirmation of the view that equal exchanges of energy were involved in all social acts.[51]

In Waxweiler's hands sociology became the study of the relations among human beings conceived as units of energy within their specific social milieu. Waxweiler also placed the concepts of fatigue and energy at the center of his "ethological" theory of society. The milieu, he argued, either supported the organism in its efforts to develop, producing a *rapport* in which the economy of energy is maximized or it discouraged the organism, resulting in a profound fatigue in which the organism fails to adjust to a new situation.[52] Waxweiler produced an endlessly self-procreating vocabulary of biosocial neologisms such as the "nutritive cycle." He invented the term *protection* to underscore the centrality of each milieu's capacity to support or reject energetic relations and to promote their constant reparation in the life of society. Because the repair of any damage to the energetic equilibrium is the normal functioning of any milieu, the social principles Waxweiler derived from his biological perspective were essentially liberal and progressive. In advanced societies, he claimed, reform legislation plays the role of a bioenergetic, protective mechanism. Reparation is realized, Waxweiler argued, through the medium of the state and through the agency of certain individuals who, as a scientific elite, are able to perceive the breakdown, and need for a redirection of the social process. Waxweiler's sociological theory attempted to raise to the level of a "grand synthesis" the basic idea of energeticism and productivism in social life.

At least as important as his rather cumbersome theory, were Waxweiler's indefatigable efforts on behalf of Solvay's Institut de Sociologie which he carried on until the German invasion of Belgium sent him abroad in 1914. Under his direction, the institute undertook hundreds of studies on a bewildering variety of theoretical and practical social themes, from the neurological origins of the will to modern transportation systems.[53] The institute also produced numerous studies of social issues, including the length of military service and the length of the working day. Among the most significant was the elaborate and well-executed study of the nutrition of 1,065 Belgian workers published by Waxweiler in 1910.[54] During World War I, Waxweiler was appointed to head the Belgian bureau of economic information in London, an agency devoted to planning for Belgian economic policy in a reconstructed Europe.[55] A pacifist, he was also a highly vocal defender of Belgian's claim to neutrality during the war, resulting in his most famous political work, *La Belgique neutre et loyale* (1915).[56] His unfortunate death in a traffic accident in London in June 1916 brought an abrupt end to his career.

The Energetic Imperative in Wilhelminian Germany:
Wilhelm Ostwald and Max Rubner

Wilhelm Ostwald (1853–1932), world-renowned German chemist and popularizer of energeticist ideas, was, unlike Solvay, *un vrai savant*; he left behind an immense literary and scientific oeuvre that included more than forty-five books and five hundred papers.[57] He shared with Solvay—whom he once called "the founder of sociological energetics" and to whom he dedicated his programmatic *Die Energetische Grundlagen der Kulturwissenschaft* (1909)—an unbridled passion for the concept of energy. He also shared Solvay's "mania" for reform movements, to which he devoted a significant portion of his later career. Named ordinarius professor of physical chemistry at Leipzig in 1887, Ostwald's scientific contribution was largely an extension of

Helmholtz's, which included a more sophisticated demonstration of the impossibility of the *perpetuum mobile* and a method of measuring the "equilibrium positions of chemical reactions" by "free energy functions." His most influential scientific work was a standard textbook of electrochemistry, translated into numerous languages, *Elektrochemie: Ihre Geschichte und ihre Lehre* (1896). But his greatest success was as a synthesizer and disseminator of the scientific discoveries of his age, and Ostwald was best known for his popularizations and collections of scientific portraits, such as *Klassiker der exakten Wissenschaft* (1889).[58] In addition to his scientific accomplishments, Ostwald was a leading German protagonist of the international brotherhood of scientists, frequently publicizing the need for international cooperation at the scientific and political level. A pacifist, Ostwald frequently attended international peace congresses (1909–1911), condemning war as a "squandering of energy of the very worst kind."[59] Ostwald was an active member of the German Monist League and in 1911 became its president. In that capacity, he published the weekly *Monistischen Sonntagspredigen*, which offered a reassuring answer to the anxieties of those who feared that the second law, entropy, guaranteed an apocalyptic future of total energy loss and a frozen planet. As Elizabeth Nesfeld explains, "he transformed for a lay public the difficult-to-grasp thermodynamics into a comforting guide to the conduct of life, combining morality with a familiar religious vocabulary close to their own experiences."[60] One of his most cherished accomplishments was the invention of a new international language, "Ida," which he believed would overcome the "errors of Esperanto" and become a "world language" by the twentieth century.[61] Ostwald even outdid Solvay's currency obsession, envisioning the internationalization of all currency and eventually of the postal banking system. But, for our purposes, the most significant result of Ostwald's prodigious theorizing was his great success in simplifying and disseminating the social and cultural implications of the doctrine of energy. For example, Ostwald's impact on early twentieth-century Marxism was considerable. In a 1924 letter to Maxim Gorky, Lenin recalled that in 1903 he and Georgi Plekhanov were engaged in a polemic against Russian Marxist followers of Ostwald, primarily Alexander Bogdanov. Those arguments found their way into Lenin's *Materialism and Empirio-Criticism*, published in 1909. But more interesting than Lenin's assault on the "philosophical blockheads" is his contention that Russian Marxist theory was indebted to Ostwald: "The methods of operation employed in the various attempts to develop and supplement Marx were not very ingenious. They read Ostwald, believe Ostwald, paraphrase Ostwald and call it Marxism."[62]

Ostwald was certainly not the only nineteenth-century German thinker to ruminate on the philosophical and social implications of the new discoveries of thermodynamics. Another was Ernst Haeckel (1834–1919), creator of the doctrine of Monism and, in 1906, of the Monist League, an enlightened anti-religion based on an amalgamation of Darwinism, scientific materialism and *Naturphilosophie*.[63] Haeckel's popular scientific works were widely read, and he devoted a significant portion of his 1899 bestseller *Die Welträtsel* (*The Riddle of the Universe*) to the idea of energy. Haeckel attacked both spiritualism and materialism for trapping man in what he called the metaphysical illusions of dualism. Only science could overcome this dualism by redefining nature in terms of "the greatest intellectual triumph of the nineteenth century," the development of the law of the conservation of energy, which Häckel renamed "the law of substance."[64]

The physicist-philosopher Ernst Mach was also an early and prolific popularizer of the new energy doctrine, and—in a carefully worded 1900 brief on Ostwald and other competing philosophical commentators on the energy doctrine—laid his own claim to primacy with his *Die Geschichte und die Wurzel des Satzes von der Erhaltung der Arbeit* (Prague, 1872).[65] Nonetheless, Mach remained aloof from Ostwald and Haeckel whose proclivities as "philosophizing natural scientists" (*philosophierende Naturforscher*) he criticized as psychologically and epistemologically naive.[66] He was also cool toward Ostwald's endeavors to secure a faculty position for Mach in Leipzig, or to win his participation in Ostwald's journal, *Die Annalen der Naturphilosophie*.[67] Mach nonetheless exerted an enormous influence on a whole generation of social thinkers and activists including the Austrian socialists, Otto Bauer, Otto Neurath, and Friedrich Adler, though largely as an advocate of rigorous epistemological skepticism.[68]

Ostwald was by far the most prominent of the German defenders of the new energetics, and without doubt the most convinced of its supreme cultural significance. His energetic writings: *Die Energie* (1908), *Die Energetischen Grundlagen der Kulturwissenschaft* (1909), and *Der Energetische Imperativ* (1912) attempted to demonstrate the implications of the doctrine of energy for the human sciences, especially sociology, "the supreme science in the Comtean hierarchy of sciences."[69] Ostwald conceived of energy as a category of perception at least on a par with, if not superior to time and space in the Kantian a priori categories of apperception: "one can represent everything in time, space, and energy, since no objective thing can exist for us without these three categories."[70] Ostwald had argued this position in his *Studies on Energetics* as early as 1891, when he proposed that energy, space and time become the absolute system of measurement, as opposed to the older "mass, space, and time." The achievement of energetics was that all matter could be subsumed under the more universalistic energy principle.[71]

Ostwald's growing interest in popularizing his views on energetics and promoting their social relevance came, perhaps not accidentally, soon after his efforts to make them universally accepted among scientists had been rebuffed at the German Society of Scientists and Physicians Congress in Lübeck in September 1895. The meeting provided the occasion for a heated controversy on energetics which pit Ostwald, and his sole supporter, the chemist Georg Helm, against growing opposition from physicists defending the "atomistic" doctrine.[72] According to the historian of science Erwin Hiebert, "Following the lectures, the physicists, headed by [Ludwig] Boltzmann, sharply criticized the energeticist position. Ostwald felt that he never before had experienced such unanimous hostility."[73] Boltzmann summed up the criticisms of Ostwald's position in a famous paper published the following year: "Probably no one holds energy to be a reality anymore; or believes that it has been proven without question that all natural phenomena can be explained mechanically."[74] Historians of science continue to debate whether Ostwald's defeat and the "demise of energetics" in natural science was due to its internal insufficiencies, especially in the realm of mathematics, or whether it died of an overdose of ontological realism.[75] Nevertheless, when Ostwald turned from energetics in science to energetics in society, his shift in audience—and style of argument—underscores his growing sense of retreat from developments in the natural sciences and the eclipse of energetics by newer scientific doctrines, such as atomism and molecular chemistry and biology, which Ostwald eventually acknowledged. Significantly, later in his career Helm too turned to demonstrating the universal applicability of energetics for economics and the cultural sciences. It would be presumptuous to conclude that the social sciences are essentially a second-hand store for ideas discarded by the natural sciences, though in the case of Ostwald, it seems inescapable.

For Ostwald, who baptized his country house in Saxony "Energie," no area of human endeavor was untouched by the laws of energy—nature, the economy, science, law, and the state.[76] Like Helmholtz, Ostwald was insistent on the absolute identity of energy; he renamed *Kraft*, or "work," *Energie* since "everything emerges from work and can be turned back into work."[77] In a universe constructed out of pure labor power, energy was essentially the source of all social wealth, and consequently, labor power was the universal "measure" through which "all products of energy and distance could be measured."[78] "Free energy," or the energy of the sun, was for Ostwald "the capital from which all living things nourish themselves, and everything that occurs, everything that makes our earth so colorful and varied, results from the transformation of free energy."[79] There were, of course, different types of energy—including kinetic energy, "form energy," heat, electrical and chemical energy—yet for Ostwald they were but forms of one single energy, as were the different types of matter which, in turn, were only the chemical and physical forms of different kinds of energy. Ultimately energy was simply everything, a synonym for "all things and events in the world."[80]

Despite its ubiquity, Ostwald recognized that energy is of little consequence unless it is "available energy" or energy that can be put to use (*Nutzenergie*). The entire effort of civilization he maintained, is devoted to converting raw energy into available energy, which requires that some form of existing power or property (labor or land) be brought to bear on the sources of energy. The evolution of mankind from the most primitive tools to the most complicated technologies could be viewed in terms of the conversion of raw energy into energy for use. The same principle that prevailed in the sphere of nature also prevailed in the domain of culture where energies normally dissipated by mankind were gradually converted into useful activities through labor and culture. For example, as Ostwald argued, the energy wasted in violence is gradually transformed into the more efficient use of available energy by the technique of law which regulates conflict. In the economy, competition for limited sources of energy results in improved conditions of existence through improved techniques and economies. In this way, culture is defined as the process by which energy is redirected toward useful purposes. All human evolution can thus be circumscribed by the gradual but irrepressible progress in the techniques of domination over the sources of useful energy. Ostwald graphically illustrated his argument, through the evolution of the domestication of "alien" sources of power, including other human beings (slavery) or domesticated animals which bring into existence property. Property then, according to its own laws of energy, expands exponentially, "the longer—in time and durability—the path is from raw energy to available energy."[81] The persistence of older forms of property, especially private ownership, Ostwald indicated, could be explained by this tendency, despite advances in the natural sciences which made them increasingly obsolete.

For Ostwald, the success or failure of energy conversion in any area of a modern industrial society was ultimately determined by the evolution of scientific knowledge. Progress can be measured by the efficiency of the process of conversion in each case, for example in the development of lighting from the most rudimentary oil lamp which gives about 3 percent of useful energy to the electric light which gives more than 15 percent efficiency. In the transition from mechanical energy to electrical energy a plethora of technical and social problems arise, whose solution determines how much energy is consumed and how much is wasted in the exchange. Especially in the industrial age, with the innumerable sources of energy available for conversion to productive use, waste becomes the paramount social issue, the actual calculus of progress.

The purpose of all social life, according to Ostwald, was to ensure the best possible methods of energy conversion—thus confirming the irresistible (even if, as Ostwald conceded, "often discredited") analogy between organic phenomena and society.[82] Despite his transparent disavowals, Ostwald, was even more predisposed than even Solvay and Waxweiler to allow the organic metaphor to dominate his image of society: "biology shows us the many-faceted levels of this increasing specialization of function or division of labor, and we can see a living being as a more advanced example of this."[83]

Progress is the story of how waste is eliminated and social coordination gradually achieved, universalized, and extended to a variety of social activities. Relying on Karl Bücher's ethnological research on the psychophysical parallel between work rhythm and body rhythm, Ostwald argued that the origin of social cooperation and adaptation was rooted in the desire of the human organism to eliminate fatigue and create a "coordination of energies" which kept the corresponding losses of energy to a minimum.[84] Society is nothing less than an arrangement for the more perfect transformation of raw to useful energy, and its imperfect organization results only in waste.

If all social life exists to convert energy to use, a single general rule applicable to all social behavior emerges from Ostwald's work: to improve the methods by which we can ensure that "the quantity of energy for use conserved from a given quantity of free energy in raw form, will be as large as possible."[85] Energetics also identified progress as a paradoxical consequence of the second law of thermodynamics. Greater efficiency and avoidance of wasteful dissipation of energy were the goals of cultural and biological development, resulting in a reduction of entropy and increased exploitation of energy. Ostwald called this principle the "energetic imperative," which he encapsulated in the formula: "don't waste energy, valorize it" (*Vergeude keine Energie, verwerte sie*).[86]

In 1910, Ostwald received an invitation from Haeckel, who he had not yet personally met, to visit him in Leipzig, where Haeckel offered him the presidency of the Monist League, which he had founded in 1906.[87] Though initially skeptical ("I was in agreement with the general direction of his thought, but not with many details"), Ostwald was charmed by Haeckel's surprisingly "friendly" and even "childlike" personality. Ostwald was also convinced that Haeckel did not have a dogmatic conception of the league's purpose: "Our personal meeting demonstrated to me that my major concern, that of a dogmatic fixation on a single explicitly detailed program, was unwarranted. Rather, the Monist League was composed of many divergent tendencies, united only in their resistance to the ever-increasing orthodoxy protected by the Kaiser."[88] Accepting the presidency, Ostwald saw the League as a public forum for promoting the scientific discoveries of Darwin and Helmholtz as the greatest achievements of a modern enlightened society, much in the spirit of Auguste Comte. As he wrote of his 1910 meeting with Haeckel: "In the meantime I had read and found convincing Comte's doctrine of the three stages of cultural development. Thus, I conceived the task of the Monist League in a very simple formula, negatively oriented toward resisting efforts to reverse the natural and necessary course of cultural development, and positively toward explicating and disseminating the scientific world view."[89] The grand lesson of science was, of course, to obtain the greatest use from the least amount of energy. Energetic utilitarianism was raised to the highest of social ideals. Even politics had to be subordinated to its overriding primacy.

Ostwald tried to steer the Monist League in a liberal direction, though he was decidedly less enthusiastic than Haeckel in making Darwin's theory the foundational science of the age. Ostwald believed that "the orientation of every monist must necessarily be *against* the right, that is against conservatism, orthodoxy and ultramontanism in any form."[90] In Ostwald's conception the sole purpose of the state was to further improve utilization of energy for the benefit of all of its members. Yet, despite his many speeches and articles on the subject, it is difficult to see what Ostwald's maxims entailed, since his proposals tended to be general statements condemning war, advocating international forms of cooperation (his Ida project), or calling for greater state intervention to preserve the national energy supply. In economics, however, Ostwald did demonstrate an odd propensity toward extreme attitudes, condemning the issuing of paper money and other forms of paper wealth by the government. Money, or capital, in his view was concentrated energy insofar as it "was the general equivalent of all value, and a general measure of all value." Paper wealth represented a false representation of "energy" which, Ostwald believed should be eliminated, along with privately sanctioned moneylending.[91] Whether the latter idea was inspired by unconscious anti-Semitism or, more likely, by economic conservatism is difficult to ascertain. In any case, Ostwald's proclivity to certain offbeat or even cranky ideas lead him to embrace a few less than enlightened solutions. In criminal punishment, for example, he favored "castration" and not imprisonment, as the "socially most utilitarian method," since "it did not diminish the criminal's labor power," but prevented murderous instincts from being inherited in the future.[92]

In contrast to Solvay, who did not admit that energy could exist independent of its milieu, Ostwald wanted to extend the concept of energy to all events in the universe. Alfred Fouillée, the French idealist philosopher, observed that Ostwald exemplified the kind of mind that "wanted to find in the notion of energy a sufficiently general principle to encompass all of the phenomena of nature in one, to serve as a systematic basis for an interpretation of the world."[93] For Fouilée, whose own philosophy was strictly opposed to energeticism, there was a legitimate scientific energetics which explained the different manifestations of force, light, electricity, and mechanical motion as variants of a single "energy," and there were those, like Ostwald and Solvay, who sought to create a "kind of metaphysical system" from these legitimate ideas.[94]

Sparing none of his ample wit and irony, Max Weber, in 1909, devoted a long review to Ostwald's *Energetische Kulturtheorien*. Weber pointed to the many affinities between Ostwald and Solvay, especially their propensity to "spillover" (*Umstülpinq*) of a scientific "world picture" into a "worldview." Weber denounced the "intemperate arrogance" of scientists who arbitrarily extended the categories of the natural sciences to the social and cultural world. Such endeavors, he said, only demonstrated what results in the "rape of sociology by purely scientifically educated technocrats."[95] Moreover, the intellectual content of Solvay's productivism was "petty bourgeois" and "epigonal" when compared to its intellectual heritage, which includes the classical French utopians Proudhon, Comte, and Quetelet.[96] Ostwald fared somewhat better than Solvay, insofar as Weber seized on his discussion of the discordance between the conquest of new forms of energy and the dogged persistence of older forms of property relations as a theme that might have led in an interesting direction, had Ostwald developed its implications, which he did not. Weber defended his own lengthy (and amusing) but overwhelmingly negative discussion of such a "wretchedly poor" book on the grounds that one often "learns more from the mistakes of an otherwise important scholar than from the correct ones of an unknown scholar."[97] Although Weber didn't hide his contempt for both Solvay and Ostwald's excursions into social thought, he recognized that the tendency to normatively apply natural scientific theories to social questions was not limited to the energeticists. In another review of the works of the liberal economist Lujo Brentano, Weber discussed at some length the impact of Gustav Fechner's "psychophysical" theory on the marginal utility school of economics.[98] Unfortunately, Weber did not touch on the more interesting side of what he called Ostwald's "error" (going far beyond his academic competence), the social impact of the doctrine.[99]

Max Weber considered Solvay to be far less in possession of "good sense" than Ostwald, although he admitted that his energeticism actually resulted in a far more coherent social program and a more effective orientation toward the economic and social issues of the day. In fact, Ostwald was far less

effectual, propagating his energy doctrine as an amorphous cultural concept. His main antagonists were unspecified "scientific materialists" who, according to Ostwald, insisted on separating matter from its sources in the
forms of energy. Instead, he generally proposed that all the properties of
matter be regarded as different forms of energy: mass as the capacity for
kinetic energy; space, volume energy; weight, positional energy (*Lagenener-
gie*); and so on.[100] Matter was nothing but the spatial reordering of the different forms of energy which, as another unsympathetic critic remarked, "could
be extended *ad absurdum*, which is no service to science."[101]

The true German analogue to Solvay in the practical realm was not Ostwald but Max Rubner, whose discoveries led to the confirmation of the law
of conservation of energy in physiology and to a remarkable transformation
of the science of human nutrition in the last years of the century. Rubner
was a student of Carl Voit, who pioneered the chemical approach to nutrition
in Germany in the 1860s and 1870s. Dissatisfied with Voit's approach, Rubner attempted to determine the precise energy values of nutritive substances, and in several studies attempted to prove that his method of calculating
animal nutrition was more accurate than Voit's. His law of isodynamics calculated the quantity of fats, proteins, or starch recruited to produce a given
amount of energy.[102]

In Rubner's view, the liberation of the natural sciences, especially biology, from the illusions of "hypermechanical" vitalism offered modern
thought the chance to find its way back to an unromanticized nature. The
discoveries of nineteenth-century physics and physiology—by Johannes
Müller, Justus Liebig, Helmholtz, Bernard, and Du Bois Reymond—
demonstrated that it was a profound error to see "physical processes of the
organism in opposition to the laws of inorganic nature."[103] With Helmholtz
and Mayer, the unassailability of the unity of "force and matter" (*Kraft und
Stoff*) was firmly established. Yet it was not until 1889 that Rubner, in a classic experiment, proved that the law of energy conservation is valid for
biology "according to all the demands of precision."[104] The importance of
Rubner's experiment was not to establish any new principle of energy conversion, but to demonstrate, by the use of a more sophisticated respiratory
calorimeter, the exact equivalent between the nourishment ingested and the
amount of heat or energy produced by a living animal.[105] In short, Rubner
was able to offer proof of the theory of energy conversion in the physiology

of nutrition. Several years later, similar calorimetric experiments conducted on human beings by the American Wilbur Olin Atwater, who had worked with Voit and Rubner in Munich, led to a similar confirmation of the calorie as a unit of measure.

Rubner's work on nutrition, which he pursued first in Marburg and later in Berlin, was far more extensive than Voit's. In addition to elaborating the nutrients in the foods, it also considered the effects of age, clothing, climate, air, and temperature on calorie exchange. Rubner was also interested in the cultural consequences of diet, and the relationship between diet and longevity.[106] In his *Laws of the Use of Energy in Nutrition* (*Gesetze des Energieverbrauches bei der Ernahrung*, 1902), Rubner treated nutrition as an example of energy conservation in everyday life. Energy and matter, for Rubner, were far more than the "slogans of a materialist philosophy," they were the basis for an experimental science of social hygiene that encompassed not only nutrition but also all aspects of social life: "My goal," he noted, "will be achieved, insofar as I can use the methodological research on the problem of nutrition as a means, but not remain constrained by the narrow framework of individual nutrition. We must attempt to understand the living being in all its aspects."[107]

The Kaiser Wilhelm Institute for Labor Physiology

To achieve his goal of extending his nutritional theory of energy equivalents to other domains, Rubner proposed that the prestigious Kaiser Wilhelm Society, which sponsored most officially sanctioned research in Imperial Germany, establish a special Kaiser Wilhelm Institute for Labor Physiology in Berlin under the leadership of Rubner. The draft proposal (*Denkschrift*), which he submitted in May 1912, outlined the goals of the new institute. His rationale was to make practicable the discoveries of the physiology of energy for the productive power of the German industry and military, by concentrating exclusively on the labor power of the individual worker. Its task would be to fulfill "the universally acknowledged need for detailed knowledge of occupational and industrial hygiene."[108]

Unlike Solvay's sociological institute, which considered the worker's milieu as well as the psychological and physiological aspects of work, Rubner conceived of his institute in terms of the productivity that could be gained from concentrating on the corporeal being of the individual worker. However, he extended the concept of work to include other aspects of performance which could he investigated from a physiological standpoint:

> Under the concept of work performance [*Arbeitsleistung*] we usually mean the performance of the human being as a work machine [*Arbeitsmaschine*]. Our cultural development has, however, relegated this form of human activity increasingly to the background. It has discovered alternative forms of work, whose realization depends more on the intellect than it does on mechanical energy in those thousands of kinds of work—the supervision of machines, the concentration on detail work brought on by the division of labor—for which attention, skill, conscientiousness, and duration of performance is most decisive.[109]

The new institute, which was founded in April 1913, was to concentrate on the "broader dimensions of human performance," on different "life tasks" among different age groups and sexes, and among individuals of different "constitution and race." In an advanced industrial society, "work" could be conceived in terms of the transition from the almost exclusive use of muscular energy to "the nervous regions and the performance of the brain, e.g., the sensual activity, the perceptual faculty and the education of the will."[110] Its research program included the nature and conditions of work in each industry, the work environment, and the diet and personal hygiene of the workers themselves. In each of these areas Rubner maintained, the elimination or prevention of dangers to health would improve performance. Above all, Rubner claimed, "the capacity to work of the human being is dependent on the standard of nutrition." For this reason, the institute was to place primary emphasis on Rubner's most coveted social ideal, "rational nutrition," since "the incongruity between work and nutrition is the most important cause of corporal decline."[111]

Conclusion

Solvay's Institute for Sociology, and Rubner's Institute for Labor Physiology marked the beginning of the institutionalization of the doctrine of energy in quasi-academic settings, and the development of extensive pro-grams for the laboratory study of "work" in the energetic sense. However, these early efforts to produce a sustained link between the science of work and state social policy did not exhaust the political and social implications of energeticism. The emerging science of work played an important role in the political debates on the length of the working day, the requirements of military training and physical education, and most importantly, as I will show in chapter 3, in the lengthy controversies over social insurance and industrial accidents.

The attraction of energeticism for nineteenth-century social reformers derived from its claim to universalism, neutrality, and objectivity, all of which derived in turn from its pedigree in physics and physiology. But en-ergeticism also derived—as Solvay and Ostwald, the first systematic protag-onists of the social doctrine of energeticism constantly reiterated—from the enormous productivity they anticipated would arise from a society reor-ganized in concord with the laws of nature. Rubner's ideas on the utility of nutritional knowledge for the expansion of labor power, embodied in his pro-gram for the new institute exemplified this confidence in the social benefits of scientific discoveries. But the most utopian hope of social energeticism derived from yet another dimension of energetics: its presupposition of an infinitely transparent and malleable world. As Félix Le Dantec, a well-known French popularizer of scientific ideas, noted in 1907: "If the principle of the conservation of energy is truly general, then man knows or can know, directly or indirectly, all of the transformations, all of the changes in the world in which energy is involved. We know how to measure the variations of energy in chemical bodies, in Colloids, in warm bodies or electric bod-ies, in mechanical systems. Therefore, because of a transformation in any one of its domains, the quantity of energy expended can be integrally re-trieved in another domain known to man. A certain quantity of energy never disappears into an unknown form beyond the limits of the world which we know."[112]

THREE

Social Knowledge and the Politics of Industrial Accidents

The origin of modern Western European welfare states is closely linked to two novel ideas that gained enormous prestige during the last two decades of the nineteenth century: The idea that an expansion of the concept of rights to include the obligations of society toward the individual reduces or minimizes risk and inequality, and the idea that social responsibility can be grounded scientifically and demonstrated by statistical laws. If risks and responsibility were both social in nature, then certain legal conceptions that still defined risk and responsibility in terms of contracts, negligence, and individual liability were obsolete. In practice, this meant that the task of the state was to regulate and enhance social bonds with the aid of an ever-expanding arsenal of laws based on information gained through statistical surveys and empirical investigations. The appearance of public and private institutions entrusted with accumulating and disseminating potentially useful social knowledge was the direct outgrowth of these new ideas, as were new professions (such as social medicine and social hygiene) and new specializations (such as labor law and insurance law) that emerged in tandem with social reform legislation in the earliest phase of European state social policy.

Toward a History of Social Knowledge

The 1880s and 1890s generated a complex relationship between new forms of sociological, legal, and medical knowledge and the political requirements of states. Yet, it is important to recognize that the state was not a single monolithic institution but a broad spectrum of agencies that fulfilled different and often contradictory requirements: a guarantor of social control, regulator of markets, and protector of rights. It would thus be a simplification to see social knowledge as either simply fulfilling the imperatives of states for instrumental purposes, or as the primary engine of the reforms themselves. Knowledge did not merely serve to justify the implementation of reform; the politics of reform also accelerated the demand for and production of knowledge. The complex dynamic of knowledge and politics in this period requires attention to both the internal development of the types of knowledge involved and the political imperatives of reform legislation.[1]

Much of the early reform legislation on the continent was the product of an unstable coalition of conservative traditionalists, liberal reformers, and moderate socialists. To consider the first state social policies as the product of a homogenous ideology or class strategy is to disregard the complex mixture of motives behind their initial inception. For example, in the case of the famous German law of 1884 which established a system of state accident and health insurance, the financial requirements of large and small industry and local governments, the political motives of the dominant political elites, and even the increasing claims of workers all contributed to the passage of the new law. It is certainly true, as Hans-Ulrich Wehler argued, that the reform policy was viewed by the iron chancellor as an effort to apply the Bonapartist methods he had observed in France to the "taming" of the workers' movement—in tandem with the antisocialist laws.[2] But other, equally important motives played a considerable role in both its conceptualization and implementation. As Florian Tennstedt points out, at the outset, the short-term electoral gains that Bismarck hoped the reform proposals might achieve far outweighed the long-term strategic goal of defusing the working-class movement.[3] Immediate pressures on provincial and local governments faced with burgeoning responsibilities for the sick and aged (returning from industrial centers), as well as fears of industrialists overburdened by increasing legal claims, also played a role in the formation of a national policy.[4]

Finally, a combination of enlightened idealism and domestic realpolitik among the political elite also must be acknowledged. The Verein für Sozialpolitik played a central role in "transforming the public view of social and economic problems" and in making socially interventionist liberalism respectable in Germany.[5] As Bismarck's liberal minister of commerce, Heinrich Friedrich von Itzenplitz, noted more than a decade before the passing of the 1884 reform:

> Interference of the existing state with the socialist movement is by no means to be equated with the triumph of socialist doctrine. Rather, from my point of view, the action of state power as it exists today appears to be the only means of halting the socialist movement in its path of error; to steer it in a more beneficial direction it is necessary to acknowledge that which is justified in the socialist demands and can be realized in the framework of the state and social order.[6]

From these broad motivating factors and intellectual premises arose an expanding role of knowledge and the availability of a new set of scientific arguments on behalf of reform policies. After 1890, European liberals, rejecting traditional laissez-faire economics and impatient with the enmity of labor and capital, frequently had recourse to a positivist calculus: that society is governed first and foremost by social laws, and that social ethics consist in fitting human behavior more closely to those generalizable laws.[7] Such reformers saw their own sophisticated methods and arguments as evidence of a higher and more scientific stage of social reflection, that of sociologized man. In France, liberal intellectuals, including the influential economists Charles Gide, Charles Rist, Paul Cauwès, and Raoul Jay, grouped around the *Revue d'économie politique*, founded in 1886, developed a set of arguments based on the interdependence of productivity, consumption, and social justice as a rationale for reform. Similarly, the Durkheimian Célestin Bouglé argued for a solidarist view of society premised on advances in social knowledge.[8] Like Max and Alfred Weber, and the other German reformers of the Verein für Sozialpolitik in the same period, these French academic intellectuals believed that the cause of reform could best be served by the results of empirical social science. In 1904, Jay summed up their arguments in this way:

> A nation that permits the destruction or reduction of the mental or physical forces of the manual workers makes one of the worst calculations. Those physical and moral forces are a part of the national capital like the sun or machines. The industrialist who, in order to reduce the costs of production, permits his machines to deteriorate . . . would be considered a fool. . . . If we do not think the same of an industrialist who imposes excessive labor on his workers or pays them an insufficient wage, that is because we know that he will never have to repair the damage caused by his criminal negligence. The damage is charged to the nation.[9]

Jay's eloquent statement, in a treatise devoted to promoting the legal protections of the working class, underscored the elective affinity that emerged by 1900 among social hygiene, economics, and reform: the labor of the worker was the "capital of the nation" that should not be misused or wastefully consumed.

Another crucial aspect of the impact of knowledge on the new reform legislation has been emphasized by François Ewald in his massive study of the debate on the accident law in France.[10] Ewald argues that the debates and legal precepts surrounding the reform legislation introduced an entirely new kind of legal framework that redefined "risk" as the central social problem and made the maintenance of an acceptable level of personal and social risk the basis of social solidarity, giving rise to what he calls the actuarial or "providential state." The notion of a "society" is thus constructed out of a myriad of efforts at the administrative and personal levels to remove, predict, and repair the damages of dysfunction. Public debate is thus confined to the calculation of the limits of acceptable risk. Devoted to the perpetuation of social solidarity, regularity, and normality, a main purpose of the state is to regulate juridically risk—a task that also requires the production and consumption of vast amounts of social knowledge.

By investigating the problem of industrial accident reform in a comparative framework, it can be shown that new conceptions of risk, responsibility, and liability did in fact emerge from the new legislation of the 1880s and 1890s. Although this survey concentrates on developments in Germany and France, its emphasis is less on the differences between conceptions of insurance (public versus private), or the class coalitions that brought reform into being, and more on how in both countries the establishment of a new legal norm or ideals of "social risk" led to a displacement of conflict over accidents from the direct relations of employer and employee to the sphere of jurisprudence and, ultimately, to conflicts among statistical and medical experts. This chapter is an analysis of how industrial work became subject to a wide range of social knowledge because of reform, but also how political and social conflict could not be divorced from the conflicting claims of knowledge, which increasingly became a field of social contestation.

Industrial Death and Dismemberment

In the last quarter of the nineteenth century, industrial accidents were increasingly viewed as a problem of crisis proportions, a perception confirmed by the shocking statistics gathered to demonstrate the phenomenal rise in workplace tragedies.[11] Between 1885 and 1908, Germany had over two million industrial accidents, and in France, industrial deaths (not including mining or metallurgy) rose from 1,562 in 1900 to 2,138 in 1905.[12] Between 1865 and 1890, 1,928 miners were killed, and 2,645 injured in over 128 accidents.[13]

As reformers sought a reversal of government policies, which almost universally placed the burden of proof of negligence on the worker, proposals for a massive restructuring of the accident compensation laws were widely debated in both France and Germany. Workers' organizations also paid greater attention to the accident issue, encouraging victims to press claims, creating private funds and associations for mutual assistance, and sometimes even forcing plant owners into expensive litigation.

For a worker, a serious accident often meant the end of the capacity to earn a living, dependence on family or charity, and in some cases, loneliness and isolation from the social milieu.[14] Yet, at the same time, the *dramatis personae* of the industrial accident expanded to include attorneys, judges, lawmakers, government officials, medical experts, and the insurance specialists. New professions emerged in the accident crisis: the accident claims adjustor, the expert physician attached to the firm, and the technical safety expert. The perception of the industrial accident as an urgent matter of public social policy, and the need for relatively precise information about accidents, their causes, frequency, and social or occupational distribution, were inextricably linked. The accident and the knowledge of the accident, while distinct for the victim, became fused in the positivist *mentalité* of the second half of the nineteenth century and influenced the acts of legislators, doctors, judges, and politicians. Situated at the intersection of working-class politics, the law, and the new profession of social medicine or hygiene, the industrial accident became the crucible of a changing relationship between knowledge and political power.

Rather than focus on the social consequences of the accident for the individual worker, or even for a specific trade or locality, this chapter is concerned with the way that accidents altered knowledge or, more precisely, restructured knowledge along different social and political axes. The industrial accident is significant, not only because of its impact on the victims, but also because it was the crucial point at which social and political forces first confronted each other to determine responsibility for the personal costs of industrialization. The concept of occupational risk, or *risque professionnel*, provided for an entirely new set of rights and obligations in the workplace. With the first efforts to exert public control over the alarming accident rate, relations among labor, capital, the state, law, medicine, and scientific knowledge entered a new constellation. Basic to this constellation were three simple questions that proved remarkably difficult to answer: What is an accident? What is its cause? Who is ultimately responsible? Protracted political, legal, and medical struggles over these questions defined a quarter century of efforts to come to terms with the accident issue.

In Europe, the industrial accident became the example par excellence for the idea that by acquiring special juridical rights labor could compensate for its more substantive inequality in the workplace. For the first time, the accident issue raised the question, to what extent do the risks of industrial life transcend the private interests of capital, as well as the formal requirements of law, and permit the state to intervene, not only to determine the conditions of work (hours, ages, sanitation) but also to guarantee safety or security? Until the mid-nineteenth century, European jurisprudence held that the firm's liability for an accident had to be proven by the victim or his (or her) family, which was financially prohibitive, even if it could be established. Like other forms of equality in the marketplace, however, the free labor contract secured legal equality while increasing the laborer's weaker economic and social position. If liability was permanently shifted to the firm or owner, as many reformers demanded after 1880, did this not, liberal jurists protested, eliminate all possible guilt or negligence on the part of the worker and destroy the free labor contract? Firm owners protested that capital should not be made to bear the full or even partial financial burden for what were simply the risks of modern life.[15] Indeed, if negligence was abolished and employer guilt presumed, would not the liberal ideal of equality before the law, or individualism itself, suffer irreparable damage?

Socialists, on the other hand, saw in these reform proposals a cynical attempt to undermine their own position: did not the willingness of state and industry to compensate the dead and the maimed demonstrate only callousness toward the living labor they so ruthlessly exploited?[16] Industrial accidents simply exemplified the normal relations between labor and capital, and the terrible mining disaster at Montceau-les-Mines in 1894 served as an example of how "owner's responsibility" was really a "capitalist crime."[17]

Apart from these broad divisions produced by class perspective, a controversy emerged over the claim that it was the industrial scourge that was responsible for the rise in accidents. Why, for example, if risk was social, should the law only apply to industry and not to agriculture? Did the rise in statistics reflect an increase in real dangers or in more accurate reporting, or, as medical specialists claimed, was the law itself the cause of an epidemic of worker fraud or "simulation"? These conflicts, perhaps even more than those based on divergent class position, brought the expertise of public and private insurance companies, legal theorists, legislators, doctors, and scientists to a sphere previously regarded as the private terrain of conflict between employer and employee. By opening the factory to the scrutiny of these competing discourses, the workplace became the scene of empirical investigation, legal theorizing, statistical review, juridical decision, and medical supervision. The legal hermeneutics, medical quandaries, and statistical conundrums arising over the nature of the industrial accident created a situation in which scientists and doctors concerned with the deleterious effects of industrial work could exercise a hitherto unthinkable influence.

One particularly important consequence of these debates is the importance which the study of worker fatigue assumed in the attempt to demonstrate the social character of industrial accidents. Scientists and physiologists concerned with the industrial laborer began to focus on the distribution of accidents according to the workday and workweek. Although the science of fatigue had already become a significant academic enterprise by the 1890s, by 1900 it underwent a political transformation in relation to the debate on industrial accidents.[18] Emerging from the confines of the laboratory, knowledge could prove that an accident was neither a willful act on the part of the worker nor the result of a malevolent entrepreneur, but a statistical fact linked to the body's relationship to the work process. The industrial accident was the product of fatigue, a physiological response to the acceleration of the work tempo and the length of the working day. It followed that the state—armed with the irrefutable truths of science and perched above rival interests—could ensure surveillance of the workplace, reduce accidents, and resolve some of the pressing dilemmas of industrial work and labor conflict.

Before the Law

Until the Europe-wide insurance legislation of the 1880s and 1890s (Germany, 1884; Austria-Hungary, 1887; Sweden, 1891; Norway, 1894; Denmark, 1898; France, 1898; Belgium, 1903; Italy, 1905; and Switzerland, 1906), the burden of financial assistance to ill or disabled workers fell largely to the private aid societies (*freie Hilfskassen* or *sociétés de secours mutuels*) formed largely after 1848 as workers' self-help organizations.[19] Throughout Europe, workers' accident protection was a confused and overlapping network of weak local, national, and craft organizations, almost all of which were inadequate to the task of providing more than minimal assistance in few and extremely needy cases.

The German Reichshaftpflichtgesetz (Imperial Employer's Liability Act) of June 7, 1871, established the conditions for compensation of accidental death or injury directly caused by a deputy or representative of the firm during the course of his duties.[20] In the French and Belgian Napoleonic Code, as well as under German commercial law, employer liability could only be claimed in cases where negligence was proven by the worker, usually only after long and costly litigation.[21] In cases where employers were inadequately insured or failed to maintain premiums, or simply when owners or insurance companies refused to pay, a worker's claims became a dead letter.[22] Accident cases were the source of enormous resentment by workers deprived of compensation, while industrialists complained of heavy expenses incurred under the voluntary private insurance system.

The first broadly comprehensive system of obligatory "public-legal" accident, sickness, disability, and old-age insurance was introduced by Bismarck in the German Reichstag in March 1881 and adopted in July 1884.[23] The German system was entirely state administered by the Reichsversicherungsamt (Imperial Insurance Office), a newly created body composed not only of civil servants, but also of parliamentary (Bundesrat) deputies, employer's organizations, and worker's representatives.[24] The state assumed two-thirds of the cost, the employers one-third through the employer corporations (*Berufsgenossenschaften*).[25] At the outset, the accident insurance covered only the most dangerous occupations, including mining, quarrying, and, of course, hazardous industries such as iron and steel. All German workers in industrial jobs were eventually insured and compensated to a maximum of two-thirds of their income in case of total disability and loss of earning capacity. Subsequent revisions extended the law to agriculture, maritime, and transport.[26]

In December 1887, Austria followed suit with a similar compulsory accident insurance on the German model. Other European countries proved far more reluctant to base their systems on the German compulsory model. An interesting case is Switzerland, which approved a compulsory system after lengthy parliamentary debate, but submitted it to a popular referendum in May 1900, where it was overwhelmingly rejected. Opponents of the law campaigned to identify accident insurance with German authoritarianism, and even distributed thousands of silk neckties with the inscription: "vote no on May 20."[27] The Swiss referendum became a symbol for the lack of popular support for the German system and its paternalist and authoritarian connotations.[28] By the beginning of the twentieth century, only Austria, Hungary, Norway, and Luxembourg had followed the German lead and adopted state-administered compulsory worker's insurance.[29] France adopted a private insurance system on April 9, 1898, Belgium in 1903, and Italy in 1905.[30] Great Britain made private compulsory insurance part of the

1897 Workman's Compensation Act, which was expanded in 1906 and 1909.[31] The United States lagged far behind European developments; most states passed workmen's compensation acts between 1911 and 1948, but the power of free trade and the free labor contract inhibited any strict liability doctrine.[32]

Despite the limited success of state-sponsored insurance, the emergence of a Europe-wide system of accident compensation law amounted to a fundamental redistribution of social risk and responsibility. To a far greater extent than any prior labor legislation including the British factory acts of the 1840s, the legal basis of the relationship between labor and capital was transformed by insurance law. In this respect, the German law was pathbreaking in its articulation of the principle that industrial accidents are caused less by the design of the plant, or by the particular owner, than by the special conditions of industrial work.[33] Though some German industrialists pressed for a radical diminution of pension in cases of gross negligence, even this modification failed on the grounds that it reintroduced employee responsibility through the back door.[34] Worker negligence was limited only to illegal and purposeful actions covered by the criminal code, while management negligence—to the dismay of the worker's organizations—was entirely nullified.

By removing the entire question of negligence from the insurance law, German jurisprudence admitted the fundamental inequity of the free labor contract. The accident insurance legislation of the 1880s and 1890s was a tacit admission, as many contemporaries recognized, that the free labor contract could only be maintained by recognizing the fundamental inequality of the two parties involved. The principle that the state or society should guarantee protection to the weaker party against the vicissitudes of industrial labor was a frontal assault on the free labor contract as a normative and regulative principle.[35] The wage was no longer sufficient recompense to warrant the risk of death or injury. Accident laws were based on "an actuarial conception of social risk," in which the causes of the accident are attributed to the greater chance involved in the social nature of the work, based on the law of statistical averages, as opposed to personal fault.[36] The risks of industrial labor were thus compensated by what Jacques Donzelot has called the "juridical requalification" of the worker.[37] The substantive consideration of industrial risk overshadowed the formal principle of the equal relations of both parties and was ultimately justified by the idea of "the state as the guardian of the moral order."[38]

The Modernity of Risk

The German law profoundly influenced other European reforms by altering the balance of risk and responsibility. Ironically, the shift to employer responsibility was justified by the assertion that the nature of modern industry and not personal negligence exposed workers to greater risk, a claim that would not be sustained by accident statistics. Although initially applauded by French reformers who pointed to its extraordinary breadth (including sickness insurance), liberal opponents of the German law characterized it as a Prussian invention designed to impose the power of the state over civil society. The proposal introduced in the French Chamber of Deputies in 1882 was supported by an unstable coalition of government officials, journalists, doctors, a small group of industrialists, conservatives, radicals, and a few Socialists. Although the Chamber of Deputies was more favorably disposed to the accident law than the conservative senate (which was dominated by the traditional propertied groups), liberal opposition to state intervention in both houses obstructed its passage for more than a decade and a half.[39] In France, as Sanford Elliott and Judith Stone have shown, the dedication of reformers to securing the social peace was resisted by the alliance of small producers and large industrialists, and by the strong republican tradition of property rights as opposed to state intervention.[40] As a radical departure from *liberté de travail*, the accident law was consistently opposed by those who warned, as did the noted entrepreneur and reformer, Émile Cheysson, that a breach of common law in favor of the workers might open the floodgates of socialism. Supporters of the law emphasized that the employer "owed the worker a guarantee of this right to subsist from the day on which an accident lowers his capacity to work."[41] But it was only after employers were won over by a narrow restriction of the law to large industry, by the promise of lower expenses, and by the guarantee of private insurance, that it finally passed on the eve of the April 1898 election.[42]

The French law removed the demand for proof of "the fault, the negligence or the imprudence of his *patron* or his representatives," and shifted responsibility to the owner of the firm, while eliminating all personal fault in determining compensation.[43] As stated in the original proposal: "When a man rents his labor to another man, and is injured in the course of performing his duty, the employer is responsible (*en plein droit*) except if he proves that the accident was the result of a fault committed by the victim."[44] Clearly reformers intended that the law take into account changes in "social evolution," and that solidarity replace individual responsibility in the industrial sphere. According to the monarchist Albert de Mun, "Bosses [*patrons*] and workers are considered as individuals with no relations in common, . . . as if the work contract was not a special kind of contract, whose conditions are necessarily subordinated to certain considerations of the social order, to certain duties, to certain reciprocal obligations."[45]

According to the doctrine of *risque professionnel*, which was introduced by Felix Faure on February 11, 1882, the owner (*patron*) was declared responsible in all cases where the industry or the dangers of the industrial setting constituted a special hazard insofar as "work is responsible for the accidents that it causes."[46] Cheysson provided the most precise definition of *risque professionnel* as "the risk assignable to an occupation which is ascertained independent of the fault of the workers or patrons."[47] However, since the doctrine of *risque professionnel* held employers responsible while simultaneously arguing for the social assumption of risk, there appeared to be a contradiction between risk and responsibility which, some advocates of the German model maintained, could only by removed by a state system. The first version of the French law was restricted to large industrial establishments where workers were servants of hazardous mechanical engines.[48] "Each invention which augments the productivity and perfectibility of industrial work," noted one commentator, "makes it more complicated to use and control machines, and thus makes the situation for those who utilize them . . . more dangerous."[49] Mechanization constituted a social, as opposed to individual, risk.

Unlike the German law, the French law did not include health insurance, and at the outset of the debate, narrowly restricted the notion of social risk to large-scale industrial production. *Risque professionnel* also implied that a work-related accident was a quasi-public event, insofar as the public well-being is enriched by labor: "The social risk of work must be distinguished from other risks, which are individual in nature," because "the worker who is injured on the field of honor of work merits a more generous insurance than the citizen who is the victim of an accident outside of work or of an illness."[50]

As in the German case, *risque professionnel* was predicated on a statistical conception of fault. In the spirit of Durkheim, the sociological regularity of the accident made its accidental character social. "Insurance," noted Cheysson, "is the compensation for the effects of risk by the organized mutuality according to statistical laws, that is to say, according to the economic laws that govern the course of things."[51] When this supreme conception came into conflict with the precepts of liberalism and freedom of contract, the ideas of free agency and will had to be modified: "Demographic facts, social facts themselves, are subordinate to inflexible rigor of the average. . . . It is that permanence which becomes the basis of insurance and which confers on it the character of scientific truth. If the individual is relieved of danger and its caprices, the masses on the other hand obey the laws of certainty and fall under the grip of calculability."[52] In 1898, *risque professionnel* prevailed and accidents were declared compensable, regardless of the cause, if they resulted from the "industrial life of the victim," except, of course, if they were malevolently induced or self-inflicted. Although the concept of "gross negligence," was ultimately dropped, force majeure (acts of God), and the somewhat ambiguously phrased *faute inexcusable* (unforeseeable causes) were substituted when it became clear, as in the German case, that any consideration of personal negligence reintroduced the possibility of firms holding victims liable for accidents. On the other hand, the doctrine of employer responsibility found only a "faint echo" in the jurisprudence because it inequitably burdened only the heads of firms with a responsibility for which there was no parallel responsibility on the part of the workers.[53] The law noted only that any boss (*chef de enterprise*) was in principle responsible and had to maintain adequate insurance if he entered into a labor contract with the victim of an accident.[54]

Rejecting the German system, France adopted a noncompulsory insurance scheme based on private insurance companies (*assurance libre*), with state financing only in case of the failure of a firm or private insurance company to pay an indemnity. An accident was designated as "all bodily injuries caused by the action of a sudden and external cause," a definition that was modified to include the phrase "inherent in the work" the following year.[55] Occupational ailments, however, were defined as the "slow consequences of fatigue or occupational drunkenness [*insalubrités du métier*]" and were not included. The law was applied to all industry, manufacturing, mining, building, public enterprises, and transportation, but did not include commercial or agricultural occupations.[56] As in Germany, the idea of social risk was considered to be a consequence of industrial modernity, recognizing that impersonal forces rather than individual wills were often the determinants of a person's destiny. With the advent of social insurance law, the positivist credo—which sees social laws as more decisive than individual passions and interests, morality and guilt—was embedded in a political context.

France was relatively slow to adopt a work accidents law because of the result of intense political conflict evoked by such novel principles. French liberals saw the various drafts of the law as threats to the very political conception on which the nation was founded.[57] "Socialism," they complained, "was being substituted for the labor contract by the introduction of *risque professionnel*."[58] The accident law was above all a subversion of freedom of contract, "a germ of destruction in our judiciary system" and a "German vice."[59] The presumption of employer responsibility amounted to "the creation of a new privileged [working] class," and conversely the creation of "a juridically inferior race," the entrepreneur. It was a return to the principle of aristocracy in the name of democracy, the reaffirmation of a special "privilege and exception" for workers in a jurisprudence only recently expunged of such notions.[60] Instead, the liberals proposed the doctrine of *responsabilité contractuelle* (contractual responsibility) based on the moral obligations of the free labor contract (which paralleled the medieval idea of a master's responsibility for his servants) as an alternative to *risque professionnel*. Advocates of *responsabilité contractuelle* agreed that the burden of proof of negligence should be transferred to the *patron*, without, however, the accompanying transfer of a priori fault.[61]

For the French firm owners, unlike the more servile German industrialists of the Second Reich, the new law represented the irrepressible growth of state control over industry in the Third Republic. In 1883, they responded by organizing L'Association des Industriels de France contre les Accidents du Travail (Association of French Industrialists against Work Accidents), devoted to resisting the new legislation. The association called upon entrepreneurs to establish private initiatives such as employee protection plans and plant safety programs, and proposed collectively assuming the premiums for the most dangerous occupations.[62] In the decade before the passage of the law, the French Patronat was remarkably imbued with a vigorous sense of Christian responsibility and a will to preserve its moral prestige, dramatically demonstrating a "note of nostalgia for the social relations of the *ancien régime*."[63]

The question that dominated the stormy debates in the Chamber of Deputies was, why should the risks of mechanization supersede all other "normal" risks? Did this not place modern industry at a disadvantage, legislating a disincentive to progress by penalizing an employer simply for introducing "the most highly developed tools"?[64] Would an employer choose to adopt modern techniques if faced with higher insurance premiums? While a few radicals claimed that the elimination of employer negligence encouraged immorality by giving him a "premium for the assassination of the worker," the most articulate opponents of the law argued that it would slow down economic progress, depriving workers of their means of livelihood.[65] One critic even suggested that the *risque professionnel* borne by the *patron* should be balanced by a *risque vital* borne by the worker, who would be required to provide a certificate of medical good health before entering the factory.[66]

Although far less effective than their French counterparts, a few German liberals, most prominently the economist Lujo Brentano, campaigned against the Bismarck compulsory insurance law.[67] The state, Brentano maintained, should only protect those persons directly in need of protection in order to ensure the sanctity of the free labor contract.[68] A liberal order, he argued, could not tolerate an insurance law which only strengthened the hand of the entrepreneur at the expense of the worker's associations and the *freie Hilfskassen*.[69] The *Kathedersozialisten*, or "socialists of the chair," on the other hand, led by the economist Gustav Schmoller, supported the compulsory insurance program as "a pedagogical instrument" which could educate the working classes in the potential benefits of the state. Schmoller appealed to the "crown and bureaucracy" as the only neutral elements in the social class struggle.[70] Most German industrialists, especially those in steel and iron, supported the chancellor, but a recalcitrant few saw the law as a wild concession to Bismarck's political ambitions and denounced the system as an "irresponsible waste of work, time, and money."[71]

A central issue in both the French doctrine of *risque professionnel* and in the German Insurance Law was the distinction each drew (in the public debates as well as in the compensation provisions of the law) between the modernity of mechanized industry and traditional forms of work that did not involve a social risk. Martin Nadaud, a former worker who became the leading defender of the insurance idea in the French chamber, emphasized that *risque professionnel* did not apply to the manual trades, still covered by the civil code, in which "the danger didn't increase."[72] For its opponents, however, the distinction between the "modern" plant and the old artisanal enterprise was entirely arbitrary and did not correspond to the specific risks involved in any particular form of work. The argument that *risque professionnel* was an imperative of modern industry and its unanticipated dangers was, in their view, historically and statistically false; modern industry with its equipment and organization was far less dangerous than the nonmechanized trades: carpentry, roofing, naval construction, wagon or cab driving, seagoing trades, and, above all, mining. The connection between modernity and risk was subjected to its most scathing critique by Leon Say, the liberal economist and leader of the opposition, when he declared that "the great *risque professionnel* of humanity is that each human being is mortal and might lose his physical or mental faculties."[73]

Were work accidents a consequence of modernity? The statistical evidence largely bears out the contentions of the opponents of *risque professionnel*. In both France and Germany, nonindustrial accidents, especially in shipping and milling, were the most serious, while the "elementary dangers" of mining, quarrying, and maritime work outstripped the hazards of industry. Mechanized industry proved only moderately dangerous, accounting for roughly one-fourth of all accidents.[74] However, the modernity of risk was borne out insofar as accidents involving machinery rose more rapidly than others, though fatalities declined.[75] Overall, accidental death remained relatively stable over the first decade of the German law, while injuries (both temporary and permanent) increased. The debates in Germany and France demonstrate that the notion of social risk prevailed, not because of any "objective" considerations, but because it was consistent with the view that modernity required a new principle of "fault" for social risk to triumph over liberal protestations that freedom of contract was being trampled on. If social risk was not truly a consequence of modernity, then the success of the German law as well as the doctrine of *risque professionnel* attest to the power of a perception of reality that far outweighed all arguments to the contrary.

What Is an Accident?

The French law passed in April 1898 underscored the definition of an accident as a sudden and unanticipated event, as opposed to a long-term illness, disability, or exposure ruinous to health. Most eloquent was Léon Bourgeois, president of the commission empowered to draft the French law, who defined an accident as "a sudden violent event" as opposed to "a sickness, which on the contrary is a continuous and persistent condition, not having a continuous and persistent cause."[76] His language, taken literally, meant that the "doors of the law" would remain forever closed, even to the most deadly of toxic emissions: "If death comes in two hours, *monsieur le ministre*, it is not an illness!," his opponents cried out in the chamber.[77] His supporters, however, ridiculed the idea that a job-related "accident" might occur over a long period of time, by pointing out that if that were true, the rampant alcoholism among waiters might as well be considered an industrial accident, since it occurred as part of normal intercourse with customers.[78] To be sure, the definition of an accident as a time-bound, sudden occurrence was problematic. In France, the moderate Socialists supported the law in the chamber, but faulted *risque professionnel* for its failure—in stark contrast to the German inclusion of sickness insurance—to provide a broader definition of accident which also included the effects of an occupational disease or disability. If special hazards of industrial life were indeed a social responsibility, then social liability could not be limited to accidents alone, but should be naturally extended to all occupational maladies.[79] The socialists thus threatened to open the Pandora's box of coverage for occupational diseases, which the advocates of *risque professionnel* wanted to avoid at all costs. Even in Germany, where the health insurance law paralleled the accident law, the relatively higher pensions paid to victims of accidents encouraged industrial hygienists to extend the notion of "accident" to include occupational diseases of a chronic nature.[80] The German expert Georg von Mayr analyzed the dilemma at the Milan Congress of Industrial Accidents in 1894: "An accident is a social occurrence, which under certain forms appears indubitably as such; but, it also takes other more ambiguous forms, wherein it approaches an occupational illness."[81]

The issue of what constituted an industrial accident was also controversial in Germany where mounting confusion over a decade of contradictory rulings by the Imperial Insurance Office called attention to the vagueness of the 1884 law. Exactly what might be included in a plant accident—what injuries, which external causes, or what time span could elapse between cause and injury—remained unspecified. For example, the German law specifically excluded all "types of plants which do not involve the risk of accident for the persons employed therein."[82] Although the German high court (*oberster Gerichtshof*) ruled that the accident had to be connected to the plant, "not only in time and place, but also causally," it did not set forth whether "only accidents connected to the special dangers of the plant in question are to be considered as plant accidents," or whether those "which simply occur as a consequence of the general danger that threatens all persons" employed in that plant should also be included.[83] Initially, the Imperial Insurance Office interpreted the law in the narrow sense (e.g., that accidents had to be causally connected to the risks associated with a particular kind of work in the plant), but by 1888 it was already shifting toward a broader interpretation that compensated victims of any accident occurring in the plant.[84] German legal experts like the noted jurist Heinrich Rosin challenged the Imperial Office on the grounds that only that aspect of the accident which was literally a social risk (for example, industrially caused) should be covered. Rosin distinguished between an accident "occurring in a plant" (*Unfall beim Betriebe*) and a "plant accident" (*Betriebsunfall*), requiring that a "special danger" (*besondere Gefahr*) exist, "caused by the particular dangers of a plant that go beyond the dangers of normal life."[85] For example, he disputed a Berlin decision on behalf of a woodcutter in a public park who was awarded a pension for a broken leg that occurred while walking from the canteen to the woodcutting area after midday break.[86] In another case, a worker was pensioned for an accident that took place while lounging in a dangerous area of the plant. Rosin contended that "neither the time nor the locality of the accident" alone was "decisive" for the "causal connection" of the accident, and the "special dangers" of the plant were not a direct cause in either case. If his distinction might appear "cold blooded," he added, the intent of the law was not simply to insure plants with a higher risk and exclude others, but rather to insure those workers "whose work exposed them to a special risk of accident."[87] However, for the *Kathedersozialisten*,

Rosin's strict interpretation undermined the very principle of the law, since the elimination of negligence made it necessary for all accidents, without exception, to be covered by the insurance. Fuld states, "The essential difference between accident care which rests on the basis of the [old] Employer Liability Act and one which is based on the [new] insurance principle, is precisely that the former can only take into account accidents which result from the special dangers of the plant, while in the latter case these limitations are removed."[88] These protracted legal and juridical hermeneutics over the meaning of "accident" were an expression of the new political principle which both the German and French law introduced: the double linkage of risk of its social causes, on the one side, and to the modernity of those causes on the other. Despite the differences between state and private insurance, and the lack of health coverage in France, both insurance doctrines shifted the political center of gravity of the issue from one of individual guilt and responsibility to the social character of risk, to time, and then to circumstance. The modernity of risk was embodied in the notion of *risque professionnel* and in the "special danger" of industry as the criteria for compensation in Germany. The debates over what was an accident were directly linked to the juridical interpretation of social risk. However, by invoking the notion of "special danger" (*risque professionnel*), legal theorists also left themselves open to an even wider challenge: if it was the nature of work that produced the risk to be borne by society, as opposed to either the employer or employee, why should liability be restricted only to the most dangerous industries, and not to all industry, to particularly risky occupations, to agriculture, commerce, or transportation? To support their claims, all sides in this legal controversy appealed to the higher law of numbers. If it could be shown that accidents were linked either to specific types of industry or even to the nature and organization of work, then compensation could hardly be restricted to either the most dangerous trades or the modern industrial enterprise.

The Revelatory Power of Numbers

After the first decade of compulsory accident insurance in Germany and the adoption of similar laws elsewhere in Europe, the question of the relationship between mounting claims and allegations of employee fraud became the center of international debate. Did not the astonishing rise in claims which the German law elicited, and which the French law also brought about, demonstrate, as some experts claimed, "the correlation between the institution of that insurance and the increase in the number of accidents," or even prove that insurance itself added to the risks of modern industry?[89] Did the new law encourage the reporting of minor or invented mishaps, and perhaps also provide an incentive to workers to "commit" an accident? Was the physician now placed in the position of judge in deciding the legitimacy of those claims? And finally, could not the assumption of risk by society ultimately destroy society's ability to bear the costs of the swelling army of maimed and disabled veterans of industry?

By 1896, the number of recorded accidents in Germany increased by 60 percent, and compensations tripled between 1886 and 1896. In Austria, claims doubled in half that time.[90] Moreover, accidental death remained relatively stable over the first decade of the German law, while disabilities (both temporary and permanent) skyrocketed. Such figures reinforced the anxiety among insurance experts, politicians, and jurists that the startling rise in less serious accident claims resulted either from growing negligence and carelessness or, more malevolently, from the desire of some workers to escape the duties of work. Critics of the liability system often distinguished between "real accidents" and the growing number of "legal accidents."[91] The statistical deluge appeared to confirm the claim already put forth in the French parliamentary debates, that compulsory accident insurance was "an incentive for the inattention and the negligence of the worker."[92]

French and German experts also disagreed about whether or not a state-administered compulsory insurance scheme on the German model, or the private scheme favored by the French, encouraged greater or fewer accidents. French supporters of the private system pointed out that if the entrepreneur and not the state assumed the greatest burden for the premiums, it would induce him to undertake accident prevention in the interests of reducing costs and claims. In 1891, for example, the French monarchist and critic of the German system, Octave Keller, argued that the frequency of accidents in Germany could in part be attributed to the fact that there were fewer incentives for German entrepreneurs to take precautions against accidents, since the state assumed the greater part of the fiscal responsibility.[93]

However, by 1891, German law explicitly required firms to enact accident prevention measures, and employers could be fined if found negligent by the state insurance system. The German system also seemed to encourage workers to press illegitimate claims since, as one expert noted, "when face to face with his *patron*, a worker might feel some shame in taking advantage of the slightest pretext to claim a pension." But in the German or Austrian systems he is confronted with "that impersonal being, the State, which anyone might exploit without scruple."[94] Von Mayr, however, rejected the conclusion that the rising numbers were a direct result of rampant negligence on the part of the workers. Instead, he pointed out that the stringent system of reporting encouraged the frequent notation of accidents of secondary importance with only temporary disability. Above all, he argued, the real difficulty was dealing with firms that maximized profits by accelerating the rapidity of machine work. Such efforts led workers "to resist as much as possible the length of the work done with a feverish pace and to obtain a normal working day that is as short as possible."[95] During a heated debate in the Chamber of Deputies in 1900, the solidarist economist Raoul Jay noted that if lesser accidents with temporary or partial disabilities increased disproportionately to deaths, the mounting number of smaller claims could be explained only by lax attitudes of the corporations, tribunals, and doctors. If, however, fatalities increased at the same rate as the most serious injuries, then "neither employers were more negligent nor were workers more imprudent." It was the nature of the work that was at fault.[96]

The rising accident statistics were also accompanied by a chorus of voices calling for an increase in state control over industry and for accident prevention schemes including worker education, stricter plant regulations, and the use of preventive equipment. Major international expositions of preventive techniques were held in Berlin (1889), Brussels (1897), Vienna (1900), and Frankfurt (1901), and industrialist associations for the prevention of accidents were founded throughout Europe.[97] By 1903, with the founding of the Deutsche Verein für Versicherungswissenschaft, an organization devoted solely to the study of insurance, specializing in workers' claims, with over six hundred members, we can speak of a "science" of accident insurance.[98] The *Kongress über Unfallschutz und Unfallversicherung* held in Vienna in 1913 was an international gathering of the crème of insurance specialists, among them the thirty-year-old Franz Kafka, whose professional writings had already distinguished him as one of the most promising young Czech experts.[99] Museums of "industrial hygiene" displaying safety devices for workers were set up in Zurich (1883), Vienna (1890), Amsterdam (1900), Munich (1900), and Berlin (1903).[100] The German Imperial Manufacturing Ordinance (*Reichsgewerbeordnung*) of June 1, 1891, stipulated that industrial firms were required to "organize their plants and its equipment *so* that the dangers for the life and health of the worker are eliminated as much as possible," and delinquent employers were subject to fines.[101] The largest German firms ostentatiously complied. The Berlin-based Allgemeine Elektrizitätsgesellschaft (AEG) set up a permanent display of photographs of dismembered limbs, with the skeleton of a severed hand prominently featured.[102]

The effect of these efforts to reduce accidents was, however, largely disappointing and often restricted to the largest firms. Smaller firms proved to be sorely lacking in even "an elementary understanding" of health and safety measures.[103] Some firm owners even refused to inform their workers of the insurance law for fear of rising absenteeism. The debate on the crisis of accident statistics grew with the expanding numbers. The direct conflict between accident victim and employer gave way to parliamentary debate; the new laws led to intensive juridical and jurisprudential duels, and the experience of a decade of rising claims and statistics led to interpretive battles over the numbers and the great controversy over the causes of accidents. Work was no longer the sphere of the simple relations between employer and employee, but the fulcrum of widely divergent moral, legal, and medical perceptions. By 1900, the charge of "fraud or simulation" in claims became the chief focus of the debate on the accidents. Medical experts on insurance fraud read in the accident claim charts the signs of a vast deception perpetrated on unprepared doctors and unsuspecting insurance administrators by the working class. In both Germany and France, elimination of individual risk did not obliterate the problem of fault, but removed it to a different plane, where abuse of the law became a new subject of medical and legal knowledge.

Fraud and Its Discontents

Almost immediately after the French insurance law was enacted, the statistics seemed to replicate the German experience. By 1900, an enormous increase of thirty-six thousand accidents over the previous year, caused public alarm from legislators, industrialists, and physicians against "the epidemic of simulations," the "professionals of industrial accidents," and the fraudulent abuse of the law by those who took advantage of naive medical practitioners not trained in "suspicious medicine" (*la médecine soup-çonneuse*).[104] German industrialists, doctors, and legal experts had already warned their French colleagues to expect an epidemic of accident fraud. Indeed, by 1891, the total costs of administration and claims in Germany had more than tripled. German employers' organizations complained bitterly of their "heavy sacrifices," charging that "workers wanted to cash in on the smallest accidents while drawing out the period of cure."[105] Some medical specialists agreed with their assessment. According to Professor Fritz Stier-Somlo, a leading expert on medical ethics, fraud was rampant in all areas of social insurance, but was most pervasive in cases of industrial accidents. Medical fraud, he said, was already "a mass experience" and "pension addiction" was an epidemic. The problem had taken on such a "terrifying dimension" that in one small section of the city of Darmstadt, for example, a study of the construction industry revealed that 125,000 marks in fraudulent payments had been made in 1905 alone.[106] Some German physicians declared the new "pension-hysteria" to be so bad that it had to be "confronted head-on" by a new collaboration between medicine and the law.[107]

The issue of industrial accident fraud became a point of contention at the intersection of work, medicine, and the law. For the first time, it brought the doctor into an intimate relationship with aspects of the law, which had heretofore been the preserve of criminal cases involving negligence. The medical expert became the acknowledged "court of last resort between the adversarial parties: worker and industrialist, as well as the judge who pronounces his final judgment."[108] French and German medical specialists agreed that clinical observation revealed that workers often fraudulently manufactured or, at the very least, exaggerated their injuries. "Today, there is unanimity among civil doctors," remarked Dr. Hubert Coustan, author of several studies of the problem in military medicine, "who almost all admit to the abuse of idleness and the epidemic character of fraud."[109] Treatises on the simulation of accidental injury proliferated, and doctors were urged to work closely with insurance experts to curb the appetites of the workers.

Ambroise Tardieu's 1879 *Étude médico-légale sur les blessures*—the first full-scale, medical-legal textbook of occupational accidents—also included an extensive discussion of the "false or exaggerated allegations and fraud employed by plaintiffs in their appeals for claims of indemnity."[110] Citing the case of a miller, who sued for sixty thousand francs plus three thousand francs annual pension for "simple contusions of the legs and arms, and an incapacity for work which I evaluated at roughly three months," Tardieu emphasized that he had been struck by how "ridiculously elevated" such claims were. He remarked that he had often been called upon by the courts to give an impartial opinion of the physical damages resulting from an accident. His patients demonstrated many different and interesting types of simulation, such as attributing the effects of old accidents to new and less serious ones, and he warned that such cases tended to "degenerate into a veritable hypochondriachal mania."[111]

Tardieu's pioneering work was only the prototype of what soon became a standard medical discourse: the elaborate taxonomy of fraud, deceit, and exaggeration in industrial accident cases. A comprehensive work on the subject published in France in 1907 contained a bibliography of no less than 2,181 items.[112] Beginning in 1905, international medical congresses were held almost annually to discuss specific issues concerning the simulation of accidents. Most medical experts admitted that "the premeditated simulation of a serious injury" was extremely rare, but cautioned that "in the very large number of cases where there is some fraud by the insured, there is an insignificant accident, imaginary pain, or simply a refusal to work even if completely cured."[113] Alfred Bienfait, a doctor at Liège, conducted an important survey that concluded that "if simulation proper is unusual, the enormous exaggeration of a real mishap is frequent."[114] French workers' argot frequently referred to the voluntary absenteeism gained by the self-inflicted accident as "hitting the road" (*faire le macadam*).[115] Though such cases of workers who inflicted real injuries on themselves to appear as the result of an accident were the least prevalent form of abuse, medical textbooks catalogued self-inflicted or phony injuries to assist doctors in identifying them. "Criminal and fraudulent abuses cannot be revealed except by the special knowledge of the doctor," noted one expert "astonished to see how great is the ingenuity of certain insured individuals in creating new lesions, more or less unknown to medicine."[116]

Henri Secretan, the leading Swiss medical expert on accidents, recounted the story of a young man, who fell from a horse onto the soles of his feet, complaining of pain in his left leg. He became so expert in mimicking the effects of sciatic back injury that he received three months' pension. He walked badly and was once even found lying in the street, after which he claimed he could no longer even visit the doctor and was treated at home. Finally, it was decided to perform an operation on his sciatic nerve. When the operation began, he was overcome by a panic attack, threatened all present, and "galloped from the hospital."[117]

The complaint of nonexistent injuries, nervous ailments, paralysis, or muscular pains after an accident was common. Even more so was the exaggeration of minor injuries.[118] It was rare for workers to continue working after incurring even a minor injury that required a dressing, and the payment of lump sums for permanent minor injuries that were not especially debilitating (such as the loss of a toe or part of a finger) was considered a special incentive for abuse.[119] The effects of old illnesses or injuries were often presented as the product of a recent accident, and doctors were especially warned to examine all hernia cases with special attention to the possibility of old afflictions (*anciennes lesions*).[120] The French law in particular seemed to encourage this kind of abuse precisely because it entirely excluded occupational illness from compensation. Ailing workers, the experts charged, often provoked or simulated an accident in order to achieve their "fair share" for uncompensated illnesses.[121] French Socialists countered such charges, however, by pointing out that the conditions of work often produced slower and less dramatic ailments that could only be denied compensation by the cold-blooded and narrow interpretation of the 1898 law and, more important, that employers often sacrificed safety measures in order to pay insurance premiums.[122]

In his comprehensive report to the International Congress of Social Insurance held in Rome in 1908, Charles Juillard graphically described what he called "the fecundity of the human spirit in imitation."[123] Where the indemnity was equal to or approximated the salary of the victim, the tendency to prolong the period of absence from work was "a constant preoccupation."[124] Juillard concluded that "provocation and simulation have reached the proportions of a plague."[125] French workers were also accused of using the half-day pay they received for convalescence "to satisfy their alcoholic passion, retarding the cure indefinitely."[126] Secretan estimated that twenty of every hundred days paid by insurance companies could have been normal workdays. These figures, he emphasized, only referred to "absolutely abusive idleness" and not to minor injuries for which claims were paid, which would "raise the figure considerably."[127] Some doctors noted false claims as high as 30 or 40 percent and, in a sensational report, a German railway physician, Dr. Moller of Kirschseeon, declared that 90 percent of all claims brought to his attention were fraudulent.[128]

In France the question of medical confidentiality (*le secret medical*) was widely debated in the interest of making doctors more responsible for reporting fraudulent claims to the state authorities.[129] Doctors were encouraged to ignore their sympathies for "some poor devil whose claims were ill founded" and to remain firmly within the law, lest the abuses proliferate.[130] German doctors too were pressed "to combat the epidemic of simulations in all its forms," and "to build a dam against hysteria and simulation."[131] Despite such stern warnings, some physicians saw it as an illusion of the legislators and jurists to believe that medical experts could be the shock troops of the "struggle for the pension."[132]

Physicians, on the other hand, sometimes complained that service on the official employee health boards (*Krankenkassen*) forced them to act not only as therapists but also as "expert medical judges of whether social services should be provided or not."[133] Often, they permitted claims to extend beyond the intent of the law. Because of the lack of health coverage, French doctors were sometimes motivated by the "desire to extend the notion of *risque professionnel* to injuries that are the indirect results of work."[134] Illnesses that result from extreme physical or mental fatigue were sometimes awarded compensation, since for the physician it was "preferable to limit the unemployment of an insured who does not show any objective injury, than to contest the unemployment of a worker whose inflammation absolutely prevents him from working for several weeks."[135]

Greater familiarity with the cases brought up for review led many medical specialists to reverse themselves and admit that the initial perception of fraud was exaggerated, and that the medical profession should not rush to judgment in the denunciation of the accident victim. Dr. Carl Thiem, one of the leading German authorities on illnesses related to accidents, noted in his oft-cited *Handbuch der Unfallerkrankungen* (Handbook of accident-related illnesses,1898) that "as a result of my most recent experiences, I can no longer maintain my earlier view of 10 percent simulation."[136] If exaggerations were common, "real simulations" or "deceit" were "uncommonly rare." He concluded that most diagnoses of fraud later proved mistaken, and with greater experience "the previously assumed percentage of simulated accidents stands in an inverse relationship to scientific knowledge." Often, Thiem added, a case worsened after the original medical report written by the employer corporation physician was made. Even when the victim produced a more favorable report from his or her own private physician, he advised doctors not to dismiss such documents, except for the most egregious cases of doctors who sought to expand their fees and practices by providing such exaggerated reports. He also counseled physicians involved in cases with the Imperial Insurance Office to act as "technical assistants," and for those who wanted to act as judges "to study law and not medicine."[137]

In his speech to the International Congress of Social Insurance in Rome, Juillard distinguished five separate types of abuse including "tolerable or excusable abuse," "inevitable abuse," "avoidable abuse," and "criminal, punishable, and fraudulent abuse."[138] For example, "precautionary abuse" usually meant the prolonged care of an injury during convalescence and could hardly be condemned; the Germans, in fact, called such necessary extensions of compensation during the period following cure, a "beauty pension" (*Schönheitsrente*). "Inevitable abuse," was systemic; it included the faking of an accident where a severe occupational ailment did not warrant compensation.[139] A German doctor even identified "honest simulation" as an abuse created by the insurance system; for example, when an accident victim confronted with a medical expert who "systematically reduces the indemnity to which he is entitled," embellishes his symptoms.[140] In short, earlier predictions of rampant fraud, drawn largely from statistical arguments, were revised on the basis of greater familiarity with the injuries themselves.

Such considerations, however, hardly balanced the bellicosity of physicians, academics, and publicists who continued to warn that the "pestilence of fraud" was "a cancer on the organism of our entire working population" and stood in "a direct and causal relationship" to the accident insurance law.[141] In his widely read polemic, *Unerwünschte Folgen der deutschen Sozialpolitik*, published in 1913, the nationalist economist Ludwig Bernhard claimed that only the British economy profited from the fact that "the [German] working class has in part succumbed to the 'pension addiction' that has crippled its energy and joy in work."[142] The ever-vigilant Coustan warned that the new law was "a clear menace to the laboring Frenchman . . . [who] upon entering the hospital or the bedchamber as a result of an occupational accident, dreams of only one thing—not of departing cured, but of departing with an income."[143]

Class Struggle for the Pension

After 1900, the physician took center stage in the "struggle for the pension," which the burgeoning insurance claims produced. In France, the awarding of a pension depended on medical certification by an expert attached to the firm; in Germany, it depended on the Imperial Insurance Office, which could rarely be challenged by the victim. Especially in France, where there was no parallel health insurance system, the certification of a claim often meant the difference between a pension or none at all. Insurance medicine was a specialization produced by social policy legislation, leading to an almost instant enmity between medical experts and worker's representatives.

In Germany, the Socialists closely monitored the problem of insurance abuse, claiming that the almost exclusive focus on abuse and fraud only diverted attention from the failure of German industrialists to introduce effective accident prevention. The Social Democrats counterpoised worker protection to workers' insurance, emphasizing protective legislation, state surveillance, and safety devices as opposed to compensation.[144] In France, the Confédération Générale du Travail (CGT) emphasized the need for more factory inspectors, a shorter work week, more rest days, and above all safety measures.[145] Victor Griffuelhes, secretary of the CGT, charged that French judges were being "counseled" on their responsibility to find cases in favor of the companies.[146] Socialists insisted that the accident issue was tied to dangerous working conditions, inadequate safety precautions, long hours, fatigue, and the intensification of work, all of which contributed to the burgeoning number of claims.[147]

Even before the 1884 law was adopted, German Social Democrats denounced the notorious passage in the *Denkschrift* (the memorandum drafted by the Bochum industrialist Louis Baare, that was the basis for Bismarck's

Reichstag speech), which referred contemptuously to the hypothetical worker who "intentionally places himself in danger" in order to "live an enviable life as a pensioner," or of the "weary of life" (*lebensmüde*) worker who commits industrial suicide "in order to secure the future existence of his family."[148] Once the German law was passed, the Socialists charged that medical experts assigned to insurance cases through the employer corporations were partisan to the industrialists. Although initial statistics showed the most serious accidents to be declining, the reality, they protested, was that compensation was being systematically reduced. Physicians attached to the employer corporations were awarding only partial disability claims in more severe cases and overburdening accident victims by refusing to acknowledge less serious claims. The Social Democrats accused the professional association of company doctors (Institut der berufsgenossenschaftlichen Vertrauensärzte) of having only one purpose: "to send the worker back to work as soon as possible."[149]

The Socialists were extremely bitter about the overall trend of judgments by the Imperial Insurance Office which, by 1906, reflected a clear "shift to the disadvantage of the victims."[150] "The employer's charges of *exorbitant burdens* and the complaints of certain doctors about *pension mania* have apparently, at least partly served their purpose."[151] German workers' slang included the term *Rentenquetschen* (pension-squeeze) to describe the behavior of company physicians who "declare every small improvement to be a major one to justify a reduction of the pension."[152] Doctors were also reluctant to challenge the opinions of their colleagues and feared that if their own judgments were challenged, "the claims of the injured would expand beyond all bounds."[153]

Accident Neurasthenia

One major area of dispute, however, was not accidents in general, but an ambiguous form of accident claim in which psychological rather than physical effects of the accident prevented workers from returning to the job.[154] Sudden accidents or near-misses that did not result in gross physical injury were those most likely to produce the symptoms of traumatic neurosis because, as Freud later explained, the anxiety that allowed the individual to "work through" the incident was often absent. Victims were haunted by dreams whose purpose was to "master the stimulus [the accident shock] retrospectively by developing the anxiety whose omission was the cause of the traumatic neurosis."[155]

Labeled *Unfallneurasthenie, Unfallhysterie, Rentenneurose,* or *Unfallneurose,* these newly discovered disorders were the subject of enormous controversy in the medical and popular press, a sort of dress rehearsal for the notoriety that they would receive some years later as "war neuroses." With accident insurance, cases of this type swelled, and institutions reported numerous patients suffering from accident-related neurasthenia and hysteria. The Sanitarium der Landesversicherungsanstalt Beelitz, near Potsdam, for example, reported a rise from 18 to 40 percent in the number of patients suffering from worker's neurasthenia in the period from 1897 to 1903.[156] "If Bismarck had foreseen what an inflation of nervous weakness and nervous suffering, including complete mental breakdown, that social legislation would cause," said one doctor acquainted with these cases, "he would have certainly prevented its introduction."[157] The most common manner of handling such complaints was a prescription of the "healing power of work" and to return the "accident-hysteric" to the scene of the mishap as soon as possible.[158] The only way to eliminate this contagion, another prominent doctor argued, was to absolutely refuse any compensation for traumatic neurosis, even if it meant that legitimate cases were deprived of a claim.[159] In fact, as Andreas Killen shows in his detailed study of traumatic neuroses among German switchboard operators, there was no consensus among the experts: one camp emphasized the occupational hazards associated with the telephone operators' work, the other with the weakness or predisposition of the women themselves.[160]

For the moderate German Socialists, grouped around the *Sozialistische Monatshefte,* this attitude was another callous form of medical abuse: "a healthy nervous system soon overcomes a serious mental shock, but an already weak or sick one will show symptoms of illness much sooner, and these are what are classified under the concepts of accident-neurasthenia and hysteria."[161] What the press failed to report, they noted, was how many cases later proved that the doctor had been mistaken and that there was indeed "a serious mental disturbance resulting from the accident."[162] Often cited was the well-publicized case of a miner in Gelsenkirchen, who, after surviving a catastrophic cave-in, complained of severe headache and nervousness and was declared a fraud until he suffered a complete mental breakdown. Echoing the view of the New York psychologist George Beard, who had invented the term, the Socialists claimed that neurasthenia was the disorder of civilization, or "American Nervousness," as Beard called it. They argued that the "increase in complaints of simulation was closely related to the growth of nervous disorders, which unfortunately have found a wide basis among the working population." "This rise of nervous suffering is not a direct consequence of social legislation," as critics of the law had argued, "but an indirect consequence of the enormous economic development which Germany has undergone in the last century."[163] In 1897, the Imperial Insurance Office confirmed their arguments: the diagnosis of "traumatic neurosis" explains "a large number of apparent contradictions, that is, phenomenological combinations that contradict our logical, scientific preconceptions and experiences, but of which we know one thing, that they are not consciously simulated."[164]

Accidents and the Triumph of Fatigue

The new role of social knowledge in the politics of the workplace provided a unique opportunity for a relatively unknown community of European physiologists and hygienists, who, since the early 1890s, had been assiduously investigating the phenomena of fatigue, energy, and efficiency in industrial work. Entropy seemed to offer irrefutable proof that society could never fully control the laws of energy and exhaustion. Until the early 1900s, advocates of the newly emerging European "science of work" (*Arbeitswissenschaft* or *science du travail*) had been confined to laboratory investigations of the impact of modern industrial tasks on worker's physiology and psychology.[165] Although new methods of measuring fatigue, most notably Angelo Mosso's *ergograph* (1884), could provide reliable data on the course of individual fatigue, few practical uses could be found for these new discoveries. The controversy over industrial accidents provided its advocates with new evidence and a new issue to demonstrate their shared conviction that fatigue was not only a scourge for the worker but also for the expenditure of energy in the nation. If fatigue could account for industrial accidents, their social character could be demonstrated.

Moreover, the science of work was becoming an international movement, assisted by the growing number of international organizations concerned with the accidents issue: The International Congress of Hygiene and Demography, the International Congress of Industrial Accidents, and the International Congresses of Social Insurance. These organizations did not merely facilitate exchanges of information, but afforded the social hygienists and physiologists advocating a scientific solution to the worker question a forum to demonstrate their approach to the accidents issue. In both Germany and France, record-keeping of the time, day, and nature of the occurrence made careful study of accidents possible for the first time. Analysis of the distribution of accidents during the day and the week would, the industrial hygienists speculated, reveal a correlation between fatigue and the cause of most accidents: "The number of accidents would increase as the workers became more tired, and the distribution of those accidents according to the hours of the day in which they occur would furnish a means to evaluate the degree of fatigue of the workers who are victims."[166] If proven, this hypothesis would finally lay to rest the charges of deception and chicanery while irrefutably demonstrating the social character of the accident as a consequence of the nature of the modern work experience. Such evidence would establish the necessity for state intervention in the workplace, for more progressive legislation, and above all for a reduction of the length of the working day.

Armand Imbert, a Montpellier physician and reformer who attempted to demonstrate the utility of scientific expertise for solving the "worker question," denied that it was either worker's simulation and greed, or negligence and callousness by management that accounted for the majority of incidents. The complaints of rising worker abuses by the insurance companies, of excessive premiums by the bosses, of duplicity by medical experts, and of the rejection of their judgments by the workers was not, he argued, "an inevitable consequence of the conflict of opposed interests."[167] It was a "profound error," he claimed, "to regard the workers and the insurance companies as natural enemies."[168] Imbert disputed the claims of the medical experts and insurance companies with the same statistics they cited to perpetrate the great fear of simulation and fraud. Exaggerated claims could also be attributed to the relationship between the indemnity and the availability of work, he noted: where there was little work, for example, among longshoremen, a half-day compensation might even amount to the equivalent of double the normal wage.[169] "A great number of accidents result directly from a state of physical or cerebral fatigue of the worker at the moment when he is victimized," he claimed, "and it is easy to provide multiple proofs of this assertion, which . . . would result in the possibility of greatly reducing the number of victims."[170]

In his observations of the dockworkers of Sète, Imbert concluded that the private insurance companies were wrong to believe that the disproportionate number of accidents, as opposed to other ports, indicated the likelihood of organized fraud and premeditation on the part of the workers. Rather, since the tonnage of merchandise handled at Sète was far greater than at other dockyards, fatigue was also more marked: "The larger number of accidents thus appears as a physiological consequence of the particularities of the work, independent of the struggle between the workers and the bosses."[171]

In order to graphically prove his point, Imbert (with the inspecteur du travail of the department of Herault, M. Mestre) undertook a series of detailed investigations of the 2,065 accident victims in that department in 1903.[172] The accidents generally climbed uniformly in the period before the midday break, repeating that pattern even more acutely during the afternoon, with the highest proportion of accidents falling in the last few hours of work. They concluded that "the influence of occupational fatigue, given our mode of organization of work, on the production of accidents" was undeniable.[173] The statistics revealed that "the number of accidents more than doubled in the course of each half-day," and conversely, showed the considerable impact of midday rest on the number of accidents occurring at the beginning of each afternoon. Fatigue, Imbert noted, "renders the worker less able to avoid an unexpected accident, because he is unable to respond with an effort as intense, or with movements as rapid, as in the normal state."[174]

Imbert predicted that a significant reduction in accidents would result from a half-hour rest pause during each half day in all industries. Society could not remain indifferent to the deterioration of the energy-producing organism, he declared: "It is dangerous, moreover, in view of the complete development of that organism and its future efficiency to extract a usage that is too premature and too intensive; it is not indifferent, on the other hand, to how many hours of work are consumed, and whether those hours are consecutive or punctuated by one or many rest periods."[175]

Statistics collected from other departments, as well as in Germany, Belgium, and Sweden, confirmed the fatigue-accident correlation: "industrial accidents occur in a definite relationship to the hours of the day."[176] An 1897 German study of the distribution of accidents showed that there were twice as many plant accidents in the three hours before midday break than in the previous three hours, and that most accidents occurred between 3 and 6 PM.[177] What was previously thought to be the result of negligence or carelessness on the part of the worker, "in the great majority of cases now appears as the consequence of the onset of fatigue."[178]

In the German case, however, the fact that the number of accidents falling on Mondays was greater than those falling on Saturdays indicated that "besides work itself, the conduct of life is of decisive importance for safety and for the question of fatigue."[179] Delicately put, reports of the disappearance of *"Blauer Montag"* (Saint Monday) were premature.[180] Even the Socialists, who rarely commented on the issue, began to complain of the high rate of drunkenness during working hours.[181] The French also noted the higher relative accident rate for Monday vis-à-vis the other weekdays. Imbert studied the accidents in Herault in 1904 by days of the week and discovered that although there was a higher accident frequency on Mondays, the figures were deceptive since "a good number of workers rest on Monday from the fatigue of Sunday, which diminishes, in a proportion that is impossible to determine with precision, the working population on the first day of the week, and increases the relative importance of the Monday accident rate."[182]

By 1900, many physicians with industrial experience agreed that the struggle against the effects of alcoholism on the workplace was an essential aspect of labor's well-being. Social hygienists trained in preventive medicine and sympathetic to the Socialists promoted the general spread of "hygienic culture," demanding the expansion of communal health services and educational programs. The German Association for Social Medicine, founded in 1905, put pressure on local authorities and fostered research into the social conditions of workers' health.[183]

The statistical data yielded an even more unexpected result. Against all predictions, as the hours of work decreased, the accident rate rose even more sharply. The German industrial hygienist, Emmanuel Roth, admitted in his detailed report to the 1907 Congress of Hygiene and Demography, that the "progressive rise in general accidents stands in a certain causal relationship to the reduction of labor time, and to some extent represents its reverse side."[184] If the reduction of labor time produced greater fatigue and accidents as a result of the intensification of work, the exclusive emphasis of reformers such as Imbert on a shorter workday or rest periods was misplaced. The shortening of the workday represented at best "the equivalent of the greater intensity of the activity."[185]

The accident question brought into focus what was already evident to both labor and capital: that the shortening of labor time created a new problem, the speed-up of the machinery to compensate for lost time.[186] As Roth pointed out: "[It was crucial that] the intensity of work, the energy expended for a given work process within a specific period of time not exceed a certain amount. The energy expended does not depend simply on the absolute amount of work, but also on the distribution of the work over time. Thus, the true art of work is not to exceed the amount of energy which the organism can tolerate without permanent damage."[187] It was becoming increasingly clear that the real issue was not simply wages and hours, but control over the speed and tempo of work, over time and motion. "The question of fatigue of the working class could not simply be limited to the question of the hours of work, or even to the organization of work and the design of the workplace, from a more or less technical point of view, but to a large number of other questions of a social, economic, personal and psychological nature."[188] Concern with fatigue, time and motion, and the quality of the work environment reflected deep social changes in the nature of the factory. "Chronic fatigue and exhaustion," noted one of the resolutions adopted in 1907 at the International Congress of Hygiene and Demography, [is] "observed in all factories where the intensity of labor is regulated by the machine."[189] The reduction of fatigue would greatly reduce the number of accidents, and science could thus provide the means to effect a profound change in the nature of work. In some occupations, for example, the amount of energy expended during a normal workday was so excessive that the fatigue accumulated did not permit the "elimination of waste" during the hours of rest. At the onset of the next day, the worker was "impregnated with poisonous substances."[190]

But even such "more or less restrained" proposals were met with the resistance of all parties concerned. Imbert's sensational findings on the causes of industrial accidents, which were cited, for example, in the Socialist

Minister of Commerce Alexandre Millerand's report to the president of the Republic and widely republished, did not remain uncontested. The industrialists' *Revue industrielle* carried a biting rebuttal by Philippe Delahaye in its October 8, 1904, issue, entitled "La prétendue fatigue des ouvriers envisagée comme cause des accidents du travail" (So-called workers' fatigue considered as a cause of work accidents). Delahaye criticized Imbert and Mestre for "a priori" applying the explanation of fatigue "to the statistics," and denounced their suggestions for reform as "irreconcilable with the conditions of industrial work."[191] Imbert and Mestre responded in kind, noting that one does not have to affirm or deny a priori the existence of exhaustion as we can form an opinion by observation alone.[192] The trade unions also resisted efforts to reduce labor time so long as they were not matched by wage payments for the lost time.

Conclusion

By the end of the first decade of the century, experts on accident claims were convinced that the efficient deployment of the energies of society could not be realized in the atmosphere of class antagonism, and that the state should provide the necessary surveillance to ensure "a permanent medical supervision of all manufacturing enterprises."[193] The work of the body had to conform to the laws of energy rather than to the imperatives of politics. The economic advantages of such supervision were evident: by reducing accidents, "the deterioration of the sources of energy on which prosperity depends" could also be lessened.[194] Such radical prescriptions naturally provoked skepticism about the practicality of the science of labor. As Hector Depasse, a member of the Conseil supérieur du travail and a liberal politician, remarked as early as 1895: "It is possible, to a certain extent, to supervise the employment of time, but how do you supervise the employment of energy?"[195] Nevertheless, the testimony of the accident experts was echoed in the French parliamentary debates on the length of the workday, particularly in the discussions of February 1912, when Catholic reformers as well as Marxian Socialists like Edouard Vaillant made use of Imbert's work to emphasize the "evident relation between the long day and the industrial accident."[196]

Certainly, this expectation that the state would perform the task of ensuring a thorough rationalization of the workplace in the interests of both capital and labor was premature. In fact, although the state in both Germany and France expanded greatly its supervision of industry before World War I, it was not until after the war that anything approaching effective surveillance became widespread. The accident issue was in many respects a laboratory for the kinds of social experiments that later began the march toward a postwar socialization of the industrial sphere and the rise of the rationalization movement in both Germany and France.

Despite the differences between state insurance in Germany and the private system adopted in France and elsewhere, the debates on the definition of the accident, on the causes of the burgeoning statistics, and on the extent of fraud and simulation were remarkably similar. The protracted debates on the causes and definition of industrial accidents, the question of the modernity of risk, the crisis of simulation and fraud, and the political debates which these issues engendered, reflected a new tendency to subject work to a wide range of knowledge: legal, medical, statistical, sociological, and technical. The abolition of negligence corresponded to a new conception of risk which no longer sought the blame for an accident in the weaknesses of individual character, but in the shared hazards of industrialization. The importance of legal experts, who debated the definition of an accident as linked to the time, circumstances, and nature of the work, as well as the appearance of medical experts who adjudicated claims attested to the new forms of professional knowledge that emerged as a consequence of new social legislation. The rise of positivism as a neutral social discourse—in the concept of social risk, in the medical mediation of disputes, in the analytics of statistical tables, and in the science of work—all represented a changed politics of knowledge.

Yet, as this chapter has shown, the politics of knowledge was hardly a terrain free of conflict. As liberals challenged the assault of the new legislation on the free labor contract, conservatives were skeptical of the linkage between modernity and risk, and socialists in both France and Germany disputed the narrow definition of an accident and challenged the partisanship of medical authorities in awarding claims. Professional experts also offered new techniques of accident prevention and new methods of ferreting out illegitimate claims. The study of fatigue as the primary cause of industrial accidents revealed the relationship between worker physiology and the rhythms and organization of work. In short, with the advent of social reform legislation, work became the object of a wide range of state-sanctioned interventions and analyses: health and safety regulation, frequent inspection, statistical surveys, legal decisions, and medical opinion. Though the scientific language of positivism was always evident, the claims of expertise were hardly immune to the political tensions that characterized the industrial arena. The subjection of work to knowledge did not eliminate social conflict, but it displaced the direct conflict of classes onto the plane of intellectual exchange, politicizing knowledge.

FOUR

Neurasthenia and Modernity

In his pioneering work *American Nervousness* (1881), the New York physician George Miller Beard identified the modernity of "neurasthenia" with an analogy: "Men, like batteries, need a reserve force, and men, like batteries, need to be measured by the amount of this reserve, and not by what they are compelled to expend in ordinary daily life."[1] Beard claimed that "nervous diseases are far greater here than in any other nation of history." Americans were especially prone to the lack of nerve force required for "brain-toil" and the "punctuality" necessary to "keep the lamps actively burning."[2] Beard believed, paradoxically, that because of their superior mental capacity, the scientific and technological genius of Americans made them less resilient to the shocks inflicted on them by their own mighty civilization.

Beard's contention that neurasthenia was a product of the culture of modernity remained a staple of theorizing for decades. However, as I will argue, among European physicians and physiologists the relationship between neurasthenia and modernity did not remain fixed. It was transformed during three decades of debate, ultimately revealing a remarkable secret: that neurasthenia could also account for the triumph of modernity.

As Beard's term swept the continent during the 1880s, European physicians challenged his social etiology and his insistence that neurasthenia was an "American nervousness." In France, Augustin Morel's theory of degeneration and Jean-Martin Charcot's emphasis on the hereditary etiology of nervous disorders, for example, competed with the view that neurasthenia had social causes. Critics of Beard also observed nervous illness in the ancient world, and some experts argued that in Europe the shock of confrontation between the old and the new exaggerated such effects.[3]

The standard textbook on neurasthenia in fin-de-siècle France, *L'hygiène du neurasthénique*, was coauthored by Dr. Achille-Adrien Proust, father of the greatest literary neurasthenic of the age, and Gilbert Ballet. The elder Proust was a prominent Paris physician and epidemiologist who served in the French Ministry of Public Health.[4] Like Beard, Proust saw neurasthenia as a disorder "least dependent on heredity," pointing to its "predominance in towns, among the middle and upper classes, in a word, in all circumstances where intellectual culture or commercial and industrial traffic are carried to their highest degree of intensity."[5]

If neurasthenia could be ascribed to the social pressures of modern life, for Proust it also approached a modernist text in its virtual maze of shifting and unreliable "objective" symptoms, and the even more unreliable "subjective" monologues produced by the afflicted. Neurasthenia often took the form of stigmata that appeared to be physiological—headache, rachialgia, neuromuscular asthenia, dyspepsia, insomnia, and sensitivity of the skin—yet for which no organic causes or lesions could be found. The chief sign of neurasthenia was the "perpetual sensation of fatigue" (muscular, energetic, mental), and patients complained of exhaustion similar to the effects of fatiguing mental activity. Frequently, neurasthenics showed a distinctive but inexplicable abulia, or lack of will.

Neurasthenia was not simply a malady, but a kind of incessant orchestration of analogies to other maladies. In fact, neurasthenic patients produced symptoms that were so close to real disorders that misdiagnosis was extremely common. Neurasthenia resembled both hysteria and melancholia, but was far more elusive and shrewdly deceptive in its plethora of physical symptoms. Freud commented on this aspect when he noted that hysteria and neurasthenia were often combined "either when people whose hysterical disposition is almost exhausted become neurasthenic, or when exasperating impressions provoke both neuroses simultaneously."[6] This similitude, combined with a frequent alteration of mental and physical states, accounts for what physicians referred to as "cyclical or circular neurasthenia;" in which hyperactivity alternated with moments of complete fatigue and immobility.[7]

Extreme confusion, even the lack of ability to remember their own symptoms, was widely reported to be a universal characteristic of neurasthenics. Proust noticed that his most intelligent patients gave an "incoherent and diffuse" description of their disorder. Charcot applied the revealing bon mot "*l'homme du petit papier*" to those neurasthenic patients who frequently appeared in his consulting room with slips of paper or manuscripts with an endless list of their ailments.[8] Otto Binswanger, the leading German expert, noted that neurasthenics demonstrated a lack of attentiveness and disturbances in memory, especially in more complicated thought patterns: "If you question the patient more closely, you will find that at the outset of this memory disturbance, the memory image of an earlier occurring sensation is not lost, nor are simple thought sequences."[9] One writer referred to "fatigue-anesthesia" as the state of being too tired to remember to feel tired.[10]

In the presence of symptoms almost completely lacking in consistency and reliability, the physician has no other means of information than the statements and lamentations of the invalid: "There are few patients whose examination demands so much patience and tact as that of neurasthenia." Like the critic confronted with a disjointed and elliptical narrative, the physician relies only on his or her interpretive authority to stabilize the chaos of appearances produced by the patient: "By proceeding thus with methodical inquiries, prudently directed and often repeated, the physician will be able little by little to check the statements of the patient, separate the true from the false, and arrange the symptoms according to their clinical importance, disentangling those of leading importance from those that are secondary."[11] As allegories of the "real," neurasthenic symptoms derive their power entirely from the amplification of other illnesses. These symptoms are elusive, fleeting and immediately lost unless invested with meaning by becoming part of a larger interpretive matrix—a phenomenon that Walter Benjamin once explained as the shock required by all allegorical representation. The meaning that such images reveal is at once quickly exhausted, leaving only a melancholic deadness in its wake.[12] We may call this allegorical aspect the second order of modernity in neurasthenia, a modernity of symptom and narrative in the "physiognomy of the disease."

The treatment of neurasthenia proved even more difficult than diagnosis, since social milieu played an important role in any cure. Proust and Ballet observed that neurasthenia could be treated by "the observance of many hygienic measures dealing with environment, alimentation and physical exercises." They singled out boarding schools as an "evil" for those children especially prone to neurasthenia and viewed as "the most serious danger" incubated there the "exaggerated development of the sexual instincts between the ages of twenty and thirty giving rise to debauchery and lubricity." Proust and Ballet counseled that the child must be "habituated to *will*," and if this fails, there "may give rise in him that moral paralysis that is called abulia."[13]

Proust discounted Mitchell's "rest cure," which demanded complete withdrawal from the demands of society, as well as Beard's famous "electrotherapy"; "hydrobaths" and a host of popular cures. These, he claimed, were secondary to the more basic "suggestion" of the physician: "the moral action exerted on the neurasthenic by the physician and his surroundings constitutes one of the most powerful therapeutic agents that can be employed."[14]

Although neurasthenics were plagued by fatigue, there was little consensus on what precisely was the root cause of their notorious lack of energy. Charles Féré, a student of Charcot, observed that at La Salpêtrière patients with hysterical disorders demonstrated intense periods of "automatism," a kind of extreme physical fatigue equivalent to the experience of arduous labor in normal individuals. Féré took this fact to be evidence that neurasthenia was not without organic origin, and that the "derangements of the mind" were produced by some form of extreme nervous excitation (*irritabilité*).[15] Féré maintained that neurasthenia could sometimes be detected by a device called an audiometer—a measure of reaction to almost inaudible sounds—which permitted researchers to compare the "states of distraction" of neurasthenics with normal "lazy" subjects.[16]

With its unreliable and analogic symptoms, its absence of lesions, and the confounding behaviors of sufferers, neurasthenia seemed to defy the laws of physiology. By the early 1900s, several prominent French psychologists began to despair of the ambiguities associated with the bewildering multiple symptoms and causes of neurasthenia, and they proposed the new classification of "asthenia" to distinguish the specific "maladies of energy" or "diseases of the will" from neurasthenia tout court. These materialist physicians believed it was necessary to separate loss of energy and inability to act from neurasthenia's confusing and secondary proliferation of symptoms. "Today, the domain of '*la neurasthénie*' is so vast, so imprecise, that it is necessary to undertake a work of revision," wrote Albert Deschamps in his 1908 *Les maladies de l'énérgie*. "In this 'vast forest,'" he continued, "it is necessary to mark out a path to separate that which is 'simple nervousness' [*névropathie simple*] from hysteria, degeneracy, and psychasthenia [*psychasthénie*], and to show that neurasthenia is not singular, and that there is no one neurasthenia, but the asthenias," which he defined as a series of responses to "a defective organization in the reservoir of energy."[17] Closely following von Helmholtz, Deschamps theorized that energy was carried along its pathways by "nervous waves" (*l'onde nerveuse*) analogous to electromagnetic waves, which created a "perpetual circulation of energy in the organism," but which might become impaired by either insufficient or excessive expenditure.

Deschamps was hardly alone in his attempt to place neurasthenia on a firmer physiological basis. At the beginning of the century, Théodule Ribot, editor of the influential *Revue philosophique*, the central organ of philosophical materialism in fin-de-siècle France, carried on a virtual campaign to provide the "diseases of the will" with a materialist foundation. For the leading "psychophysiological" psychologists—which included Ribot, Charles Richet, and Wilhelm Wundt—"desires, passions, perceptions, images, and ideas" were the product of bodily sensation. Ribot wrote, the "'I will' has no efficacy" without the complex "psycho-physiological mechanism, in which alone resides the power to act or restrain."[18] It followed, therefore, that all irrational beliefs could be attributed to the defects of the will. Ribot dedicated his major 1884 treatise on *Les maladies de la volonté* (The illnesses of the will) to exposing the connection between reactionary religious or political ideas and disturbances in the will. Like Charcot, who also drew a parallel between the psychic states experienced by hysterics and those experienced by religious mystics, Ribot traced these experiences to an "annihilation of the will."[19] Religious "ecstasy," in which all energy is concentrated and the will seems to evaporate, was seen as being analogous to somnambulism or hypnotic trance, in which consciousness is temporarily abolished. These atavisms recalled an earlier and "automatic" stage in the evolution of the will, while the conscious will, the highest stage of physiological and moral development, was a shield against these primitive states of mind.

The pathological will is evident, Ribot contended, in "two great classes," impaired and extinguished. The impaired will might exhibit "morbid inertia," usually accompanied by intense feelings of fatigue. The extinguished will is characterized by abulia; as Ribot explains: "[The] 'I will' does not transform itself into impelling volition. . . . [These patients] know how to will interiorly, mentally, according to the dictates of reason. They may experience the desire to do something, but are powerless *to act* accordingly."[20] If the treatment of neurasthenia required the careful disentangling of physical analogies and mental representations, so too the "diseases of the will" required that mental ephemera be distinguished from the material foundations of the disorder. The pathologies of the will—pessimism, irresolution, morbid fear of action and above all the refusal to engage in any productive activity or work—are not states of consciousness but consciousness of an inner state of depletion.

Characteristically, materialist physiology prescribed work or energy as a therapy as opposed to the moral or "suggestive" treatment of Proust and Ballet. Weir Mitchell's "rest cure" merely capitulated to the disorder's demands. Patients who withdrew from their demanding lives into the infantile passivity of "Dr. Diet and Dr. Quiet" did not, as a rule, return to their former pursuits. Theodor Dunin, a German physician, noted that neurasthenia was an "aversion to work" (*Unlust zur Arbeit*) and that "activity was the greatest enemy of neurasthenia." The neurasthenic's proclivity to "do nothingness" was exacerbated by the "lifestyle" of the "higher classes," and was even more serious among wealthy women who "had no preoccupation and could find none."[21] Though neurasthenia could be found equally among men, Proust and Ballet, following Weir Mitchell (who treated women almost exclusively), considered the "neurasthenia of women" especially intense: "The dominant feature of this neurasthenic state is profound discouragement, powerlessness to exert the will, in one word abulia, joined to a degree of muscular asthenia that is hardly ever seen except in this form."[22]

Ribot's analysis of abulia touched on an aspect of neurasthenia not immediately evident to early investigators such as Beard who simply equated its onset with the social pressures of modernity. Neurasthenia now appears as an inverted work ethic, a resistance to work, productivity, and modernity in all its forms.[23] The cumulative effect of mental fatigue was to create a society lacking in "inhibitive power."[24] Whereas Beard or Proust saw excessive social and moral pressure as the source of inhibition, Ribot and Deschamps placed primary emphasis on the inhibiting power of the will as a material force. Neurasthenia was responsible for what might be called a traditionalism of the psyche, a profoundly conservative inertia that threatened all progress. Yet Ribot's theory also gave credence to an alternative possibility—to wit, that neurasthenia, rather than resisting modernity's enormous energies, contributed to their success. The long-forgotten debate over inertia in French ethnography reveals that Ribot was ultimately won over to this view.

In his classic treatise *La Fatica* (1891), the Turin physiologist Angelo Mosso demonstrated that the course of fatigue could be objectively charted by means of an ingenious invention he called the ergograph. Mosso's experiments showed, moreover, that fatigue even performed an invaluable function by ensuring an optimal state of equilibrium in which the body's energy economy was syncretic with the imperatives of civilization.[25] According to the "law of least effort . . . first discovered by Helmholtz, all organic life sought the shortest path to its goal." The body's natural rhythms—for example, the course of fatigue, pulse, and heart rate—determined the pace of work and eliminated waste in human labor. Fatigue governed the expenditure of labor power, as a governor mechanism prevents a machine from exceeding its efficient speed. From this perspective, fatigue is indispensable in restoring the equilibrium of the body and allows the human motor to operate at optimum efficiency. For adherents of a psychophysical approach to pedagogy and psychology, it was thought that fatigue research might even profitably apply its insights to the factory, the school, and a variety of other social domains.[26]

In 1894, the noted Italian anthropologist and psychologist Guillaume Ferrero published a sensational article entitled "Les Formes primitives du travail" in *Revue scientifique*. Ferrero claimed that recent ethnological research proved that in primitive cultures idleness or inertia was the natural state of the human species.[27] The "horror of mental and volitional effort," the "repugnance" that savages display toward work confirmed that the major portion of humankind did not engage in social labor without constraint or force. Even in the modern world, entire social groups—thieves, vagabonds, prostitutes—were motivated solely by the avoidance of productive labor. Modernity was a violation of human nature. The only question, Ferrero concluded, is "why does mankind progress at all, why does inertia not rule the species, eliminating all incentives to progress, productivity, and civilization?"[28]

Two years later, the German economist and musicologist Karl Bücher published *Arbeit und Rhythmus*, an extremely popular book that challenged Ferrero's conclusion that the primitive was a prisoner of idleness and inertia. It was not work per se that the primitive avoided, but rather "tense, regular work." In fact, the labor of primitives was "extraordinarily toilsome," accomplished with inadequate technical means and often achieved with extreme artistry. Primitive labor, Bücher observed, was governed by its own natural rhythm—for example, the beat of a blacksmith's hammer or the work song or chant. The body's tempo guaranteed "thrifty energy use." This natural order, however, was consistently undermined by civilization, which systematically destroys the rhythmic element in work, making it externally imposed. Rhythm—the source of all economy in work—not external constraint, was at the origin of both culture and production.[29]

Seizing on Bücher's work, Ribot argued that Ferrero had confused the pathological asthenia investigated by Deschamps and by the psychologist Pierre Janet with the normal state of mankind.[30] Rather, society's *asthéniques* demonstrated the pathological form of the law of least effort in their obsessive desire to avoid activity and to sleep and rest. Janet had noted this "horrible exhaustion" and "aversion to all novelty" in his asthenic patients, a pathological traditionalism he called *misonéisme*, an opposition to anything new.[31] Rather than contributing to a pathological avoidance of labor, Ribot held that the law of least effort was socially adaptive, leading to greater efficiency, simplicity, and productivity. Indeed, social life was unthinkable without the kind of "shorthand" ubiquitous in the arrangements of society— language, morals, daily life, political institutions, religious belief, science, and art—which benefited from "inaction or the minimum of action."[32] Linguistics, for example, has long understood that there is a kind of "principle of laziness" (*principe de paresse*), which gradually eliminates excessive sounds, at work in phonetics. Similarly, the history of religion shows that the law of least effort brings about tolerance, since the fanaticism dividing hostile beliefs ultimately "surrenders to the analogy" that can be found between all systems of belief.[33] Ribot thus claimed to have discovered the productive side of *misonéisme*, the disposition of the psyche to find the shortest path in any endeavor. The pathology of neurasthenia revealed the paradoxical secret of progress, efficiency, and the order of productivity.

The modernity of neurasthenia is not simply the effect of excessive pressure, but rather the *misonéisme* inherent in all analogy—not unlike the propensity of neurasthenics to produce analogic symptoms as a kind of visible shorthand of their pathological fatigue. The pathological resistance to modernity of the energy-afflicted and the primitive are, ontogenetically and phylogenetically, evidence of an atavistic stage in the evolution of the will. These pathologies expose the secret of modernity: if *misonéisme* signaled anxiety in the face of change, modernity depended on it to bring about a "rupture with habit." Because the human will was characterized by "mediocre perseverance and vigor," because of its rapid fatigue, *misonéisme* is the protective instinct of the species to reduce excessive action, to regulate physical and mental activity and to find new means to achieve its ends. The law of least effort produced not inertia but innovation.

At the outset, neurasthenia was identified by Beard and his European followers as the inability of mind and body to resist the onrush of modernity's stimuli. By contrast, Ribot and Bücher made fatigue indispensable for the great achievements of modern civilization. Only in its most pathological forms—neurasthenia and psychasthenia—did the will exhibit an impairment or extinction inimical to rationality and social progress. In normal circumstances, though, just as survival of the fittest was the mechanism that explained the emergence of new and viable species, *misonéisme* guaranteed that the law of least effort functioned as the regulator of economy and efficiency in mind, body, and society. Anxiety about fatigue was misplaced in the modern era, the materialists reassuringly concluded, since normal fatigue did not threaten modernity but defined the threshold of excessive labor and energy expenditure. Insofar as it "presupposes a balance between debits and receipts, between useful activity and rest," fatigue conserves energy and regulates its movements according to the law of least effort. Fatigue does not threaten civilization—it ensures its triumph.

Psychotechnics and Politics in Weimar Germany: The Case of Otto Lipmann

Academic or quasi-academic subdisciplines and professions with applied or practical interests regarding labor (such as industrial physiology, industrial medicine, industrial psychology, and industrial sociology) emerged in almost all European countries after World War I. Industrial psychology, in particular—although rooted in the pre–World War I sciences of work— first achieved professional legitimacy in the interwar period.[1] This chapter looks at some of the professional, intellectual, and political controversies that surrounded the establishment of industrial psychology as a discipline in the Weimar Republic by focusing on Otto Lipmann, a pioneer of industrial psychology in interwar Germany.

In France, the science of work occupied an ambiguous position vis-a-vis both labor and industry before World War I. In the earliest phase of industrial physiology and applied psychology, several of its advocates, especially Armand Imbert and Jean-Marie Lahy, were sympathetic to the workers' movement, attempting to demonstrate the superiority of a scientific approach to the deployment of labor power as opposed to both exploitative capital and working-class resistance. Imbert, for example, tried to enlist the support of workers for his experimental approach and Lahy was a resolute critic of Taylorism and its consequences. However, other advocates of the new scientific approach to labor saw the possibilities of compromise, as did Jules Amar and Josefa Ioteyko, who advocated collaboration between the Taylor system and the workers' movement in the interests of raising "social efficiency."[2] These divisions did not, for the most part, survive the war. After the war, there was a rapprochement between the different political camps. Differences were muted, and even those who, like Lahy, remained fellow-travelers of the Communist Left, did not use their positions as the leading French proponents of the science of work to promote discord between those who were more inclined to see its benefits as complimenting the economic rationalization plans of industrial managers. These methods were far more successful in Britain and the United States, where the National Institute of Industrial Psychology and the work of Elton Mayo (and Hugo Münsterberg before World War I) in the Department of Industrial Research at Harvard University, promoted a close affiliation between industrial psychology and industrial management.[3]

In Germany, too, industrial physiology and psychology rapidly won wide acceptance as both a theoretical and applied discipline after World War I. This success resulted in the rapid proliferation of several competing schools of "psychotechnics" and a plethora of methods of aptitude testing and industrial psychology. But it also resulted in a deep division between those who saw the new approaches as an adjunct of the "rationalization" of industry, and those who conceived of these scientific approaches as a means of reducing the power of industrial management over labor. By the 1930s, the increasingly political tenor of these controversies demonstrates that psychotechnics and industrial psychology cannot be simply understood as "technical" instruments at the disposal of industry or management, but rather as a field of contestation between different approaches to social knowledge.

In Germany (as in France and Great Britain) industrial psychology emerged from the wartime military uses of "psychotechnical" methods to sift out "the best-suited" candidates for gunners, drivers, pilots, and other military jobs.[4] Psychotechnics soon won academic respectability as a practical "technique" and figured in the training of engineers and "industrial experts" (*Betriebswissenschaftler*) who would, in turn, train those who would put these methods into practice. The professorship in applied industrial psychotechnics, established at the Institut für Industrielle Psychotechnik at the Technische Hochschule Charlottenburg shortly after the war and occupied by Georg Schlesinger, attests to this newfound acceptance. Unlike the United States, where industrial psychology encompassed a broad range of academically anchored managerial approaches, in Germany industrial psychotechnics was considered a basic lynchpin of government-sponsored efforts to improve the efficiency of industrial labor. In 1920, for example, the Prussian Ministry of Science promoted the idea of increasing productivity by personnel selection and training techniques.[5] Increasingly, the field divided into those who trained practitioners for industry and those who believed that a scientific discipline might be established with greater attention to the social consequences of these methods, and with greater scientific legitimacy than the psychotechnical approach alone afforded.

The case of Otto Lipmann, who represented this second alternative in Germany from 1906 until his death in 1933, is instructive because it allows us to focus more closely on the professional, intellectual, and political circumstances that prevented this alternative approach to industrial psychology from becoming hegemonic. Rather than examine the history of this profession either from the traditional standpoints of the internal history of applied psychology, or from the Marxist standpoint as an ideologically motivated compensation for the problems of advanced capitalist industrial organization, I propose to examine how the formation of the professional field, the intellectual assumptions and premises of Lipmann's theoretical activity, and the political environment in Prussian state circles circumscribed the emergence of industrial psychology in Weimar Germany.[6] Although Lipmann's work and career was in some ways unique, perhaps idiosyncratic in his perseverance to keep the "science of work" distinct from direct industrial applications, and because of his insistence on the political neutrality of his science in class conflict, his case challenges, some basic assumptions about how new forms of social knowledge become established, or perhaps fail to do so. The case of Lipmann thus offers a new perspective for evaluating the role of political and professional conflicts in the process of disciplinary formation.

Otto Lipmann and the Origins of Applied Industrial Psychology

Otto Lipmann was one of the pioneers of practical or applied psychology as an independent discipline in Germany.[7] A student of the "second generation" of German experimental psychologists, Hermann Ebbinghaus and William Stern, Lipmann together with Stern, founded in 1906 the *Zeitschrift für angewandte Psychologie* and the Institut für angewandte Psychologie und psychologische Sammelforschung in Berlin-Wilmersdorf (which shortly thereafter moved to Klein Glienicke). At the outset, Lipmann was secretary and Stern director, but after Stern moved to Hamburg in 1916, Lipmann assumed the sole directorship. Privately financed from his income, the institute became the "center of his life's work." It was never a laboratory or research center in the conventional sense, but a library encompassing an enormous collection of materials relating to the psychological aspects of work and occupations. The institute compiled data, transmitted scientific information, and promoted the use of applied psychology for particular economic problems, especially standardized aptitude tests and statistics.[8] In his obituary for Lipmann, Stern underscored his "indefatigable and prolific efficiency," embodied above all in his editorship of the "forty-five volumes, sixty-eight supplements (*Beihefte*) and forty-seven research papers (*Schriften*) of the journal.[9] In addition to his editorial activities, Lipmann published studies on a wide array of psychological subjects like memory proficiency, perception, intelligence, sex differences, and even a short tract on an important although neglected subject: the lie.[10] Lipmann pioneered the use of applied psychology to study the "higher" professions. His 1918 *Frageliste zur psychologischen Charakteristik der mittleren (kaufmännischen, handwerklichen und industriellen) Berufe* (Checklist of psychological characteristics of midlevel [salesmen, craftsmen, and industrial] occupations) was renowned, but he also contributed monographs on the use of applied psychology in law (*Grundriß der Psychologie für Juristen* [Foundations of psychology for jurists], 1908), psychiatry (*Handbuch psychologischer Hilfsmittel der psychiatrischen Diagnostik* [Handbook of psychological methods for psychiatric diagnosis], 1922) and pedagogy (*Grundriß der Psychologie für Pädagogen* [Foundations of psychology for teachers], 1909). He was one of the first to advance the importance of statistical methods in applied psychology and he served as scientific secretary of a Reichstag commission to investigate the problem of labor time, resulting in his most important book, *Das Arbeitszeitproblem* (1926). This work, and his textbooks on industrial psychology (*Grundriß der Arbeitswissenschaft* and *Lehrbuch der Arbeitswissenschaft*) made him the most important pioneer of applied industrial psychology in interwar Germany.

The Professionalization of Industrial Psychology and Psychotechnics

The beginnings of applied industrial psychology as both an academic discipline and as an industrial practice can be traced to the early years of the twentieth century. As early as 1910 Hugo Münsterberg attempted to extend the results of Wilhelm Wundt's applied psychology to industry and the professions, first in the United States where he was professor at Harvard University, and then in Germany.[11] The first aptitude tests were developed by Münsterberg in 1910, at the behest of the American Association for Labor Legislation, as a means of selecting tramway conductors to avoid tram accidents.[12] Münsterberg's *Psychology and Industrial Efficiency* (US, 1913; Germany, 1913) affirmed the superiority of the American Taylor system as a method of organizing industrial work while providing one of the earliest critical evaluations of its lack of a psychological orientation.[13] In his influential *Grundzüge der Psychotechnik* (Fundamentals of Psychotechnics), Münsterberg elaborated the concept of *psychotechnics* to describe the broad range of social and cultural phenomena which could benefit from psychology. He also emphasized the economic potential of advertising, marketing, and productivity in industry.[14] In 1912, Münsterberg observed—somewhat optimistically—that "consulting psychologists" could be found in American firms while in Germany such practices were virtually unknown.[15]

William Stern, who was professor of Psychology in Breslau (1907) and in Hamburg (1916), conducted experimental studies of the psychology of individual and group differences with an eye toward their potential uses for industry. Stern invented the term *psychotechnics* in 1903 to describe the uses of applied psychology for investigating "the diverse external conditions affecting human work in the school and in the occupations." Stern included in this category the study of worktime and its division; pauses, holidays, piece and hourly wages, monotony and diversity of work, performance, motivation, adequacy of the workplace, and even the psychological effects of tools and machines.[16] In contrast to Münsterberg, Stern also distinguished between the theoretical component of applied psychology and its direct application as psychotechnics.[17] Stern also warned against the indiscriminate instrumentalizing of applied psychology, and above all, against its social misuse. Rather, he cautioned, applied psychology "must contribute assistance to the creation of significant goals and must permit its activities to be limited by the ethical evaluation of these goals."[18]

Despite the efforts of Münsterberg and Stern to found an academic discipline of industrial psychology with practical implications, the success of industrial psychology in Germany was the work of a very different, but equally dedicated group of psychologists and practitioners. Unlike Stern and Münsterberg, who were academics, the new generation was composed of men with a great deal of industrial experience such as Schlesinger and Walther Moede (his successor at the Institut für Industrielle Psychotechnik), who conceived of psychotechnics as a practical *"Heilslehre"* (therapy) that could compensate for some of the "irrationalities" of capitalist production by rationalizing work methods, evaluating behavior in the firm, and by preselecting individuals for tasks from "youth to old age."[19] World War I opened the path for the success of psychotechnics, offering a practically unlimited field of activity for as yet wholly unproven methods that had thus far been developed only in laboratory contexts.[20] The war did not so much further the invention of new techniques of testing aptitude, combating fatigue, diagnosing and treating psychological illness, and improving efficiency and boosting output, as much as it extensively employed these already established techniques for the first time and provided those trained in psychotechnical methods with a vast laboratory to demonstrate the utility of their knowledge. As Fritz Giese, one of the leading German psychotechnical experts in Weimar Germany remarked of his own wartime service: "the war not only presented psychology with new knowledge, it also created new subject matter that, without that sad occasion, would surely have remained estranged from it."[21]

Psychotechnics made its wartime debut as a technique for selecting the best-suited candidates for tasks requiring a high degree of technical skill and other aptitudes in the military, above all drivers, pilots, and gunners. In 1915, Moede and Curt Piorkowski established the first testing station for automobile and truck drivers in Berlin, establishing standardized tests of physical and mental capacities (vision, hearing, attention, motivation, fatigability, and nervousness).[22] In addition to promoting the use of women as truck drivers, they established fourteen similar stations in all reserve divisions (*Ersatzabteilungen des Heeres*), performing between ten and thirty thousand tests by 1918.[23] In 1915, Piorkowski also developed a general test to predict success in "middle" and "higher" occupations, according to "desirable or necessary psychological functions."[24]

In addition to the selection of military personnel, industry also began to make use of the aptitude test during wartime, especially to determine the vocational aptitudes of women and students rapidly entering industry. By 1917, several large German firms—including the AEG, Loewe, and the Zeiss optical works in Jena—had established "psychotechnical divisions."[25] In November 1917, the German women's vocational agency (*Frauenberufsamtes*) promoted occupational counselling, including psychotechnical aptitude testing, as did similar agencies set up for younger workers.[26] Also in 1917, Lipmann and Stern developed psychotechnical methods for the selection of workers replacing those sent to the front.[27]

The war also furthered the scientific study of what was termed "human economy," the point of intersection between production techniques, mobilization of national resources, and the politics of demography.[28] Well before World War I, the political and economic goals of national self-assertion were linked to new scientific methods of organizing production in a coherent and well-planned strategy of improving the biological and productive power of the population. In this respect, the Kaiser-Wilhelm-Institut für Arbeitsphysiologie in Berlin (KWI/A), founded by the world-renowned physiologist Max Rubner in 1912, assumed a position of prominence. At the outset of the hostilities the institute was enlisted by the Ministry of War to undertake studies of wartime nutrition requirements and the optimal use of labor power employed in the munitions industry.[29] In 1915, Gerhard Albrecht, an employee of the KWI/A, identified the practical consequences of the institute's industrial research as "determining the limits of labor power, the influences on work performance on the minds and bodies of the workers, and determining how, in the future, work can not only be structured to be profitable but also economical and without damage to the worker."[30]

The KWI/A also claimed to be able to provide a more scientific and more reliable method of achieving industrial output than the Taylor system which rested on "less secure foundations." As Dietrich Milles has pointed out, even before 1914 the institute was oriented toward placing the Taylor system on a more scientific footing and considered fatigue research to be the most important component of a more "progressive" scientific management.[31]

Although the KWI/A clearly did not envision its role as competing either with private or military research agencies dedicated to industrial hygiene (*Gewerbehygiene*) to protect workers' health or with the practically oriented psychophysics testing stations, the war greatly extended the range and scope of the institute's activities. These included, in addition to the nutritional studies pioneered by Rubner, the development of psychophysical aptitude tests for evaluating the distance perception of military drivers, pilots, and railway personnel. By 1917, the experimental psychologist Carl Stumpf reported that although psychotechnics was still in its infancy, "the measurement of reaction time, and the refinement of. sense perception for military purposes have led to practically useful results and instruments." He predicted that psychological testing, especially the more sophisticated use of psychophysical aptitude tests, could result in the "selection of the most fit forces for industrial work."[32] Rubner too saw the promise of psychotechnics for the postwar world: "The opportunities for the application of psychological methods in everyday life are certainly more numerous than one had previously imagined. During the war, the measurement of the rapidity of tasks modeled on actual techniques performed by an automobile driver has proven very practicable in excluding unsuitable persons from this occupation. Psychological processes can never be entirely separated from their physiological basis and foundation, and a sharp differentiation between them is therefore impossible."[33]

As Rubner anticipated, the postwar period afforded new opportunities for the psychotechnical methods developed under wartime conditions. After 1918 they were extensively applied to reintegrating returning soldiers into the peacetime economy, for improving the productivity of industry and for improving the health and well-being of a war-weary populace. Psychotechnics became a European-wide movement and in Germany, under the slogan "the right man for the right job," psychotechnical aptitude testing became a virtual craze. Adapting techniques they developed during wartime, Moede and Piorkowski (founders of the privately funded *Berliner Begabtenschule* [Berlin school for the gifted]) used psychotechnical examinations to retrain veterans for a variety of civil occupations, such as street-car conductors, typesetters, typists, and clerks. Moede developed a battery of tests to determine physical and intellectual aptitude, somewhat later shifting his interest to tests of character and motivation. In addition to these specific tests of ability, other, more general basal tests were developed to determine rapidity of learning, attention span, judgment, and a host of psychological attributes.[34]

These military and industrial successes also paved the way for academic acceptance. Although many universities established institutes or departments of applied psychology, it was the technical colleges and commercial schools which almost universally established psychotechnical laboratories and institutes by the mid-1920s.[35] Most prominent among these new psychotechnical institutes was the showcase Institut für Psychotechnik at the Technische Hochschule in Berlin-Charlottenburg, founded by Schlesinger, whose efforts to combine the American system of Taylorism with scientifically designed aptitude testing earned him a reputation as "the German Taylor."[36] By mid-decade, engineering students in German universities were required to complete a course in scientific management and scientific factory organization, including the latest developments in applied psychology.[37] In 1922, Prussian officials complained that there were no less than "five psychological and psychotechnical institutes" competing for the same financial support.[38] Several newly established psychotechnical journals— including *Industrielle Psychotechnik*, *Praktische Psychologie*, and *Psychotechnische Zeitschrift*—were testimonies to recently acquired academic legitimacy (and professional differences).

The success of psychotechnics was in part due to the massive restructuring of the labor market immediately after the war, but it was also a consequence of the generally positive reception accorded to it by the trade unions, who regarded its scientific neutrality as an equitable and objective basis for "achieving the best relation between labor power and the labor process."[39] The use of psychotechnical aptitude testing for choosing officers candidates in the Army and Navy, for example, was especially welcomed by Social Democratic Party officials as a way of breaking the traditional hegemony of aristocratic elites in those careers.

In 1919, a Prussian law decreed that occupational counselling and employment agencies be set up with the aid of psychologists.[40] By 1922,

Germany had no less than 170 psychotechnical "testing stations," causing the Ministry of Labor to create a special agency to deal solely with psychotechnical problems.[41] Employers also found psychotechnics an efficient method of deploying labor according to vocational skills (as well as screening for political reliability). According to the journal *Industrielle Psychotechnik*, sixty-three firms established testing stations in the early 1920s.[42] Psychotechnical methods were extensively adopted by the German railway and postal system, and by nearly all large metalworking, engineering, and electrical firms.[43] In addition to its industrial uses, psychotechnical aptitude tests were also used for the selection of candidates for occupations as diverse as office work and hairdressing.

Between 1920 and 1923 an intense rivalry developed between engineers and academic psychologists over which profession was best qualified to develop and administer the new testing methods in industry.[44] Among the academic psychologists, only Moede wholeheartedly sided with the engineer's claims to preeminence, while Lipmann, and most other professional psychologists criticized the dilettantism and amateurism of the engineers.[45] Some psychotechnical experts, including Giese, acknowledged that despite their claims to expertise, extensive academic training was not really necessary to administer aptitude tests and that university training might be superfluous. Lipmann, Stern, and most of their academic colleagues were opposed, maintaining that the instrumentalization of psychotechnics as a "management science" (*Betriebswissenschaft*) was short-sighted and unscientific. The dispute between engineers and academics became widely publicized in the pages of Lipmann's *Zeitschrift für angewandte Psychologie*, which carried a long series of attacks and rebuttals culminating in Schlesinger's attempt to achieve a rapprochement by acknowledging the achievements of each discipline and calling for better training in scientific methods among practitioners of psychotechnics.[46]

The controversy between plant engineers and the psychologists also revealed a division among the academic experts. Whereas Moede was clearly oriented toward industry, Lipmann and Stern were oriented toward the intervention of the "neutral state" in the labor market, and toward securing governmental support for their own "scientific" methods of aptitude testing and vocational counseling.[47] At stake was not so much whether industry might or might not make use of such methods, but whether government agencies would support one or another group in distributing funds, establishing University chairs, and dispensing other forms of political largess. In this regard Lipmann and Stern, and their supporters, were concerned with establishing psychotechnics in cooperation with state labor agencies and educational authorities, while the group around Moede and Schlesinger favored cooperation with industry, management scientists, and engineers.[48] Lipmann demanded that a "much sharper line [be] drawn" between commercial and practical psychologists, severely criticizing their lack of experience, and unscientific and "lay" use of these methods. Moreover, from the standpoint of the industrial psychologists, the proposal to turn Moede's Charlottenburg Institute into a "Central Institute of Psychotechnics" with state support met with strong disapproval from Lipmann, not in the least because he entertained very similar ambitions. But there were more substantial differences emerging. Lipmann believed that the scientific credibility of industrial psychology would be sacrificed if, as Moede proposed, industrial profitability was the only criteria of success, and if the new science was "not compatible with the interests of the working class.[49]

Despite the apparent success of the Lipmann-Stern group in securing professional approval for their standpoint at the seventh congress of the Deutsche Gesellschaft für Industrielle Psychologie (German Society for Industrial Psychology), the Moede group prevailed in practice. By 1923, most industries routinely used such psychotechnical methods, usually administered by engineers or administrative personnel for the selection of fit or unfit workers and not, as Lipmann would have had it, in the interests of general economic goals or to restrict the excessive demands of industry on the workers. Although psychotechnics was well established in industry, not a single psychologist was employed by industry in any permanent capacity.[50] Government employment practices also used psychotechnics extensively in the railway and the postal systems, but did not employ any psychologists.[51] The polytechnic schools, and to a lesser extent the universities, were the bastions of the psychotechnically oriented psychologists, whose greatest success was in training plant managers and designing testing materials. By 1923, moreover, it no longer seemed plausible that the state would achieve the ends of the psychologists by using public funds to create neutral research institutes (as Lipmann's own efforts demonstrate).[52]

After 1930, as the economic crisis began to erode interest in the psychotechnical movement it became clear that the instrumental and productivist side of psychotechnics could only be maintained at the expense of the more abstract and expendable general economic and social utility promised by its earlier advocates, and upheld by Lipmann and Stern. By siding with the needs of industry to "sort out" the most unproductive workers and maintain those who were both reliable and effective, psychotechnics became a tool of the harshest of management practices. One such example of this "ruthless" side of psychotechnics appeared in the scandal resulting from an article that Moede published in *Industrielle Psychotechnik* in the Summer of 1930. In the article, he indicated that plant managers might use such methods to distinguish between "superior" and "conspiratorial" workers. Moede obliquely suggested that managers, plant experts, and engineers ally themselves with the "superior" workers to "unify in the struggle against these bad elements and support the selection and education of superior [workers]."[53] Although mild when compared with some of the more radical political schemes proposed by Catholic conservative and National Socialist industrial policy only a few years later, negative reaction to Moede's comments arrived swiftly. The Socialist *Vorwärts* called it "scientific baseness," the Hamburger *Echo* termed it "management chicanery as science," and the *Weltbühne* spoke of the "deepest moral vacuum."[54]

Lipmann's own reaction was more reserved than these journalistic barbs, but he was apparently no less shocked by Moede's politically partisanship in recommending methods for "excluding or neutralizing unpopular or unsuited members of the firm."[55] Given Moede's position as professor at the Technische Hochschule in Berlin and as head of one of the most prestigious German psychotechnical institutes, Lipmann said, it was entirely understandable that his "recipe" for dealing with unreliable workers was greeted with such an uproar. Although Lipmann conceded that "Moede did not intend for such a misuse of his collection of methods" it was evident that this particular collection of principles was full of "tricks" that were not only "immoral" but impractical. Moede, had in fact "discredited" psychotechnics with his publication, and the "damage" to its scientific legitimacy was, despite Moede's disavowals of partisanship, irrevocable.[56]

Lipmann's public controversy with Moede ultimately led to his becoming a professional pariah among those who believed that the time had come for psychotechnics to declare its partisanship for industry. But, the contro-versy also had a profound effect on Lipmann's conception of psychotech-nics, which he now entirely disassociated from applied psychology: "a technique is not a science."[57] Industrial psychology, he argued subsequently, had to become entirely nonpartisan, offering to both capital and labor a means of evaluating competing claims, without adopting the political stand-point of any party.

In subsequent years, Lipmann found himself increasingly beleaguered in his chosen profession. Having secured neither a university appointment nor an officially recognized institute, he was neither identified with pure aca-demic psychology nor with the practical, industrial wing promoted by the engineers and psychotechnicians. In 1932, Giese—who, along with Moede, was one of the most prominent defenders of psychophysics, and who was increasingly attracted to the more metaphysical and romantic conceptions of labor that led him to embrace National Socialism—attacked Lipmann in his 1932 *Philosophie der Arbeit*.[58] Lipmann's definition of the science of work was, according to Giese, "inelegant," "hardly useful and correct," and ig-nored the "cultural goals" of science. Although Lipmann responded by dis-tinguishing his own definition from "the much broader one of Giese," his reaction to the attack can be read in the distinctly anxious tone of his *Leh-rbuch der Arbeitswissenschaft* published in the same year.[59]

Lipmann's Conception of Arbeitswissenschaft
as a Nonpartisan, Liberal Discourse

After his public dispute with Moede, Lipmann concluded that the scientific legitimacy of *Arbeitswissenschaft* could only be achieved by a strict demarca-tion of the field from the practical techniques of psychotechnics. He now defined psychotechnics as a technique that could be distinguished from a larger technology or apparatus of methods available to firms, and equally, from broader theoretical concerns. Psychotechnics could not be concerned with ethical issues, or with any general scientific considerations since it was purely a practical method in the service of a specific purpose.[60] But this new emphasis represents more of a change in tone than an alteration of Lipmann's fundamental position. As early as 1918 he had proposed that the broader implications of psychophysical aptitude testing (in education, vocational counseling, etc.) be separated from its practical uses.[61] He criticized the popular slogan "free path to the talented" as overly simplistic and naive since an adequate psychological profile had to take into account "not only what requirements each job demands but also what requirements each worker can fulfill."[62]

For Lipmann, "the working person" was always at the center of consideration.[63] He defined the science of work as the "science of the conditions and effects of human labor," effects that he saw as either material and external or psychic and internal (joy in work, motivation, boredom, fatigue).[64] In contrast to *Betriebswissenschaft*, or "management science," which he saw as another, albeit distinct practical branch of economics (*Wirtschaftswissenschaft*), the science of work was concerned less with profitability, than with the impact of the conditions of work on the productivity of the enterprise and the health and cultural well-being of the individual worker. A crucial aspect of the science of work was therefore to distinguish between those situations in which the interests of the firm and workers were compatible, and those in which they radically diverged. For example, in the case of the Taylorization of work tasks, it may be in the interest of the firm to create a greater division of labor, although the consequence for the individual worker is that greater monotony significantly reduces the sense of fulfillment (*Arbeitsfreude*) that could be derived from work. Such considerations cannot merely be considered from the "objective" standpoint (for example, from the standpoint of productivity and profit), he averred, but had to "take into account the capacities of the workers." Their interests, however, according to Lipmann, ultimately corresponded to the long-term interests of the firm since the "worker works better, and longer, with machines and methods adapted to him, and because such measures, which may appear as purely humanitarian, also contribute to raising the joy in work of the worker and tie him more closely to the firm, reducing the frequency of uneconomical job switching."[65]

Lipmann's conception of an interest-neutral and equitable science of work was an attempt to counter what he called "the thoroughly subjective demands of, for example, a political party."[66] But it was not entirely naive. He acknowledged that the "management science solution to the labor time problem did not always coincide with the solution which the science of work proposed."[67]

If management science was entirely one-sided in its approach to the labor process, taking into account only the productivity and profitability of the firm, the science of work had to propose general principles that also took into account the effects of the organization of work on the worker. If Taylorism demanded the transformation of work into externally imposed uniform procedures, "from the standpoint of the science of work, we are led to the demand that the worker be permitted the free choice of the means of labor and the methods of labor to the greatest extent possible, and that this principle be broken only on the basis of firmly grounded economic considerations. And even when it is broken, the regulation of the labor process must be undertaken according to human economy, for example, to preserve the long-term performance capacity of the worker."[68]

Lipmann did not ignore the fact that labor and capital had divergent, even diametrically opposed, interests. Nor did he believe—as did Catholic conservative "work scientists" such as Willy Hellpach and Richard Lang, who called for return to small scale organic production communities or "*Gruppenfabrikation*"—that industrial harmony could be artificially created by schemes that "would return the organization of work to a condition which it found itself in 100 or 150 years earlier."[69] Rather he argued that in a liberal polity, where divergent social interests reigned, conflict between labor and capital had to be treated not as something to be eliminated (a point at which both radical socialists and authoritarian conservatives seemed to converge) but institutionalized. Lipmann's "science" assumes the existence of a liberal public domain in which social conflicts cannot be resolved by science, but in which political arguments could be examined by scientifically informed experts.

Nowhere is this undiminished liberal faith more evident than in Lipmann's most important work, his study of the eight-hour law, *Das Arbeitszeitproblem* (The labor time problem), published in 1926 and culled from the material assembled by the parliamentary commission on the eight hour day, on which he served as scientific secretary.[70] From the outset, he conceived of the problem of the length of the working day as a "humanitarian" and "national economic" problem, as opposed to a "private economic" problem. Although he was skeptical of the Marxist view that the worktime problem could be solved by the transition from capitalism to socialism, he argued that the conflicting social and economic standpoints converged in the premise that "labor time should be constructed so that that the life-long performance of the worker is maximized"[71]

Lipmann recognized that the labor time question was neither a purely economic nor a humanitarian problem but a point of political contestation dominated by "de facto political motives." If, for the socialist the eight-hour day was "the symbol of their power and the achievements of the [1919] revolution," for the employers it was a matter of maintaining the international position of the German economy. In addition to the standpoint of the employers, who wanted to maintain higher productivity at all costs, Lipmann distinguished between two different labor standpoints: that of the German trade union representatives and that of the representatives from France, Belgium, and England. The German trade unionists (majority SPD) required—as did the employers—that the reduction in labor time be accompanied by an intensification of labor and by the maintenance of earlier (ten-hour) productivity levels. The leaders of the British, French, and Belgian unions, on the other hand, did not at all recognize the requirement that workers produce as much in eight hours as in ten. For them the eight-hour day is a purely "social political" measure, not an economic one. For the German employers, of course, maintenance of production at prior levels was of paramount importance, requiring not merely greater effort but improvements in technology and in methods of management. From their point of view—the postwar depletion of German capital and the inability of German workers to maintain a higher work tempo—the eight-hour day endangered the competitive position of German industry.[72]

Lipmann did not deny the validity of these contradictory perspectives. Rather, he argued, that the purpose of his investigation into the requirements of different industries was to "remove the struggle over the labor time problem from the sphere of political conflict, and raise it to the level of scientific precision."[73] In Lipmann's view, a peaceful solution to the controversy "would spare the economy something of a far greater value" than that which might be lost by a few hours of work.

We cannot here consider the methodological implications, statistical calculations, laboratory data, psychological factors, and historical dimension which Lipmann brought to bear on his careful consideration of the relations between productivity or performance and worktime in a variety of industries.

Characteristically, he did not dismiss the employers demand that productivity and competitiveness be taken into account. But he affirmed the workers' claims that shorter hours reduced fatigue, accident risk, and poor health, while providing greater cultural advantages. These competing claims had to be weighed against each other and evaluated individually in each case. Lipmann concluded that ultimately there could be no definitive answer to the question what is the optimal worktime for industry: "for every kind of work there is an economically optimal worktime that can be theoretically, and sometimes even practically, calculated, although the data is not yet fully satisfactory. The eight-hour day is perhaps the optimum worktime, which is the average of the optimum for all industries, but the degree of divergence from the optimum in individual industries and between different kinds of work both higher and lower is considerable."[74] Paradoxically, despite the gradual lengthening of the working day in Germany after 1919, the hourly productivity of labor increased not because of the length of the working day per se—but because the general productivity of labor began to recover from lower (because of physiological, psychological, and economic difficulties) immediate postwar levels. There are different optimal worktimes for different industries, and for different work in the same firm. The same is true even of different workers whose psychological and physiological capacities are different.

Such considerations, Lipmann recognized, could obviously not resolve the conflict between labor and capital since the human being is "not a machine" and optimal labor time could not be reduced to a simple formula. Though fatigue represented a clear external limit to the maximal use of the worker from an economic standpoint, the cultural requirements of workers also had to be taken into account in assessing the effects of different kinds of work on the mood and psychology of the worker. Nonetheless, he concluded "we can objectively investigate—and this is the purpose of this study—if these changes in labor time born of cultural-political (or any, for that matter) considerations have indeed, as many claim, been a nightmare leading to 'catastrophic' economic effects, or what actual economic, hygienic effects, they in fact have had."[75] The advocates of shorter worktime would, he argued, improve their position if they conceded that for certain industries, longer worktime was required, while their opponents might benefit from recognizing that their apocalyptic visions of ruin in the face of any reduction in labor time were exaggerated.

To be sure, Lipmann's position between "the stools" was not, especially in the later years of the Weimar Republic, an enviable one. The economic crisis, the eclipse of the rationalization movement in German industry, growing unemployment, and the declining position of organized labor strengthened Lipmann's conviction that there was a "collision of interests" between "the economy of the firm" and the national economy.[76] Moreover, he recognized that "that an ideal balance" between the "best design of work" from an economic point of view, and the "best construction of work," from the standpoint of the working person was no longer "thinkable."[77] But, precisely because an "equilibrium of the opposing interests was no longer possible, and because every compromise can be no more than a compromise which satisfies neither of the opposing interests," the interests of capital and labor "must be fought out."[78] Precisely because such conflicts are inevitable in this economic system, he observed, all attempts to "radically resolve" these antagonisms "must be rejected."[79] Such attempts to end the conflict between capital and labor must of necessity result in an end to democracy and liberty as well. The position of the science of work as a discourse was defined not by its lack of political insight, but by the political insight that it was above all imperative to maintain the terrain of conflict, and not, as the radical parties of the Left and the Right threatened, to eliminate it: "This defines the task of the science of work. It cannot itself intervene in this conflict, and can do nor more than remain neutral and coolly demonstrate what is taking place."[80]

Lipmann thus defined the discursive position of the science of work: against partisanship for capital and labor; without a naive faith in the ability of science to intervene in, or resolve, the social conflicts raging around it; and against the radical parties which saw in the removal of conflict the cure that always was far worse than the disease. There can be little doubt that Lipmann felt personally threatened by these radical currents, and in the end, especially as a Jew and something of a socialist, his investment in their failure was far greater than most of his colleagues. These considerations make him less a naive practitioner of neutral and objective science, than a "cool" observer of what is taking place.

The Politics of Official Recognition

Lipmann encountered his first difficulties in establishing a secure position in the emerging field of industrial psychology during World War I. As early as 1911, Carl Stumpf, who (along with Wilhelm Wundt, Stern, and Hermann Ebbinghaus) had pioneered the introduction of experimental psychology in Germany, had appealed to the Kaiser to establish a state-supported research institute in applied psychology sponsored by the Kaiser Wilhelm Society. In December 1916, after Rubner's KWI/A was established, Stumpf renewed the appeal, pointing to the new situation created by the war, and to the "practical possibilities of applying psychological methods of investigation" which had "appeared far more strikingly than could have been anticipated."[81] It can be assumed from the subsequent correspondence that at the time Stumpf considered Lipmann's Berlin Institut für Angewandte Psychologie und Psychologische Sammelforschung (Institute for Applied Psychology and General Psychological Research) to be the leading candidate for official recognition by the Kaiser Wilhelm Society, and Lipmann's proposal followed shortly thereafter. Naturally the establishment of a Kaiser-Wilhelm-Institut parallel to Rubner's Kaiser-Wilhelm-Institut für Arbeitsphysiologie provoked intense interest on the part of Rubner and his associates, who, already one year earlier, had defined the "working goals" of their own Institute to include "enlightenment and the dissemination of knowledge" concerning "the physiology and psychology of work."[82] In May 1917, Rubner responded to a request to evaluate Lipmann's proposal:

> Professor Lipmann in Klein Glienicke has put forward the proposal . . . to establish an institute for applied psychology with the funds of the Kaiser Wilhelm Society. . . . There is no doubt that experimental psychology and its methods can be useful for many areas of practical life. One only need think of Münsterberg's activities and publications in Cambridge, whose ideas and orientation have many points in common with those of Lipmann's in the accompanying report. . . . It appears to me, however, that such a schism of psychological experimentation either leads to a division of labor that is not entirely desirable in practice, or to an exaggerated narrowing of the purely physiological method of work, and of its practical results.[83]

According to the internal discussions of the advisory board of the KWI/A, it was agreed that the new techniques of psychological aptitude testing ("for railway employees, distance assessment, automobile drivers, or pilots") "belonged to the mandate of the labor physiological and brain institutes." "A separate research institute, like that desired by Professor Lipmann," the board concluded, "is not necessary at this time."[84] Lipmann's proposal, which in any case, was to take effect only after the war, was tabled.

After 1918, with the establishment of the Republic and, in an entirely new set of circumstances, the Prussian Ministry of Science, Art, and Public Education began to entertain new proposals concerning the establishment of an institute for applied psychology in Berlin. At the outset, it was not clear whether this would be a larger enterprise, including industrial medicine (*Gewerbehygiene*) as well as labor science. But, in May 1920, discussions took place between the representatives of several government ministries (including the Ministries of Commerce, Labor, and Economics, and the Postal Service) and several prominent psychologists (including Lipmann, Stumpf, and Hans Rupp of the Berlin Institute of Labor Physiology). The new methods of applied psychology, vocational psychology, and aptitude testing had proven useful in the war and could be applied to the new circumstances of economic want and dislocation. Moreover, they could serve "as a means of the contemporary democratic and socialist epoch, and to overcome the legacy of the authoritarian state (*Obrigkeitsstaat*) insofar as "the free path to talent was universalized." Stumpf's proposal to include applied psychology in all university institutes met with general enthusiasm.[85]

Until the mid-1920s, the success of psychotechnical methods of vocational selection, counseling, and testing, and the establishment of psychotechnical institutes in most polytechnic colleges, and some major universities, enhanced the prestige of applied psychology. Lipmann, however, still found himself in a difficult situation, having been able to secure neither a teaching post nor official support for his institute. Moreover, his ability to sustain the existing institute through private means was by 1921—presumably as a consequence of the inflation—in serious jeopardy. In May 1922, Dr. Alfred Beyer, a Socialist member of the Prussian provincial parliament, proposed that the Landtag (State Diet) grant Lipmann's institute official status as a "state-sponsored Institute for the Science of Work and Industrial Hygiene" (Staatliches Institut für Arbeitswissenschaft und Gewerbehygiene) under the supervision of the Ministry of Welfare. According to Beyer, not only was Lipmann the "only psychologist who after the war published in foreign professional journals," but his purpose was always to "develop applied psychology as a recognized science."[86] Moreover, Lipmann had always placed the future of applied psychology above self-interest and "personal vanity":

> It should particularly be recognized, that Lipmann never attempted, as an abuse of his scientific and social conscience, to use his institute as a means of earning any income [*Erwerbsunternehmung*], even though the institute, up to this point, has not only brought him no material gain but also has been supported by him from his private funds. It is to be feared that this can no longer continue under the current changed economic situation, and that in the future not only his personal labor power but also that of the scientific effectiveness of his institute and its materials and experiences will be lost to the public, if the state does not intervene.[87]

The socialist *Vorwärts* published Beyer's appeal to prevent the "deterioration" of the institute.[88] The Minister of Welfare responded positively to the proposal, noting, after consultations with the Landtag, that the creation of a state-supported Institute for Labor Science and Industrial Hygiene (Institut für Arbeitswissenschaft und Gewerbehygiene) was approved, and that the Institute would henceforth come under the authority of the medical division of the ministry. Moreover, the minister added that such an institute was justified by the fact that "it was a matter of natural course that a firm owner, by aiming at the *maximal* performance, leaves significant social and health factors out of consideration . . . which make the creation of such a state institute a necessity."[89] The fact that Lipmann already had an existing institute, whose library and facilities would simply be transferred to the state, facilitated the decision.

Lipmann's apparent success was short-lived. Only a few days later, the Minister of Finance, von Richter, in a sharply worded reply criticized the Welfare Ministry for establishing an institute that in no way represented an "essential function of the state [*lebenswichtige Staatsaufgabe*]" and called the 250,000-reichsmark budget a "rapidly expanding permanent burden on the state treasury."[90] The apparent collision between the two ministries required delicate negotiations, which were scheduled to take place before the upcoming vote on the budget in the Landtag. In these discussions, at which Lipmann was not present, but was represented by Beyer, the liminal status of Lipmann's institute was a deciding factor in the negative outcome.

According to the representative of the finance ministry, the Landtag had already decided against the nationalization (*Verstaatlichung*) of Lipmann's institute in February; moreover, such an institute would naturally compete with several already existing institutes established in the polytechnic colleges. A representative of the cultural ministry, Dr. Kruß, attacked Lipmann's institute for "not being a scientific institute in the sense of a university institute," but a "collection and information point." At best, the finance minister proposed that a small one-time support be granted to the private institute (125,000 reichsmarks). Although Beyer attempted to defend Lipmann on the grounds that there was no duplication between his and the other institutes, and although the Welfare Ministry pointed to the advantages of supporting "an already existing Institute," the negative mood prevailed.[91]

Throughout the spring of 1922 Lipmann's proposal twisted in the wind as his prospects in the ministerial councils worsened. The commerce and trade minister complained of the fact that the "need for a sixth psychotechnical and psychological institute in Berlin" could not be demonstrated, and proposed instead, a "condominium [*Arbeitsgemeinschaft*] of the existing institutes."[92] Since only the socialists in the Landtag supported Beyer's initial proposal, he added, it would be dangerous to create a state agency (presumably Lipmann's institute) which might exercise control over other institutes, especially given the "opposition" between Lipmann, the university institutes, and the "men of practice," such as Moede and Piorkowski,[93] were the psychotechnicians marking out their domain, to the exclusion of their nemesis, Lipmann? It seems clear that his ties to the Socialists via Beyer, and the marginality of his self-financed enterprise played a role in dooming his efforts to achieve state sponsorship. Added to suspicion of Lipmann's "opposition" to the university institutes and the "men of practice" we can perhaps discern yet another factor, only *sotto voce* at this point, which sealed his fate. To what, except anti-Semitism, can we attribute the remark of Dr. Kruß: "To convey state authority to Liepmann [*sic*] provokes concern [*errege Bedenken*]. The Cultural Ministry is opposed to Lipmann being given authority over others in a supervisory capacity. In this way, the process can be stopped, since it is questionable that Liepmann is the most suitable person."[94]

Lipmann quickly realized that the decision had fallen against him. In August, he wrote to the Ministry of Welfare to request a small sum to maintain the institute which was now in dire straits. In subsequent years, the institute operated on a shoestring, essentially as a one-man operation with no public funds.[95] In 1929 the Institut für Arbeitswissenschaft was established under the direction of Otto Graf. Ironically, in December 1932, Lipmann who had never held a university position, was offered an appointment by the University of Berlin to offer a course in the psychology of work. It came too late for him to assume the post.

In February 1933, the editors of the *Psychotechnische Zeitschrift*, proclaimed their allegiance to National Socialism. In June, Moede's *Industrielle Psychotechnik* also announced the support of all those "practitioners of applied psychology and psychotechnics who affirm the new state." In fact, the psychotechnical experts "as in no other branch of psychology" were quick to embrace the new order.[96] Apart from those Jews and Socialists who were officially proscribed from performing their functions, most academic psychologists soon followed suit, proclaiming in many different and creative ways their ideological allegiance and the usefulness of psychology for the Nazi state.[97]

In October, the *Zeitschrift für Angewandte Psychologie* was placed under proscription by the National Socialists. Lipmann's offices were occupied and sacked by students belonging to the SA. He committed suicide on October 7, 1933, at the age of fifty-three. His obituary appeared in the last issue of the *Zeitschrift* to carry his and Stern's names on the masthead. In the following issue (February 1934), the new editors—Otto Klemm and Philipp Lersch, two lesser practitioners of psychotechnics—published an editorial in which Lipmann and Stern (who had emigrated to the United States) were not mentioned, but, in which the "struggle of the Führer," for the "soul of the German people" became the leitmotif of Lipmann's journal.[98] It would remain so for twelve years as an industrial psychology entirely different from Lipmann's was established, as a university discipline, in industry, and above all in the military.

Conclusion

The story of Lipmann's lifelong campaign to secure professional and official recognition for industrial psychology, and to convince Prussian authorities of the need for public support for his institute demonstrates the extent to which applied psychology was not, as historians of the professions would have it, the natural or logical outgrowth of the practical successes of aptitude testing and psychotechnics in post–World War I Germany. Rather, Lipmann and his mentor and coworker, William Stern, represented a distinct counterpoint to practitioners of psychotechnics such as Giese, Moede, and Pierkowski, who played a predominant role in the establishment of psychotechnics as an adjunct of the rationalization of German industry between the wars, and who continued to do so under Nazi rule. In contrast to the psychotechnical experts who were based in polytechnic institutes, Lipmann never held a university or official post. Moreover, although Lipmann and Stern were victims of National Socialist policies and their notion of industrial psychology was unacceptable to the authorities, the psychotechnical approach continued to thrive in the environment of the Third Reich.

Lipmann's vision of a neutral science of work, predicated on the results of theoretical psychology, was an attempt to carve out an intellectual domain for applied psychology between, or perhaps above, class conflict. This effort was not, as Marxist historians have claimed, entirely based on the naive illusions of an objectivistic scientific ideology. To attribute the success or failure of the interwar sciences of work to the vicissitudes of the conflict between capital and labor underestimates the significant intellectual conflicts within the discipline itself. It also neglects the existence of what might be called contestable discourses, which Lipmann's discourse exemplified. Lipmann's view that science could in fact reflect on its own relationship to the struggle between labor and capital, and even render service to both, calls into question the assumption that all sciences of work must in fact become management techniques. Lipmann was one of the first practitioners of industrial psychology to argue that in order to become a scientifically legitimate discipline, *Arbeitswissenschaft* had to make explicit what social interests it could serve, and not simply take into account the organization of industry. Even if it could not be completely neutral, he believed industrial psychology could make its results available to both capital and labor, and in this way, contribute to a clarification of what was an unavoidable terrain of conflict. His protracted campaign against the preeminence of psychotechnics and its limited industrial applications, from 1917 until his death in 1933, exemplify his attempt to create a competing discourse against what he perceived as illiberal and ideological assumptions of the psychotechnicians.

Finally, as a Jew, and a liberal with distinct sympathies for the socialists, Lipmann's fate in the political culture of interwar Germany cannot be attributed to his professional, intellectual, or discursive circumstances alone. Rather, the documents of the inner ministerial debates concerning the fate of Lipmann's institute in the 1920s, and, in his own fate at the hands of his fellow professionals in the early days of the Nazi seizure of power, attests to the significance of this directly political component in the story of why industrial psychology, as opposed to psychotechnics, was not able to sustain itself in Germany until after World War II.

SIX

The Aesthetics of Production in the Third Reich

During the Third Reich, the utopia of labor took the form of a systematic attempt to legitimize political rule through aesthetic symbolization. Aesthetics and politics were integrated not only in mass festivals and public architecture, but in the sphere of production as well.[1] The attempt to legitimize political rule through aesthetic symbolization is perhaps the most unexplored characteristic distinguishing twentieth-century fascist regimes from other forms of authoritarian domination.

Aesthetics as Social Policy

Founded on November 27, 1933, the Amt Schönheit der Arbeit (Bureau of Beauty of Labor; hereafter the bureau) was a branch of the "Strength through Joy" (Kraft durch Freude) leisure organization of the German Labor Front (DAF).[2] It was entrusted with the physical improvement and beautification

of Germany's industrial workplaces. Under the slogan "the German everyday shall be beautiful," it attempted to radically transform both the interior
and exterior landscape of the German industrial plant. The National Socialist labor decree (*nationalsozialistische Betriebsordnung*), adopted in January 1934, dissolved all workers' organizations and placed enterprises under
the absolute hegemony of management. After 1934, intensive efforts to
persuade management to remodel and renovate the workplace became a
central focus of the German Labor Front. According to its leader, Robert
Ley, prior to National Socialism workers had been systematically convinced that their activities served no higher purpose, that their labor was
only a commodity, and that they were proletarians.[3] The bureau would return to the worker "the feeling for the worth and importance of his labor."[4]
Albert Speer, the bureau's initiator and director, envisioned the emergence
of "a new face of the German workplace" and a "new epoch that no longer
considered factory architecture inferior."[5] Once degraded to a "joyless
compulsion," labor itself would now give way to "a new spirit," manifested
in obedience, self-sacrifice, and furthering the "Volksgemeinschaft" through
the "new formation of the environment."[6]

The bureau combined social policy with cultural policy in a single administrative unity. Its function, the creation of social harmony, was to be
achieved through aestheticization of labor relations. Aesthetic illusion was
integrated into concrete social forms, motivated by political goals. As such,
the bureau is a paradigm of the aestheticized politics characteristic of
National Socialism. Moreover, factories were not simply beautified by improvements in their external appearance; the subordination of human sub-
jectivity to industrial processes was itself expressed in an aesthetic form. If
Nazism had brought about the political subordination of labor, it returned to
it a cultural image that "would liberate physical labor from the curse of
damnation and feelings of inferiority which had imprisoned it for hundreds of years."[7]

The bureau's ideological function was underscored by the limitations
which the 1934 law regulating national labor placed on the Labor Front by
establishing the absolute hegemony of management within the industrial enterprise.[8] The resulting dual structure of authority separated possession of
the means of production from the instruments of political control and
legitimation.[9] Through the bureau, the control of management over labor

could be furthered, while still maintaining the appearance of Labor Front activity in the interests of labor. The aesthetic transformation of the workers' environment was to result in a political transformation of the German worker.

Beyond its specific ideological function within the Labor Front, the development of the bureau also reflected the profound change in Nazi culture and ideology that emerged after the seizure of power. Increasingly, Nazism was forced to reconcile its earlier program and ideology to the demands of an industrial society in crisis.[10] Especially after 1936, when Hitler's Four-Year Plan and "war economy in peacetime" became the ultima ratio of Nazi industrial policy, and when full productive capacity and the labor shortages brought about a greater effort to raise industrial output and efficiency through rationalization and the intensification of labor, the bureau embodied a reversal in the traditional ideological substance of Nazi cultural policy. By combining industrial psychology with a technocratic aesthetic that glorified machinery and the efficiency of the modern plant, Beauty of Labor signified the emergence of a new dimension in Nazi ideology. In its modernist emphasis on technology and design, in its architectural principles, and above all in its growing functionalism in all areas, the bureau is a striking example of the Nazi modernism and cult of productivity and efficiency that coexisted uneasily with the *völkisch* traditionalism of earlier Nazi ideology in the late 1930s. As Jeffrey Herf has shown, "reactionary modernism" was not confined to the Labor Front; Fritz Todt, leader of the Labor Front's Amt der Technik (Bureau of Technology) exhorted engineers to favor both "revolution and tradition."[11]

According to Speer, the idea for Beauty of Labor originated with Ley himself who, during a trip in the province of Limburg, was impressed with the neatness, cleanliness, and well-tended gardens of the Dutch mines.[12] From the outset, extensive plans were developed to encourage German plant managers to beautify and remodel their factories and work rooms. By the end of 1935, over one hundred million reichsmarks had been spent on the remodeling work.[13] The external appearance of more than twelve thousand plants was improved; rubble and unkempt areas were cleared away, lawns and parks turned into rest and recreation areas, walls were painted, floors washed, work clothing repaired and new washing and sanitation facilities installed and improved.[14]

These initial efforts only anticipated the broader effort to redesign Germany's industrial landscape after 1936. This first "cleanup" phase was superseded by a greater emphasis on technical campaigns to improve plant facilities.[15] In May 1935, a campaign against excessive plant noise was carried out, followed by the often repeated "Good Light—Good Work" program for improving plant lighting. Information centers were set up in all major cities to provide technical and scientific information on proper lighting and to advise employers in making the necessary changes.[16] In February 1937, the campaign for "Clean People in Clean Plants" was inaugurated, resulting in large-scale renovations of washing and wardrobe facilities. In May of that year, the bureau launched its campaign to improve air and ventilation in work rooms, followed by the campaign for "Hot Food in the Plant" in September 1938. This greater emphasis on technical changes was also reflected in an important change in the leadership of the bureau. Speer himself had always been too occupied with other duties to concern himself with the day-to-day activities of the bureau and entrusted the task to his deputy director. In August 1936, Karl Kretschmer, a Labor Front ideologue who had been the first to occupy this post, was replaced by Herbert Steinwarz, a specialist in plant engineering with an orientation toward functional aspects of plant design.

These efforts coincided with intensive work on aesthetic aspects, especially the development of model designs for the interiors of offices, canteens, and work rooms. Designs for furniture, light fixtures, tableware, and other interior furnishings were completed. Moreover, a 1936 agreement between the bureau and the Reichskammer für bildende Künste (Reich Chamber of Fine Arts) facilitated the extensive employment of artists by "plant leaders" (employers) for purposes of painting mosaics in community houses built for leisure time activities, designing furniture, and occasionally decorating the workrooms of handicraft enterprises. Particularly in rural plants, these decorations depicted *völkisch* scenes or reflected traditional workmanship and simple materials. The most extensive application of preindustrial forms to the plant environment, however, was the widespread use of wall sayings, either from historical figures, or from Hitler and other Nazi leaders. A strong emphasis on the redesign of the entrance and gate of the plant, often done in detailed wrought iron with medieval figures, also carried a strong *völkisch* symbolism.

Steinwarz's appointment signaled the shift to greater concern with the technical design of work spaces and architectonic questions. In each national district, specially designated "trusted architects" were appointed to carry out architectural and design projects undertaken by employers in accordance with the bureau's specifications. Administratively, the bureau expanded from a staff of four, housed in a Berlin apartment house in 1933, to five fully staffed subdivisions by the end of 1939: (1) administration; (2) artistic plant design; (3) technical plant design; (4) research and enlightenment; and (5) beautiful village. The artistic plant design division was concerned with the development of models for both industrial interiors and for the small number of "model plants" designed and constructed by the bureau annually. The division of technical plant design was charged with the practical evaluation and application of scientific and engineering research on light, noise, ventilation, and dust in the work environment. The enlightenment section promoted the various projects of the bureau, and more important, created initiative among "plant leaders" to adopt the proposed measures, while making available the technical and cultural information gathered in the other divisions. Special departments for sea-going vessels and plant transportation were included in the second division, and the fifth division, concerned with beautifying the German village, was established as a separate organization during the "Beautiful Village" campaign of 1936.[17]

By 1938, the annual expenditure by German employers on projects inspired by the bureau reached two hundred million reichsmarks. The bureau's expanding functions included constructing sports facilities and designing kitchens, canteens, community houses, dormitories, and resort homes. By the end of 1938, sixty-seven thousand plants had been visited and inspected by the bureau, twenty-four thousand new wardrobes and washrooms were installed, seventeen thousand park areas were provided, and three thousand new sports facilities were built, at a total cost of over nine hundred million reichsmarks.[18]

These accomplishments are all the more impressive in light of the bureau's lack of any legal authority to impose changes on the owner of a particular enterprise. The bureau could only advise management on remodeling work undertaken at their initiative and expense. Restricted by the new labor law, the bureau was limited to a variety of methods developed to persuade German industrialists that their interests would be served by adopting its recommendations. Even unsolicited visits to plants were blocked by statute. As a result, throughout 1934, the bureau appealed to the factory inspectors (*Gewerbeaufsichtsbeamte*) to extend their support for its activities by informing plant leaders of the purposes and goals of the bureau, cautioning, however, that the undertaking remained a "voluntary beautification of the workplace," and in no way infringed on the jurisdiction of the factory inspectors.[19] In July 1935, the Ministry of Labor issued a six-point declaration promising the cooperation of the inspectors by bringing employers into contact with the bureau, advertising its efforts, and informing the bureau of those employers already engaged in remodeling and construction activities. At the same time, however, the bureau was required to inform the factory inspectors of any deficiencies in the facilities of the plant.[20]

These methods were gradually supplemented by the "enlightenment campaigns," which promoted the bureau's projects through exhibitions, films, and the periodical *Schönheit der Arbeit*, founded in 1936 to depict successful plant alterations and to "win over plant leaders to the dignity with which labor is viewed in the Germany of Adolf Hitler."[21] A series of technical brochures produced along with the major campaigns, included fifteen titles by 1936.[22] A number of films were also made to publicize the work of the bureau, including a 1934 dramatization of the physical and psychological transformation of a plant as a result of the efforts of both workers and their employers to introduce the bureau.

In addition to these campaigns, less subtle methods of coercing management were also employed. The bureau consistently emphasized the economic return that improvements in lighting, noise level, dust, ventilation, and hygiene could bring. From the outset, the promise of an increase in the performance of the individual worker was a major incentive for the introduction of these changes, and the bureau's literature emphasized the increased productivity and efficiency which could be gained from the same or even less energy expenditure.[23] There were also tax incentives which often provided reimbursement for expenses in the same year, and extended credit opportunities were provided for firms renovating according to the bureau's specifications.[24] Moreover, private industry was often promised "the recuperation of the sums invested to a certain degree as a result of the publicity which accompanied particularly successful projects."[25]

Probably more effective, however, were the directives which compelled state and party enterprises to adopt the bureau's specifications, and which ordered the sixteen federal plant communities (*Betriebsgemeinschaft*) to include speakers employed by the bureau in the mandatory morning plant assemblies.[26] Party organizations, particularly the SA, decreed that "it should not be discovered that an employer who is an SA member heaps his followers into unworthy workplaces and housing in his enterprise."[27] Industrial and military construction also provided opportunities for incorporation of bureau designs, as did the temporary workers' housing built by the Labor Front.[28] Furthermore, the position of "trusted architect" gave industrial architects complying with the bureau's specifications the advantage of commissions and employment in the Labor Front's extensive building programs, as well as in private industrial construction.[29]

Above all, benefits for management were formulated in terms of Ley's statement that "the best social policy is also the best economic policy," and could be measured, not only in calculations of profit and loss, but by the "comradeship and joyful work spirit of the employees."[30] Full-color cartoon films made these points with Disneyesque figures: the "renewal" of the "plant leader" (an elephant) was paralleled by the joy of the employees (giraffes, cats, and hippos) resulting from the enlightened introduction of the bureau.[31] The official handbook of the bureau justified its activity as carrying out paragraph 7 of the new national labor law, which asserted that "the German Labor Front secures labor peace insofar as it creates an understanding in the plant leader for the just claims of his following, and in the following an understanding for the situation and possibilities of the plant."[32] According to Kretschmer, "politics, economics, and art went together in the effects of the bureau. From the political viewpoint, we want the community of men; the economy wants the best performance; and art wants to beautifully form the life of the community."[33]

The direct advantages for labor were less easy to demonstrate. The crackdown on the legal trade unions, suppression of working-class organizations, and the freezing of wages at depression levels throughout the Nazi period only underscored the compensatory function that motivated these measures. Despite the bureau's assertion that "the basis for joy in work and genuine satisfaction can only be created when work can successfully be removed from the sphere of purely material considerations, and given a higher, ethical meaning," reports of the factory inspectors often indicated the reluctance of workers to make use of new facilities.[34] Worker's resistance did not diminish when it became evident that the efforts of enlightened management meant that labor had to be provided as "voluntary overtime." The bureau's modifications often met with the remark that "money spent on the water closet should have been distributed among the workers."[35] Nevertheless, Labor Front officials (*Vertrauensmänner*) and plant stewards could not only exert pressure on a recalcitrant "plant leader," but on the reticent "following" which might exhibit reluctance when faced with the prospect of being compelled to endure uncompensated overtime to install new shower facilities or even to build a factory swimming pool.[36] Plant task force members (*Werkscharmänner*), SA, SS, and other party members were expected to demonstrate an exemplary attitude toward the other workers in creating "the spirit of comradeship and solidarity that would serve to defeat the antispirit of the class struggle."[37]

However, the success of the bureau's efforts to legitimate Nazi policy toward the industrial worker should not be underestimated. The skepticism which often accompanied the bureau's initial efforts to enlist the support of both employers and workers was, according to official Labor Front publications, largely overcome, and its ideological benefits were, according to Otto Marrenbach, head of the Labor Front's personnel office, reaped: "At the beginning of the activity of the bureau, 'Beauty of Labor' was an unknown slogan for the working man, which many thousands did not believe could be realized, a propaganda slogan which even many plant leaders thought impossible. And today? A knowledge that gives every working German the certainty that everything is being done in order to keep his working life and workplace, as well as his free time, beautiful, worthy and healthy."[38] Community activities provided by management and integrated into the plant with the aid of the bureau paralleled, and often improved upon, the facilities provided by Social Democratic, Christian, and trade unions. Community houses were built, canteens and dining halls were added or remodeled, small factory roof gardens and lawn areas were provided for rest periods, and plant flower gardens "were cared for with careful hands."[39] For workers unable to make use of "Strength through Joy" travel opportunities, the bureau encouraged plants to provide holiday homes. For women workers entering the labor force in increasing numbers after 1936, the bureau proposed that day care facilities be established or shared among a few enterprises.[40] Providing for these needs did not, however, always lessen the burden imposed by them: "The comrades of the kitchen department are voluntarily assisted by the women and girls of the factory in the rapid distribution of the well-prepared food."[41]

Above all, sports and entertainment was a major consideration. Plant leaders were advised on the design and construction of sports areas, accommodating a growing demand for sports activities during work time. Sports could, it was hoped, combine the discipline and comradeship necessary for developing an esprit de corps within an enterprise while restoring stiff muscles. Storage rooms were turned into a "little paradise of indoor sports."[42] Group exercises and gymnastics were regularly scheduled for afternoon pauses and boxing, football and ping-pong were popular diversions. Between August and September 1938, a national "sport appeal" (*Sportappell*) was held to encourage athletics in all German plants. By 1938, some ten thousand plants had established sport clubs and intra-plant sports were greatly expanded.[43]

Combined with the community activities provided by the Labor Front's Cultural Office (*Kulturamt*) and the Bureau for After-work Activities (Amt für Feierabend), and linked to the travel network of Strength through Joy, the bureau's community ideology reflected a strong utopian image of nonalienated and nonproletarianized labor. Even popular Social Democratic symbols, such as Karl Kautsky's 1904 vision of the "worker [who] will one day drive his own car, cross the oceans with his own ships, climb the alpine regions, and find bliss in the beauty of the south and the tropics," became recurrent motifs in the Labor Front.[44] Bourgeois imagery notwithstanding, the real powerlessness of labor in economic and political life was counteracted by the authoritarian administration of an objectified appearance of socialism, combining the promises of emancipation with an extensive depoliticization of industrial relations.

The bureau promised to provide an environment in which all consciousness of "proletarity" would disappear.[45] In contrast to Marxism, which was accused of exploiting the ugly and gray everyday life of the worker in the era of liberal capitalism for its own ends, Hitler referred to the bureau as the "socialism of the deed." The historical experience of the proletariat was to be dissolved in the plant and national community. According to Wilhelm Lotz, the editor of *Schönheit der Arbeit*:

And when another saying of the Führer goes: "in the future there will be only one more nobility, the nobility of labor," this shows that the proletarian coloring of the concept "laborer" and the fighting attitude toward another rank has been extinguished. Accordingly, all literary attempts to construct a proletarian culture have become pointless and forgotten. There is only one culture and one life form, that of the German people. Clearly, from all the efforts to transform the plant into a cell of community life, a life style of the German worker must emerge.[46]

The embellishment of the factory in the bureau was to be a demonstration of the "palpability of the socialist idea."[47] The objectification of the image of community in the external forms of the German industrial landscape was intended to reconstitute the soul of the German worker.

Attractive Labor

The creation of the bureau as an element of state social policy was unique to National Socialism. Its attempt to produce a "more joyful transformation of the everyday environment" was anticipated, however, by the nineteenth-century tradition which identified the beautification of the workplace with the "deproletarianization" of labor.[48] More than a century earlier, Fourier envisioned "attractive labor," in which "the workshops and husbandry offer the laborer the allurements of elegance and cleanliness."[49] James Silk Buckingham's imagined model town and the garden cities movement of the early 1900s were also predicated on the view that "air, light and sunshine could heal the damages of industrial labor."[50] By dissociating industrial processes from the image of human degradation in an inhuman and squalid environment, enlightened paternalistic entrepreneurs wanted to restore the social balance.[51] Similarly motivated was the *cité ouvrière napoléon*, the workers' housing built by Napoleon III in the 1850s, the model English villages Bournville and Port Sunlight built by George Cadbury and W. H. Lever in the 1880s, and Alfred Krupp's industrial settlements in the 1870s. Open spaces, low density, and aesthetic designs were merged with political considerations. At the root of these projects was the trepidation candidly expressed by Krupp when he began the extensive construction of industrial settlements comprised of "small houses with little gardens," in the hope that "when a general revolt goes through the land, an uprising of all classes against their employers, we may be the only ones spared, if we can get everything into motion while there is still time."[52]

After 1900, the integration of specifically aesthetic motifs took on increasing importance. In Germany, Heinrich Tessenow, Speer's teacher, designed the gymnasium and dormitory buildings for Wolf Dohrn's experimental garden city, Hellerau, built between 1911 and 1912 to institute a German educational reform.[53] Tessenow's theoretical writings, even more than his designs, reveal his concern with the relationship between aesthetics and the industrial process. For Tessenow, architecture had to affirm the principle that "the prosperity of industrial labor demands a health or strength that is composed of simple bourgeois character."[54] These bourgeois virtues of simple diligence, seriousness, persistence, love of order, and cleanliness, were to be embodied in architecture and symbolized in respect for the economy of technical form, order, symmetry, and external cleanliness. In England, the values objectified in the design of the model cities were extended to the plants themselves. At Bournville, the Cadbury chocolate factory distributed a brochure to its visitors entitled "the factory in the garden," describing its lawns, trees, wooded areas, and canaries and flowers in the work rooms. In 1931, the English Industrial Welfare Society promoted the slogan, "beauty and success in work go hand in hand," and the Glasgow machine factory of Wallace Scott & Co. painted its machines blue, its girders gray, its railings green, and other parts of the plant red and gold so that the colors would reflect light and "make the plant lively."[55]

These efforts gained remarkable currency in Germany because of the variety of schools of industrial psychology that grew out of Hugo Münsterberg's work on the subjective dimension of the labor process in the decade before World War I. Münsterberg was the first to recognize the advantages for industry of psychotechnics, the scientific measurement of the effects of "fatigue, temperature, dampness, body positions—including seating and the position of work materials—the influence of overeating, flower aromas, colored lights, dance music, and other external factors on emotional life."[56] Despite the proliferation of approaches, from Münsterberg's psychotechnics to more metaphysical schools which called for "the renewal of the soul of production," all shared the goal of reintegrating the individual into an industrial work process that, as a result of Taylorization, had been reduced to the carrying-out of predesigned detailed tasks. Through the manipulation of the objective milieu, means could be found to reduce the overt and remediable dissatisfaction of the worker toward what was regarded as an irreversible "petrification" of the work process.[57]

These attempts to placate the worker were increasingly politicized in a conservative direction by class conflict, and by resistance to the intensive rationalization movement that swept German industry between 1924 and 1928, introducing Taylorism, technification, and the standardization of parts and goods on a large scale.[58] Of particular importance was the influential school of industrial sociology developed by Catholic philosopher Götz Briefs and his coworkers, L. H. Adolph Geck, and Rudolf Schwenger. Briefs combined the insights of earlier theorists with a political strategy aimed at the practical transformation of industrial relations through direct managerial intervention. In Briefs's view, the industrial plant was a completely isolated "social sphere," distinct from both the economic and technical aspects of production, which could be organized and directed by a conscious policy in line with demands for discipline, adaptation, and hierarchy.[59]

Despite Briefs's emigration in 1934, his work was carried on by his students, particularly Geck, who provided the bureau with its theoretical basis in his textbook *Soziale Betriebsführung* (Social industrial management, 1938), and in a series of articles on the examples of Beauty of Labor in other countries.[60] Modern industry, Geck argued, could not rely for its stability on the moral bond between subservient workers and paternalist management which he so highly praised in the nineteenth-century enterprise. On the contrary, by adapting the aesthetic dimensions pioneered by the English model cities and American attempts to domesticate labor through Taylorism and Fordism, Geck integrated the concept of Beauty of Labor into "scientific" industrial policy. As a member of the Briefs's school, he believed that "the maximum of work efficiency and the comforts of human relations in the workplace" could be guaranteed. Geck distinguished between two aspects of "plant leadership": personnel and functional. While the former was concerned with questions of administration, wages, labor time, training, and education, the latter was the domain of the bureau. For Geck, the bureau's work encompassed three essential areas: the exterior of the plant, the interior, and the individual workplace.[61]

He pointed to the importance of a sleek and unpretentious factory ar-chitecture, and called for the extensive introduction of glass in industrial construction, as well as for the aesthetic importance of lawns and gardens in the factory surroundings. Color and cleanliness, good lighting and ven-tilation, and the remodeling of washrooms and canteens were all singled out for their "practical importance as well as for the coexistence between the work comrades and the employer" which they promoted.[62] Throughout the 1920s and 1930s, modern lunch rooms, health facilities, rest areas, gymnasi-ums, athletic fields, parks, and special housing were established in many European and American factories to improve plant relations.[63] Geck's hand-book clearly established the bureau's role as an extension of the science of industrial relations developed in that period. Yet Geck believed the bureau had gone further. In Germany, it had realized the project of domesticated labor rooted in the Garden Cities idea. The industrial plant was "privatized and turned into a comfortable living room."[64]

This new conception of social policy demanded a strong state which granted management the right to intervene in industrial relations to secure the new "occupational ethos," which would also "win over the worker to the state and for the preservation of traditional national culture."[65] At the same time, however, fertile terrain for the potential success of this approach was provided by the general disregard of pre-1933 trade unions for the work environment, and their frequent willingness to abandon fundamental ques-tions about the nature of work for wage settlements in periods of high pro-ductivity. Social Democratic theorists, such as Otto Bauer, denounced "lamentations over the spiritlessness of labor" as "nonsense," while embrac-ing the idea that "labor is our fate."[66] Communist theorists too, following Lenin's endorsement of Taylorism, fully assimilated the cult of technoc-racy.[67] Only rarely was the problem of "joy in work" approached from the socialist standpoint, as in Hendrik de Man's critique of those "Marxist doc-trinaires ignorant of psychology and out of touch with the actualities of life, [who] fail to see that the workers" prevailing discontent is due quite as much to the loss of pleasure in work as to the (problematic) loss of concrete acquisitions."[68]

The myth of an organic and nonalienated form of industrial production, proclaimed by politicized industrial sociology, was concretized in the Na-tional Socialist concept of a deproleterianized and economically peaceful

plant. Nevertheless, its appeal to labor was always overshadowed by its promise to management. The allure of "scientific" plant policy for both employers and the National Socialists was clearly enhanced by the Briefs's School's
militant opposition to trade unions, and its extreme antisocialism. Even the
redefinition of management as the "plant leader" in the new labor law not
only ensured the hegemony of the entrepreneur, but also redefined management along the general lines which industrial relations had almost universally established in most advanced capitalist countries. The struggle for
survival and the pursuit of self-interest had been superseded by an image of
cooperative teamwork.[69] The bureau shared with industrial psychology this
faith in the potential transformation of industrial relations in the epoch of
mechanical production, Taylorized work processes, and the depersonalized
modern factory. With the elimination of the trade unions, labor relations
were merged with ideology in the interests of social control.

Nazi Sachlichkeit

Of course, the concept of "Beauty of Labor" contained several fundamental
ambiguities, endemic to reactionary modernism. It pointed to a return to
the "community of enterprise" characterized by the unity of workman and
employer, reestablishing "the organic unity which existed in the Middle
Ages."[70] At the same time, however, it integrated aesthetics into contemporary industrial production, deriving its impulse from the latest stage
of industrial psychology. Its nineteenth-century paternalism was clouded by
real utopian tendencies aimed at the abolition of genuine discontents. These
antimonies were eventually superseded by a cult of technology and production that gradually took precedence in both the propaganda and practice of
the bureau after 1936. The machine, which in the early propaganda of the
bureau was assaulted as "God and Lord over the working man," lost the neg-
ativity ascribed to it.[71] What had in fact been a virtual "demonization" of
technology, in which machinery alone was held responsible for the failure
of liberal capitalism and the social ills of the pre-Nazi era, turned into its
opposite—the glorification of technical rationality through aesthetics.

    At the center of this change was the emergence of an aesthetics of tech-
nology and rationalization, derived from the Neue Sachlichkeit (New

Objectivity) movement of the 1920s, in which Beauty of Labor signified the aesthetic reflection of technical rationality and industrial production. Aesthetics not only intervened in the sphere of industrial labor, but industry itself was elevated to an aesthetic principle. The new technical aesthetic represented the culmination of a historical development that interpreted the industrial sphere as the source of aesthetic norms. In a direct assault on the Kantian premise that defined beauty as "purposefulness without purpose," occluding the "great majority [who] provide the necessities of life, as it were, mechanically," a new aesthetic emerged which heralded mechanical processes and made utility into a religion.[72] To be sure, nineteenth-century romantic artists, particularly in England, found beauty in the industrial landscape, even in the darkest and most exploitative workrooms.[73] But the real world of work and machine production was not yet the paradigm of aesthetics itself. The mythologized image of industrialization stopped at the door of the "satanic mills" where "man returns to a cave dwelling, which is now however contaminated with the pestilential breath of civilization."[74] Even the Great Exhibition of 1851, which placed industrial machinery on exhibition as an object of aesthetic contemplation, did not yet fully anticipate the transvaluation of aesthetic value granted to the instruments of production in the twentieth century. After 1907, the Deutscher Werkbund, formed to display the best of German art and design, indicated that technics would thereafter not only be considered aesthetic, but—especially after 1914—that industrial forms and machines would themselves shape the concept of beauty which informed contemporary design. At the annual meeting of the Werkbund in 1914, Hermann Muthesius, the leader of the Neue Sachlichkeit movement, defined the principle of the new aesthetic: "Architecture and the entire sphere of activity of the Werkbund tend towards standardization. It is only by standardization that they can recover that universal importance which they possessed in ages of harmonious civilization."[75] This new technological aesthetic became firmly rooted in Germany through the efforts of the Werkbund, and in architecture through the Bauhaus; it determined the fundamental principle of the "modernist movement." Beauty was identified with a "second nature," with mechanical adequacy and technical form. Especially in the artistic and literary Neue Sachlichkeit, which gained extraordinary popularity in pre-Depression Germany, the new aesthetic celebrated "the concrete," the thing alone, autonomous of all social relations. The mystique of technical rationality, productivity, efficiency, and "romantic faith in the speed and roar of machines all belonged to the cult of the *sachlich*."[76] Paralleling the intensive rationalization of German industry, during the upswing of German capitalism between 1924 and 1928, everything from frying pans to industrial gears were exhibited for their pious adherence to the principles of economy of form, efficiency of design, and mathematical precision. With the extension of modern design to all aspects of everyday life, social relations became mediated by an image of the world derived from technical rationality.

The new aesthetic absorbed the technocratic assumption that the expansion of technical rationality would automatically lead to a more rational social order. Like the theorists of Fordism and rationalization that had influenced them, the advocates of Nazi rationalization reflected a deep dissatisfaction with the instability of society and the perseverance of preindustrial social structures and values.[77] The utopian dimension embedded in the new aesthetic was a vision of society in which "a badly functioning social machine had been exchanged for a more perfect one."[78] This belief in the beneficent telos of rationalization was exemplified by writers such as Franz Kollman, whose book *Schönheit der Technik* (Beauty of technology, 1927) saw in machine parts, industrial buildings, structures made of steel, railroads, and submarines "the root of the power of future beauty and culture."[79] The new cult of technics contained, however, yet another, perhaps more significant aspect. It reduced real progress to technological progress, and the rational constitution of society to the rationality of machine production. By excluding the relations of production, its forces were ontologized. All reminders of the irrationality of what was judged to be the pretechnological epoch were exorcised, as if the old order would simply disintegrate when confronted with the power of the technical form. The rationality of technics, embodied in modern architecture and design, promoted the value of industrial forms without regard for the nature of industrial society. The attempt to repress even the most unobtrusive historical residues, expressed in the attack on ornament, revealed the extent to which this deep hostility to history was translated into a myth—"a rationalization without ratio."[80]

Continuity between the aesthetics of the Neue Sachlichkeit movement and Beauty of Labor is apparent in the bureau's personnel as well as its principles. It was an open secret that the bureau was a kind of sanctuary for former Bauhaus architects and designers. Wilhelm Lotz, the editor of *Schönheit der Arbeit*, was previously editor of *Die Form*, the most influential organ of the Werkbund and Bauhaus in the late 1920s and early 1930s.[81] Despite his 1928 stand against the Bauhaus's narrow reliance on "ideas attuned to industrial production," Lotz perpetuated its fundamental themes. Although most Bauhaus architects and designers were forced into exile in the early days of the regime, the work of modern architects, such as Ernst Otto Schweizer, were approvingly displayed in *Schönheit der Arbeit*.[82] Earlier propaganda that, under Kretschmer's directorship, had criticized the "functionalist boxes of the Republic," gave way to praise for the principles of modernism in industrial architecture. The machine aesthetic was assimilated in its entirety: "It can be ascertained that machines, technics, are capable of producing aesthetic satisfaction: they must, however, only submit to the laws of their own style."[83] In an article describing the reorganization of a motor factory according to the latest plant designs, one writer exulted: "As opposed to the old there is line, there is style, there is Beauty of Labor."[84] Kollman's theories were cited as evidence "that aesthetic forms no longer stand in contrast to the functional technical form."[85] Even if it was questionable that workers shared this taste in relation to the beauty of their own environment, they could be educated to acquire an appreciation of the new style.[86] The models of tableware and office furniture, designed to conform to standard industrial forms, also reflected—though somewhat subdued and unoriginal—aspects of the 1930s style. This affirmation of the new aesthetic did not go unnoticed. By 1937, the bureau found it necessary to defend itself against critics who accused the bureau of promoting Neue Sachlichkeit and constructivism.[87]

The bureau's emphasis on the hygienic and rational design of the workplace, on lighting, ventilation, and other environmental factors, derived its impetus from the rationalization movement of the 1920s. Moreover, even the most technical aspects of the bureau—the intensive campaigns to improve lighting, air, and hygiene—were not simply means of increasing output and social management. The concept of light took on ideological significance, for example, through its opposition to the image of darkness associated with the industrial workplace of liberal capitalism. For Marx that "dwelling in the light which Prometheus in Aeschylus designated as one of

the greatest boons by means of which he made the savage into a human being ceased to exist for the worker."[88] In the bureau, the lighting campaigns
attempted to signify the reversal of this situation. The film *Light*, produced
by the bureau in 1936, began with a "cultural-historical" introduction describing light as the "creative power of all earthly life, reproducing the wish
of mankind to illuminate the darkness of night."[89] The darkness and blight
of the liberal industrial landscape, "the plants of the thoughtless sacks of
gold" where "the work is sullen, done behind window panes blinded by dust,
in cold unfriendly rooms, because it must be done," was contrasted to the
selfless anticapitalism of the bureau.[90] Nevertheless, the symbolism of illu-
mination as the antithesis of capitalist industry occasionally contradicted the
dark image of work romanticized by Labor Front artists. Otto Hamel's dimly
lit painting *Eisenwerk*, shown at the Munich exhibition of 1937, appeared in
Schönheit der Arbeit with the following caption: "Unfortunately the roman-
ticism of the old workplaces attracts the eye of the painter more than what
we understand as Beauty of Labor."[91]

Cleanliness and order also externalized the model for an internalized
work discipline and routine demanded by the rationalized labor process.
"Cleanliness and order in all externalities, as well as in the inner attitude of
all members of the plant, are the living cells whose gradual growth reaches
its high point in the realization of the National Socialist model plants."[92]
The inordinate amount of attention paid to the most modern conve-
niences in washing facilities, cleaning of the workplace, personal hygiene,
modern toilets, faucets, lockers and changing rooms, cannot solely be explained by Teutonic fastidiousness in these matters. Long rows of clean and
modern washing facilities were displayed as if modern sanitary equipment
extinguished the effects of the working day. The bureau's slogan "Clean
People—Clean Factories" had moral associations as well. The elimination
of that dirtiness, which for Freud was "incompatible with civilization," took
on ritualistic character in Beauty of Labor. The "low instincts" and immorality which were said to have been bred in the industrial plants of the eighteenth and nineteenth centuries could be erased by removing the unhygienic
sources of disease and depravity.[93] Tied to the goal of "securing increase in
happiness by elevation of the moral tone," hygiene had always been important in the garden cities movement.[94] Tessenow believed that "everyday work

and our industrial worker should not only be clean materially, but clean in whole character and form as well."[95]

These attitudes were also reflected in the cult of the body, which took the form of the plant sports and gymnastics, which the bureau helped introduce into three thousand German factories.[96] Drawing on the nineteenth-century tradition of gymnastics as political training and adopting methods derived from François Delsare's "aesthetic gymnastics" (introduced to Germany at Emil Jacques-Dalcroze's school for physical culture in Tessenow's gymnasium at Hellerau), body movement was transplanted to the factory in the interests of discipline and greater productivity.[97] What had begun as a revolt against mechanization became, by 1936, an adornment of industrial production itself.

The Architecture Bureau

Above all, however, it was in architecture that the bureau most decisively established what might be termed Nazi Sachlichkeit. Before 1936, while the economy remained below full employment and productivity, architecture had been largely limited to public building in the monumental, neoclassical style, or to the *Kleinsiedlung*, the garden plot houses for workers reminiscent of rural cottages and early Krupp settlements. The Four-Year Plan, launched in October 1936, meant not only the extension of state control over labor and industry, but intense concentration on preparation for military mobilization.[98] Less practical *völkisch* residues such as the *Kleinsiedlung* were abandoned in favor of new apartment blocks in urban areas or temporary housing.[99] Demand for new industrial plants, as well as housing for those workers "uprooted" and transplanted by state intervention in the labor market, brought about new tasks for the bureau. The bureau was entrusted with the design of "simple and purposeful" houses for workers, particularly in rural areas.[100] Usually these new construction efforts were undertaken by the Labor Front for large industry or by agreement with the military. By 1939, a great deal of the new construction in Germany was either for private industrial purposes or in the hands of the Labor Front's enterprises and housing program. Industrial architecture eclipsed the monumental designs of the pre-1936 phase, incorporating principles derived largely from modernism that underscored the primacy of rationality and efficiency in the sphere of production. By 1938, a special Bureau of Architecture emerged from the bureau.[101] A conscious distinction was carefully maintained between "representational" architecture in official party buildings and industrial architecture. Moreover, buildings were required to fit their surroundings. Hitler himself recognized this distinction between the monumental public style and the factory, and according to Speer, could even become enthusiastic over an industrial building in glass and steel.[102]

The distinction between the increasing modernism of Nazi architecture and design and the traditionalism that characterized its earlier ideology was accentuated by the public rooms and buildings designed by the bureau for specifically political functions. In larger factories, these distinctly political spaces were in the "Comradeship Houses," which were built in the style of a small rural church, cloister, or feudal manor house.[103] The flags and Nazi insignias conspicuously absent in other areas of the plant were present here. Yet this facet of the bureau's work, which also included the "dignified decoration" of plant assembly places, only served to emphasize the conscious separation of "purely political" spaces from the politicized functionalism of the bureau.[104]

Avowedly modern architects were employed by private industry and their designs approvingly displayed in the bureau's publications. Peter Behrens, the teacher of Gropius and Mies van der Rohe, was commissioned to design the AEG electrical company administration building on the Berlin Grand Boulevard for Speer's famous redesign of Berlin, Germania, outraging Alfred Rosenberg, who protested against the assignment to a precursor of architectural radicalism.[105] Not only was Behrens praised for his prewar industrial designs, but occasionally even exiled architects such as Gropius were openly credited with influencing the bureau's architectural tastes: "Even more decisively than Behrens, Walter Gropius was drawn to the construction of contemporary industrial facilities. . . . Gropius had at that time recognized the economic importance of the beautiful industrial plant buildings."[106] Unlike the Bauhaus architecture of the early 1930s, however, there was little attention to classical proportions or to the radical use of new materials in most designs. Facades and entrance halls were eclectic and often reflected monumental and neoclassical elements, in sharp contrast to the buildings in the *sachlich* style. Moreover, in contrast to the Bauhaus, which endowed the rejection of ornament and its classical proportions and cubic forms with a utopian vision of total social rationality, Nazi industrial architecture retained only the utilitarian form, subordinating imagination to the demands of production and efficiency. Nevertheless, the motifs of Nazi industrial architecture are decisively modern in inspiration and were in fact largely indistinguishable from non-Bauhaus modernism of the interwar period.[107]

In early 1937, *Schönheit der Arbeit* began to publish a series of contributions by "plant leaders" and architects explicitly advocating the new style in industrial construction.[108] Pre-1933 Nazi propaganda that attacked modernism as architectural "bolshevism" had to be neutralized. Industrial architecture was proclaimed as "the most important monument of our time."[109] The old architecture which reflected the "sins of the past" was condemned—it reflected insufficient cooperation between engineers and architects. Beauty of Labor architects were required to assure the integration of technical achievement and artistic elements. Above all, historical allusion and ornament were to be eliminated: industrial buildings were not to be "palatial constructs." Monumental factory architecture which did not "form an organic whole with the entire plant" was to be replaced by architecture conforming to reality and corresponding "to the seriousness and importance of the work performed behind its doors."[110]

Among the most significant examples of National Socialist industrial functionalism were the glass, brick, and exposed structure buildings constructed for the Deutsche Versuchsanstalt für Luftfahrt (German Experimental Station for Flight), completed in 1937 by the architects Hermann Brenner and Werner Deutschmann in Berlin-Adlershof.[111] The modernism of these buildings is evident in the use of glass, brick, exposed structures, modern lighting, and neatly laid out lawns and streets. The wind tunnels and explicitly geometric patterns of the buildings were praised as the greatest examples of Beauty of Labor architecture and as illustrations of the principle that "a high degree of purposefulness and true beauty are not opposites which exclude each other."[112]

The crowning achievement of the bureau was the *"Wunderauto"* (wonder car) plant near Fallersleben, built to house the Volkswagen project, the showpiece of "strength through joy." "The Volkswagen works was to become the most powerful and beautiful automobile factory in the world."[113] In addition to the auto works, a new city was also envisioned, planned for thirty thousand auto workers and their families in the first stage alone.[114] In May 1938, ground was broken, and by December of that year the frame of the buildings, particularly the production centers, were visible. *Schönheit der Arbeit* devoted a special issue to the new plant. The four great halls, including the energy plant and machine works, were displayed as monuments to the aesthetic superiority of industrial architecture and progress under National Socialism: In fact, the celebration was premature—like most social promises of the regime, the car was never delivered. Unfinished by the beginning of the war, the works were converted to the production of arms and military vehicles. No Volkswagens were delivered for private use.[115] The new attitude toward technology was reflected in Nazi institutions as well. In 1936, under the direction of Oskar Stäbel, the National Socialist Association for German Technology was founded to bring about a harmony between *Volk* and technology by increasing scientific and technical labor power for conscripts. In March of that year, the bureau concluded an agreement to cooperate with the association in all technical aspects of the alteration of plant environments.[116] Above all, discontent with technology and industrialization, often stressed in pre-1933 *völkisch* theory, had to give way to a concept that emphasized the "good intentions of rationalization" and the "virtues of mechanization."[117] Even artisan production, still significant in Germany as late as 1939, when one third of all industrial workers were employed in shops of less than ten persons, was forced to increase efficiency and carry out technology improvements. Those artisan shops which survived the state directed "combing out" of inefficient and one-person enterprises remained under government restriction and were to a large extent turned into subsidiary repair shops for large industry.[118] These measures against small industry were echoed in the bureau's campaign for the rationalization of artisan production throughout 1938 and 1939.[119] After 1938, the productivism of the bureau was the consistent theme of its publications. The romantic image of the handicraft shop, venerated in the early days of the Nazi movement, was scrutinized and purged of preindustrial characteristics: old tables, rotten from wood worms, had to be replaced so that craftsmen could "understand the needs and demands" of the "epoch of the machine."[120] Technology was also aestheticized as the extension of handicraft production. A series of photographs displaying the aesthetic qualities of hand motions in both mechanized and unmechanized production illustrated the point that "handicraft work is not eliminated but transformed."[121] For the bureau, the enormous gears of modern industry became the objects of aesthetic contemplation, and rows of shiny oil cans became a symbol for "the hand tools of the machine masters."[122] The mistrust among German artisans provoked by the technocratic revival was condemned as *"Maschinenstürmerei"* (Luddism).

In the National Socialist New Order, the cult of technical rationality embodied in Beauty of Labor represented a significant effort to legitimize state regulation and the intensive rationalization of industry. Production and efficiency were idealized as qualities divorced from commercial considerations, the market, and imperial military aims. The myth of an abolished market society was most apparent in the bureau's successful campaign to remove all traces of commercial advertising from the plant environment.[123] Implicit was the notion expressed in the bureau's ideology of "noneconomic" production: "We do not consider the factory as an association for economic purposes."[124] At the same time the purely inward focus on the productive apparatus coincided with Germany's actual withdrawal from the world market and its attempt at industrial self-sufficiency through an autarchic arms economy. The glorification of Architectural modernism and the technocratic cult could be celebrated apart from any political and social aims which it might serve. Social realities could be eliminated by a symbolic reductionism. Modern materials became identical with the epoch itself: "reinforced concrete and steel construction are closely related to the spirit of our time."[125] Yet practical purposes were not lost—the green areas for workers' rest periods could also serve as camouflage in air raids.

Nazi Productivism

The industrial considerations that took priority in the bureau dominated not only its ideology, but its practical work as well. The intensive "struggle for productivity," announced by Ley in late 1937, directed the bureau's technical agencies to concentrate on the development of programs to reduce wasted energy and increase productivity going forward. The standardization and functional design of work processes and environments became a crucial component of the new situation. Not only were the workplaces themselves to be redesigned for maximum output, but workers too had to carry out their work in a "correct and functional manner."[126] New developments in ergonomic research were applied to furniture design to produce modern innovations such as the "norm chair," with an elastic vertical and horizontal adjustable back to benefit the assembly line worker by "preventing premature fatigue" while increasing output.[127] "Flowing work" was the goal of the efficiency expert who applied the lessons of electro-technical mass production to the development of "a psychologically grounded formation of the workplace."[128]

Although the bureau emphasized the principle that "the higher the output the greater the joy in work," it was the former that received greater attention in the information directed at management. Speaking at the National Conference of Beauty of Labor in April 1938, Ley gave assurances that plant leaders had provided him with statistical evidence that Beauty of Labor "was not a luxury or a gift, but in the last analysis had been transformed into an increase in production and surplus value."[129] For business, this meant higher profits, but for workers reductions in consumption, wage controls and longer hours were combined with the intensification of work in the plant.[130] At the same time, however, the almost exclusive focus on productivity pointed to the failure of the bureau's earlier efforts to achieve a lasting integration of the German working class. The 1938–39 struggle for productivity reflected an actual decline in the productivity of labor and growing discontent over the low wages and shortages that accompanied state direction in the labor source market.[131] Already in 1937, the voluntary overtime that was often the source of labor for the bureau's projects was publicly condemned and officially terminated because it represented, in light of the already lengthened workday, an "almost unbearable burden."[132] Nazi productivism was an indication of the growing authoritarianism of state control over labor which, having ultimately failed to "win over" the working class, was now subjecting it to the increasing domination of productivity and output.

The bureau's attempts to increase output and efficiency were designated as "steered rationalization," distinguished from the profit oriented rationalization of the 1920s by its "subordination to political leadership and social policy."[133] In fact, "steered rationalization" differed from the older variety, not in its system, but in its spirit. The changes which the bureau initiated were "completely within the meaning of rationalization, the scientific penetration of productive factory labor."[134] All aspects of Taylorism—the degradation of work, the dissociation of skill and mental labor from the worker—were accepted by the bureau as axiomatic. It was not concerned with rationalization per se, but with its disadvantageous consequences. The new design of the workplace was in fact a compensatory or remedial form of rationalization, designed to adapt labor to already technified production processes: "Machines and operations must be so functionally built and arranged that the work can be accomplished within the smallest spaces with the least possible movement and expenditure of energy."[135] Even the physiology of the worker had to be rationalized. This was the motivation for the bureau's campaign for "Hot Meals in the Plant." Plant managers were instructed that "plant leadership in nourishment means a further important step toward the rationalization of labor power; the sums invested are—if the comparison is admissible—equally as productive as the expenses for technical improvements in the plant, for construction and machine maintenance, protection from corrosion and so forth."[136] The bureau's unabashed modernism and *Sachlichkeit*, and its focus on the transformation of labor through environmental changes, were contested by a competing Labor Front agency, Karl Arnhold's Amt für Berufserziehung und Betriebsführung (Bureau of Vocational Education and Industrial Management) in October 1936. The controversy underscored the decline of traditional ideology in the Labor Front under the Four-Year Plan. Arnhold, whose Deutsches Institut für technische Arbeitschulung (DINTA) represented the extreme right wing of industrial and plant engineering in the 1920s, had criticized the criteria chosen for granting the "model plant" award, announced in August 1936 to spark initiative among industrialists.[137] Instead of the proposed "social, technical and economic" categories that were proposed, Arnhold demanded that criteria be established that followed his own program for increasing efficiency and "mobilizing the performance reserves of industry" through a heavily ideological program of quasi-military training and indoctrination for managers and trainees. Above all, Arnhold challenged the bureau's emphasis on the "material obstacles" to increased productivity at the expense of "spiritual obstacles." Neither Strength through Joy nor Beauty of Labor, not even higher wages, could decrease the "resistance and exhaustion of a worker who worked with psychological blinders."[138] Although he did not entirely disapprove of the bureau's efforts, he decisively rejected its functionalism and proposed that the "tempo of the machine be brought into harmony with the rhythm of the blood" through "the organic formation of the plant" and the militarization of the leadership.[139] The results of the controversy indicated even more clearly the primacy of the bureau over Arnhold's more traditional ideological schemes. Technical rationality, not indoctrination, rather the idea that "each kind of work determines where and how it is to be formed" guaranteed that the criteria for the "model plants" would correspond to the principles of the bureau.[140]

After 1939, the bureau was severely limited by reductions in its operating budget brought on by the war. Its activities of the previous half decade were largely abandoned in the interest of contributing to the war effort, mostly by providing technical information on the construction of shelters, troop entertainment centers, methods of improving blackout techniques, and energy saving measures.[141] But in its six years of activity almost eighty thousand factories were transformed by the bureau's projects.[142] Lighting, ventilation, and noise levels were improved; wardrobes, washrooms, and gymnasiums were provided or remodeled; lawns and parks were built surrounding the plant. Flowers, decorations, and new coats of paint appeared. Factory canteens were provided with newly designed tableware, and "community rooms" and "comradeship houses" were constructed in numerous plants. Architectural modernism and contemporary design were furthered in industrial construction. The German factory had indeed received a new face.

Conclusion

In Beauty of Labor, the utopian promise of an industrial society where work was beautiful and the class struggle abolished was given political and administrative form. Its goal was the domestication of labor, to be achieved by treating the plant as a "sphere of life," detached from the social relations that enclose the world of work and removed from the specters of working-class culture and autonomous organization. The bureau was to integrate the German worker, deprived or political and economic representation, into the "facade" socialism of the Labor Front. As objectified ideology, it signified a critique of liberalism, in which concern for hygiene and aesthetics in the environment restored the value and meaning of work. But if the bureau presented itself as a radical break with the aesthetic deficiencies of industrialization in the liberal epoch, it solidified and strengthened its political-economic basis: management was supreme, the bureau had no power to enforce its policies—its ultimate goal was the depoliticization of industrial relations. As industrial psychology, Beauty of Labor extended the domination of material nature to the nature of the worker, whose consciousness was reduced to an environmental "factor," to be transformed in the interest of productivity and habituation. As social policy, Beauty of Labor subjected labor to the intervention of techniques derived from the politicized science of industrial relations of the 1920s and 1930s on an unprecedented scale.

Perhaps most important, the bureau not only integrated aesthetics into the world of production, but derived from production a technocratic aesthetic that combined with the *völkisch* and preindustrial imagery of pre-1933 Nazism into a new legitimation based on the autonomy of technical rationality. If Nazism did not display the veneration of machinery that characterized Italian fascism in the early 1920s, or the Soviet Union in the early 1930s, this was true only before 1936, when Germany's condition could be attributed to the ills of modernity, and the support of the *Mittelstand* (small manufacturers) could be secured by the image of its dissolution.

As early as 1935, the philosopher Ernst Bloch contrasted the widespread rejection of contemporary society by a German middle strata which "sought transcendence in the past," with an exaggerated faith in the power of "neutral cleanliness, new architecture and its comforts, manufactured goods, technical functionalism and the standardization of products," as a dialectic of "noncontemporaneity and contemporaneity," specific to Germany's historical development.[143] The shift from one extreme of this dialectic to the other took place once Nazism could no longer rely on the simple legitimacy of *völkisch* ideology and an agrarian utopia. Policies directed at the *Mittelstand* were abandoned. The expansion of technical rationality to all aspects of the production process in the Four-Year Plan was extended to ideology as well. The goal of full employment, an end to the economic crisis, and industrial supremacy and military expansion, led Nazism to abandon its "utopian antimodernism" to the institutional and ideological requirements of war production.[144] If Nazism's mass support was rooted in its promise of a Germany free from the discontents of capitalism, rationalization, and the eclipse of traditional values, its historical function was to exorcize the traditional patterns of culture which conflicted with modern modes of production. In the bureau, this shift in cultural values was objectified ideologically and administratively. Its emphasis on production and the glorification of technology as ends in themselves was affirmed by persons and principles derived from the Neue Sachlichkeit movement that swept Germany in the mid-1920s. The aestheticization of machine technology, Taylorized work processes, and efficiency provided the new requirements of the regime with a cultural *raison d'être*.

It is the image of the worker, however, that most clearly illuminates the unity that binds the extensive range of the bureau's efforts between 1934 and 1939. The worker, like all the subjects of National Socialism, becomes an ornament of technically preconceived and constructed environments. As objects of management and production they are subordinated to the tempo of machines: "At machine four stands a punch operator, she activates the mechanism, moves to and fro, places plate after plate in the devouring jaws of the monster."[145] The small geometric roof gardens organize workers into prescribed patterns during rest pauses; sports areas organize their physical activity; newly cleaned machines organize them for greater productivity; neat rows of washing facilities order their cleanliness. The image culminates in the neat rows of happily producing workers who adorn the factory itself. Devoid of intentionality, the workers themselves are abstractions. Unable to reflect on their own condition, they are never permitted to speak in the pages of *Schönheit der Arbeit*. Nevertheless, "the fact that hygienic factory rooms and all that goes with them, Volkswagen and sport palace, ruthlessly liquidate metaphysics would be of no consequence, except that in the social totality they too become metaphysics, an ideological veil, behind which the real calamity gathers itself."[146]

SEVEN

Metaphors of the Machine in the Post-Fordist Era

During a flare-up of chronic anxiety over the alleged lack of the productivity of American workers, one commentator admitted in 1992 that "The work ethic may be slipping. But laziness isn't the reason; alienation is." Significantly, this remark appeared in the *Wall Street Journal*. The crisis of productivity, the author contended, was not due to any decline in hours or will to work, but to the residual effects of the disciplinary workplace. Experts blamed the lingering consequences of the Taylorist-Fordist workplace, for example, firms sticking to an outdated model in which management distrusts the autonomy of workers, prescribes dull routinized tasks, curbs creativity, and creates a workplace ill-suited to "literate, independent-minded workers."[1] In the 1990s, this criticism of American industry was cogently expressed by MIT economist Lester Thurow, who argued that American industry was hopelessly product-oriented while Europe and Japan focused on "process" improvements. American individualism and the ethic of entrepreneurship, so the argument went, restricts creativity, and inhibits cooperation, collaboration, and communication. By contrast, Thurow wrote, the capitalism of the future is "Communitarian Capitalism."[2]

This diagnosis was greatly strengthened by the almost simultaneous collapse of the Japanese economy between 1995 and 2007, demonstrating the unsustainability of Japanese firms with rigid organizational models. Nonetheless, both productivists (who saw the future of capitalism in terms of expanding technologies and innovation) and their critics (who advocate a reduction in labor time or even a guaranteed minimum income [GMI] as the solution to overproduction) almost universally shared the argument that standardized manufacturing practices—carried on in highly struc-tured environments by organized, disciplined, and unskilled workers—was not only outmoded but also an obstacle to productivity. Moreover, it is only one among many developments that have challenged our conventional un-derstandings of work, the workplace, and modern capitalism. Since the 1980s it has been commonplace to predict that computer-driven technolo-gies will dramatically change what we mean by work. In his 1986 book, aptly titled *The End of Work*, Jeremy Rifkin argued that automated tech-nologies are not only diminishing the proportion of manufactured work available, but are also rapidly shrinking the need for human labor in the white-collar sector as well.[3] According to Rifkin, the specter of automa-tion, raised a half-century ago, has become our nightmare: in both man-ufacturing and service work, workers are increasingly displaced by new technologies, and with the shift from mass employment to elite employment, joblessness will become globally endemic. Some went so far as to predict that "the work society has begun to transcend work" and that industrial labor is becoming "the agriculture of the twentieth century."[4] People-free robotized factories conjure up images of a future in which "workless work" is the norm. At the height of the 1992 German unemployment crisis, the sociolo-gist Wolf Lepenies asked whether it might not be "worthwhile to reflect on whether a change in values ought to be promoted, in which work is trans-valued, and as a result, whether unemployment ought to be less drama-tized."[5] In Rifkin's vision of the future, all governments will have to cope with what some economists called "castoffs," an unemployable labor force as opposed to cyclical "layoffs." Are we rapidly approaching the end of the work-centered society?

The Work versus Leisure Debate

In her book *The Overworked American* (1992), economist Juliet Schor answered this question with a sobering analysis of how Americans were working more rather than less. Despite overall gains in productivity, instead of enjoying expanded leisure time as the prophets of automation predicted in the 1950s, worktime had increased substantially since 1948. Americans in the 1990s worked 320 more hours than their West European counterparts. (In 2015, Americans worked 34.40 hours per week, whereas Germans worked 26.37 hours.)[6] Schor proposed a radical rethinking of the money-time tradeoff, one in which more (and better) time might be regarded as a viable alternative to what she called "the work-spend cycle." Among her practical suggestions were: (1) a fixed employee time "standard" that would allow flexibility within a given time allotment; (2) "comp" time in which extra hours are repaid with increments of time, not overtime wages; and (3) a productivity "dividend" translated into future time off. Rifkin too asks whether future gains in productivity might not be translated into more leisure time and consequently whether a transformation in consumption aspirations and behaviors might result from such a reevaluation of the choice between time and money.

Suggestions for more and better leisure, for ways to permit people to choose time over income, to curb consumption, and to achieve a slower, saner pace of life with more time for their own creative pursuits are a welcome counterpoint to high-tech productivism. However, the emphasis on self-restraint, on "opting for the time alternative" demands a program of austerity, however self-imposed and dependent on free choice it might be. Such propositions also assume, as did the advocates of the eight-hours workday a century ago, that increased leisure will be productive: "Many people would like to devote more time to the churches, get involved in their children's schools, coach a sports team, or help out at a soup kitchen."[7] Such nurturing activities might indeed be the result of more free time, but not necessarily. A great deal depends on what will happen to both work and leisure. Quality leisure, the counter-argument goes, depends on quality work. If future workers will be required to acquire more skills in knowledge and communication, the old patterns of mass consumerism may well come to reflect the class behavior of those still excluded from the new workplace.

Among late twentieth-century Marxist theorists, André Gorz (1923–2007) was unique in his consistent interest in science, work, and work time as the source of both critical and practical insights. Gorz's *Stratégie ouvrière et néo-capitalisme* (1964), translated in 1967 as *Strategy for Labor: A Radical Proposal* became a classic of the European and American New Left. Drawing on the experience of labor struggles in Italy in the late 1950s and early 1960s, Gorz offered the novel argument that an upsurge of labor militancy calling for the abolition of repetitive work, regimentation, and the authoritarian division of labor could potentially resuscitate a moribund labor movement. Such "radical reforms," he claimed, would challenge organized labor's bureaucratic constriction of vision, while reorienting it toward the democratic "conquest of popular centers of power and democratic self-rule from below."[8] Gorz drew extensively from the theoretical model developed by the French "sociology of work" in the 1950s and 1960s, and whose dominant figures were Georges Friedmann, Pierre Naville, and Alain Touraine.[9] In their view, the automation of work processes would increasingly make physical labor and the laborer obsolete; the "new worker" was the regulator and supervisor of complex mechanical systems. Squeezed by an ever-increasing tension between the creativity of technically trained universalists and the limited scope afforded by capital, these "knowledge workers" represented a subversive potential at the very heart of the most technologically advanced sectors of capitalism.

By the 1980s, Gorz had dramatically reversed the conclusions he had articulated a decade and a half earlier. In *Adieux au Prolétariat* (1980), translated in 1982 as *Farewell to the Working Class*, Gorz traced the steps that had led him to what he now acknowledged as an impasse: "Sooner or later, according to Marxist theory, the proletariat is to become conscious of its being as both labor power and collective productive worker."[10] This is so because the immensely productive power of labor leads not only to the recognition that the surplus serves no real needs, but to ever-greater mastery of the social process writ large. In the end, and neither sooner nor later will this revolutionary consciousness in fact materialize. Gorz's explanation is, as might be predicted, that the fragmentation of work—Taylorism, scientific management, and, finally, automation—has destroyed whatever consciousness of "practical sovereignty" might have existed. The very same labor process that for Marx made possible the creative potential of labor systematically extinguished all autonomy and consciousness of that potential in the worker. Gorz acknowledged that historically there once was a working-class culture with its own values, traditions, and organizations, capable of contesting and negotiating from a position of relative power. In retrospect, he says, what is striking about that culture is the "identification of workers with 'their' work and 'their' factory." However, the experience of the workers' control strikes in Italy and France during the 1960s demonstrated that once a norm has been decided upon by workers and accepted by management, it becomes no more than a new form of imprisonment for the workers themselves. At the end of the 1970s, Gorz broke off relations with the Confédération Française Démocratique du Travail (CFDT), the trade union that exemplified the program of *Strategy*, conceding that modern forms of power are a network of "subjectless," instrumental, and functional imperatives. The "heteronomy" of modern industry makes all claims to democratic self-determination in the workplace obsolete. *Adieu au prolétariat!*

Despite his abandoning of the working class as a political force and his questioning of "working-class humanism," Gorz remained remarkably faithful to the original Marxian theory. In *The Critique of Economic Reason*, Gorz reiterated Marx's famous distinction between the realms of freedom and necessity: "The realm of freedom actually begins only where labor which is determined by necessity and mundane consideration ceases."[11] The creative capacity of labor is destroyed by the imperatives of capital, whose productivist logic recognizes only labor power and labor time. Economic rationality cuts productive labor off from meaning, work from needs. This conclusion, however, negates Marxism's principal truth: the true personality, desires, and needs of the individual are most fully realized in labor as a creative act—Hannah Arendt's "auto-poiesis."[12] In the Marxian ideal of "working-class humanism," the labor movement, not labor per se, carries the utopian ideal of a "rationality which will give meaning to the whole of the development that precedes it." This rationality runs counter to the instrumental rationality of means and ends: it is another rationality, the rationality of planning, of full development of the means of production. Gorz concluded—as did the later Marx—that work is the realm of alienation; non-work, the realm of freedom. For Gorz's "post-Marxist" man liberation within nonalienated work has become "an unsustainable utopia."[13] But the second utopia in which the "electronic civilization" will eliminate millions of jobs, increase disposable labor time, and free political energy to "discover a sphere of nonquantifiable values, a 'time for living,'"[14] showed, he observed, ever greater vitality. Still in tune with Marx, Gorz asserted that "the emancipation of individuals, their full development, the restructuring of society, are all to be achieved through the liberation from work."[15] Work is no longer defined as the uniquely anthropological activity, as Marx's reference to *animal laborans* would have it. In Gorz's view, labor is one activity among others; it constitutes only one dimension of human existence and, with the technology available to modern society, it is becoming increasingly irrelevant to either human needs or human self-realization. Given his impressive theoretical sophistication, Gorz's reformulation of a "radical reform" is strikingly simple. Reduced worktime challenges economic reason by requiring only "the frontier of the sufficient" in which individuals could "adjust their hours of work to the income which they felt they needed." Worktime, he argues, has always been subjected to the imperatives of both self-renunciation and economic rationality. To the free market's demand for self-renunciation in favor of "unlimited maximization" of productivity, the labor movement responds with its own "humanism of need," a wage sufficient to live adequately and comfortably, with "time for living." Thus, the critique of economic rationality restores the worker's "existential sovereignty," a concept obviously indebted to Jean-Paul Sartre, the figure whose subject-centered Marxism dominated the early years of Gorz's intellectual career.

If Gorz criticized Marxism for its assumption that the development of the forces of production automatically brings about liberation, he remained convinced by its logic: economic rationality makes possible a reduction in both worktime and consumption, so that needs can be fulfilled in a minimum amount of socially necessary labor time. Yet Gorz was also aware that this economic rationality has reached its limits, that it is ontologically incapable of satisfying real needs, and that it presages ecological catastrophe. For this reason, Gorz may have been the last authentic Austro-Marxist, combining ecological concern with a conviction that an expansion of free time and socialism is compatible with full employment and full productivity. Nonetheless, Gorz's account is instructive in clarifying why Marxism had to choose between the "humanism of labor" and the program of liberation from worktime. Gorz's *Critique* points directly to the diametrically opposed notions of liberation that have dominated the utopias of the labor movement: liberation within work (the program of the 1844 manuscripts, the council communists of the 1920s, and the workers' control movements of the 1960s) and liberation from work (the program of *Capital*, the eight- and ten-hour movements).

Despite their differences, both productivists and asceticists—Gorz would have to be included among those who counseled self-restraint—advocated the "self-management of time" as opposed to managerial determination of work schedules.[16] Both regarded the future form of work as an individual choice, whether for increased competitiveness (foregoing union membership) or for "stepping off the consumer treadmill."[17] Yet, in two German cases where shorter hours solutions were seriously proposed or even put into effect (e.g., at IG Metall union and Volkswagen) short-term crisis responses were either imposed by a corporatist union or by corporate fiat (in 1994, Volkswagen saved thirty thousand jobs by cutting the work week to thirty hours and reducing salaries by 10 percent).[18]

As I have shown, the shorter hour's option has a distinguished ancestry. Just as today the prospect of reduced labor time as an antidote to structural unemployment is no longer connected to utopian socialist economics, 125 years ago, the British socialist John Rae denied that the demand for the eight-hour day had "anything of socialism in it at all." Rae predicted that the potential benefits of the "glad decree" were considerable: "In some trades it is probably a simple necessity for protecting the workpeople in normal conditions of health; but above all its sanitary benefits would confer upon the workpeople of every trade alike the much grander blessing admitting them to a reasonable share of the intellectual, social, domestic, religious, and political life of their time."[19] The shorter hours movement was arguably the most universal demand of labor before 1919. Advocates of reduced work time pointed to the potential benefits of less fatigue, greater longevity, and above all, higher cultural achievement. Supporters included those who believed it would raise wages (redistributionists), those who claimed it would increase productivity and prosperity (productivists), and those who imagined a working class whose education and cultivation would be elevated far above the philistine culture denied to it.

The struggle over work time was a fiercely contested issue worldwide and labor historians largely agree that the ultimate decision for "money" over "time" was by no means necessary or natural.[20] There is, however, considerable debate over why money eventually triumphed. Schor explains its success in terms of the classical Fordist model: in the 1920s a new consumer ethic that required money to buy into the social goods just becoming available to workers became hegemonic. During the depression decade, the trauma of mass unemployment devalued the time option and the New Deal was unable to secure any further reduction in hours. Other historians point to the failure of alternative models of mass leisure during the 1930s in both Europe and America. Organized efforts to institutionalize a more ennobling popular leisure—such as the Austrian socialist experiment of "Red Vienna," the French Popular Front's leisure organizations, and the English Labour Party culture in the 1930s—promised community, solidarity, and mass educational uplift but also required a relatively homogenous party and class subculture.[21] Gary Cross has persuasively argued that it is far too easy to underestimate the symbolic significance of money as conferring power and democratic access to the market when individuals are largely excluded from civic participation. The "cycle of earning and spending" justifiably triumphed because common access to goods is far preferable to, and more democratic than, an intellectualist vision of "ascetic sociability."[22] Note also that the triumph of the eight-hour day in 1919 came about as a result of the postwar political convergence of a powerful labor movement that had gained strength through cooperation with capital and the state during the war, international fear of Communism, and the dynamics of the peace settlements.

The Fordist Social Contract after 1945

The alternatives of work time versus free time, time versus money, do not fully address the remarkable change that work has been undergoing since the 1980s. As this book has argued, we are witnessing the disappearance of the great productivist utopias of the 1920s and 1930s. This crisis of productivist systems and ideologies may be far more significant than even the more narrowly defined crisis of Fordism that many critics have identified. As I will argue in the concluding section of this chapter, the metaphors that defined work during the epoch of industrialization have withered away. In the debates over the collapse of communism it is often forgotten that it is not only in Russia and Eastern Europe that one of the most compelling ideas of the last 150 years, what Gorz called the "humanism of labor," has collapsed.[23] This ideal, which can be traced from the utopian socialists of the early nineteenth century to Stalin's Five-Year Plan, envisaged a transformed work, and a transformed worker as the goal of socialism. Freed from the constraint of fulfilling needs, labor would be transformed into the central human need, its existential and meaning-giving activity. As Marx famously predicted, the shortening of the working day would bring about the end of the realm of necessity and usher in the realm of freedom.[24] Communism was the "productivism that failed" both as a utopia and as an alternative model of industrialization. In the end communism offered a minimalist social contract based on low pay, low productivity, and high job security.

In the West, too, productivism has undergone a profound transvaluation. The Fordist system established in the 1920s was not merely a new system of factory organization or a more efficient system of technical innovation, but "a socio-political regime, a set of institutionalized relationships between the social organization of production on the one hand, and social self-understanding and political organizations on the other." During the golden age of Fordism after World War II, Western capitalism rapidly recovered from the depression and was characterized by a highly successful "intensive regime of accumulation" that combined mass production with steady innovations in production techniques and a coupling of real wage increases with increases in productivity.[25] A more equitable distribution of social goods was secured by collective bargaining agreements guaranteed by Keynesian governmental controls, corporatism, and national economic policy.[26] Big profits, high wages, and high productivity, guaranteed by big unions and big government, were the hallmark of Fordist distribution policies in the heyday of the welfare state.

In America, and even more so in Europe, from the end of World War II to the late 1960s, the Fordist social contract guaranteed high wages, high purchasing power, a comfortable old age, and above all, the relative security that each generation can expect to achieve a higher standard of living than the previous one. Today, none of these assumptions can be taken for granted. The promise of a secure future, more than "consumerism" per se, defined the Fordist utopia, and the fact that it can no longer be guaranteed or expected has resulted in what Barbara Ehrenreich called the new middle-class "fear of falling."[27]

The classical Fordist model that linked increases in productive potential to more equitable distribution of wages and social goods after World War II appears to be in its terminal stage. In fact, as Eric Hobsbawm pointed out, "it was not until after the USSR and 'real socialism' collapsed, that the global nature of the crisis could be recognized."[28] The "crisis decade" of the 1980s proved that increased production technologies could "shed" human labor far more quickly than reabsorb it. Theorists of post-Fordism pointed out that this crisis bears certain similarities to the one that produced the depression: "uneven early development" of the new system produced an imbalance between expanded productive capacity and traditional consumption norms.[29] Under the rapidly "degenerating regime of intensive accumulation," Fordist systems were no longer capable of sustaining the rough balance between a high output of producer goods and the expanding consumer economy.[30] The Taylorist/Fordist constellation of growth, prosperity, and social equity reached its limit, forcing capital to adapt new and more flexible consumer-oriented strategies of production and distribution.[31] Instead of standardized mass production, firms now stress flexible batch production, smaller inventories, and niche markets. Instead of the integration of big production and centralized labor systems, outsourcing and decentralization is now preferable; rigidly time-bound factory labor is giving way to flexible work schedules combined with brutal "purposeful Darwinism" in the workplace.[32] Finally, instead of top-down control over un- or deskilled routinized industrial labor, management finds skilled, educated workers capable of working in tandem with management far more desirable. The disappearance of this disciplinary ideal may be one of the most salient features of the new post-Fordist productivism.

From the nineteenth-century industrial workplace (described by E. P. Thompson and a generation of social historians) to the totalitarian model of the work society (in both Soviet Russia and Nazi Germany), "disciplinarity" reigned supreme. Taylorism, it should also be noted, was but one among many scientific approaches to labor that shared a fetishism of corporal rationalization, and promised the end of class conflict through the greater productivity achieved by conserving the workers' energy.[33] The mobiliza-

tion of labor power in the totalitarian states of the 1930s was unprecedented. And as Paul Kennedy reminds us, these "challengers" (most notably
Italy, Japan, and the Soviet Union) were capable of extraordinary spurts of
productive energy.[34]

Although the totalitarian alternative was eclipsed by the 1960 and as my
opening quote from the *Wall Street Journal* shows, the traditional association of work and discipline is on the wane in the West. Instead of top-down
industrial discipline, democratic and communicative communities of fewer
but more elite workers are in greater demand. Before the fall of the Berlin
Wall, it was assumed that American economic hegemony could be maintained if capitalism adopted a flexible strategy toward work and worktime.[35]
The commonplace that increasing productivity and economic expansion
leads to general material well-being, including lower unemployment, has
also been called into question. One of the most sacrosanct elements of
Fordism, despite regional and national discrepancies, has always been the
close connection between politics and economics. However, in the new
global framework, economy and society are no longer linked: the economy
has become emancipated from the society and from the state: success on
Wall Street is no longer well-being on main street. And vice versa, what is
good for main street, is not necessarily good for the economy.[36]

Post-Taylorist industrial relations specialists rejected the ideal of a homogenous workforce composed of a dull, uneducated worker subjected to
hierarchical control and prescribed tasks. The disciplined rule-bound
worker, they maintained, will give way to the ideal of a "flexible, internally
motivated, continuously learning work force." Obsolete bureaucratic structure will be reborn as "a strong internal culture to support information sharing and participation in problem solving," commands will give way to
"balancing dialogue and discussion," hierarchy will be redefined as the "delegation or shared responsibility in recognition that dispersed activity requires local action and flexibility."[37]

The Metaphors of Productivism

The crisis of productivism brought about by the eclipse of the work-centered
utopias of the first half of the twentieth century also brought about a crisis

of the metaphors mobilized to frame and embody the nature of modern work. This dimension has received far less attention than the crisis of the Fordist and totalitarian productivist models.

I have proposed a rather general schema for discussing the metaphors of the laboring body for which I do not claim much more than a limited and alterable validity. The metaphor of the body as machine/motor can plausibly be compartmentalized into three distinct types: mimetic, transcendental, and allegorical. These correspond to the dominant technologies of the era which each circumscribes. During the eighteenth century, gifted artisans such as Jacques Vaucanson and the Droz family produced extraordinary automata, albeit lacking in self-moving power. The steam engines, automobiles and Taylorist-Fordist worker that convert energy to produce motion were represented by the discoveries of thermodynamics and labor power. Today's metaphor derives its inspiration from computers, and "digital organisms." What I am interested in asking is whether shifts in the forms of metaphor and the technology of work that are taking place call into question traditional notions of the biopolitics of work. The new information-ruled workplace, based on the algorithmic symbol manipulation that makes computers work, is neither based on the generation of things nor on the conversion of force, but—not unlike the duck—on the precise simulacra of other processes.

As discussed in chapter 1, Vaucanson's world-famous duck, which toured England and Germany in 1744, pecked grain, drank water, and evacuated a smelly pellet which passed through its system after being ingested was, by all accounts, a sensation. As technical fictions, the automata were epistemological machines, functioning illustrations of a biomechanical mode of explanation and simulacra of the self-moving power and capacity for generation which inevitably eluded them.[38] Yet, however much he had "endeavored to make it imitate all the actions of the living animal," Vaucanson stopped short of identifying life with the machine. This distinction was noticed by Kant when he enlisted it to refute Descartes's famous claim that living organisms can be reduced to a machine, since as Kant asserted, "no machine can replace one of its own missing parts."[39]

For Descartes, no matter how superbly produced, automata are lacking in self-moving power—a soul, emotions, language, spontaneity—and thus remain mimetic beings, correspondences to life. As Jessica Riskin notes, "rather than to reduce life to mechanism, he meant to elevate mechanism to life: to explain life, never to explain it away."[40] Even the staunchest materialists, such as Julien Offray La Mettrie, author of *L'homme machine* (1747), considered machines the "living representation of perpetual motion." But he admitted that "living machines are more than machines."[41] In his indispensable study of the automata, Jean-Claude Beaune rightly insisted that the proper definition of an automaton is "a machine that contains its own principle of motion."[42] Eighteenth-century automata were not "working" machines. On the contrary, their work was performed by their creators, and they served as entertainment, or at best, as devices to illustrate the principle of self-moving power which they failed to embody.

The productivism of the industrial revolution was governed by the realization that human society and nature are linked by the primacy and ultimate interchangeability (convertibility) of all productive activity, whether of the body, technology, or nature. Its social imaginary presupposed the metaphor of the motor which first appeared during the first quarter of the nineteenth century.[43] In 1824, Sadi Carnot demonstrated that all the forces of nature are essentially different varieties of a single, universal energy or *Kraft*. The laws of thermodynamics revealed the mimetic machine to be an epistemological dead-end, since energy is always universally available.[44] Unlike the metaphor of the machine, the metaphor of the motor is productivist: it refers not simply to the mechanical generation of movement but to the industrial model of energy converted from nature to society.[45]

As I have shown, Marx shifted his focus from the emancipation of mankind *through* labor, to the emancipation *from* productive labor by an even greater productivity. Marx became a productivist, as Agnes Heller argued, largely because he no longer considered labor to be an anthropologically paradigmatic mode of activity, and because, in harmony with the new physics, he saw labor power simultaneously as an abstract magnitude (a measure of labor time) and a natural force (a specific set of energy equivalents located in the body). The distinction between the two concepts of labor is crucial: for the generative view of labor, emancipation occurs in labor itself; from the point of view of conversion, it occurs only apart from labor, in the form of shorter hours or reduced physical and mental exertion. Consistent with the energeticist view, freedom, in Marx's famous formulation, begins where the realm of necessity ends, and not in a utopian realm where the two are fused. That crucial distinction was elaborated by a generation of German Social Democratic theorists, most notably Karl Kautsky. Work did not necessarily limit creativity, Kautsky noted, but truly productive labor in art, science, and human well-being could be achieved because of a reduction of the working day.[46]

Helmholtz was also aware of the social implications in the idea of self-moving power: redemption from painful and exhausting labor, a society of perpetual idleness. "Perpetual motion was to produce labor power inexhaustibly without corresponding consumption, that is to say, out of nothing."[47] The inventors of the automata envisaged a body without fatigue, without discontent, and without aversion to work. But they also revealed their ignorance of how the motors convert the supply of nourishment into heat, and heat into force. Perpetual motion could never be replicated, since no novel source of energy was ever produced in nature. Conversion of force did not merely solve the problem of mimesis, it superseded it by reducing the mimetic machine to the illusion of a body that "creates energy out of itself.[48] The "transcendental materialism" of the nineteenth century produced a powerful metaphor of how nature, technology, and the human body operate under the same dynamic laws of force—a homogeneity that is much more than the reduction of the life process to the model of industrial technology.

Taylorism was the first "scientific" approach to work in which the conservation of energy and the universal equivalence of the laboring body and the laboring machine was made explicit. Taylor's system—and the work of his disciples Henry Laurence Gantt and Frank Gilbreth, as well as its European competitor, the science of work—shared a preoccupation with rationalization of the body, with economizing motion by reducing each task to a series of abstract and mathematically precise movements. Taylorism rigidly separated knowledge from action by transforming the sentient knowledge of the worker into a formalized procedure monopolized by management, and depriving the worker of authority over the work process.

Although worlds apart ideologically, Helmholtz's characterization of the universe as *Arbeitskraft*, Marx's theory of the relentless transformation of labor power into the powerful engine of capital, and Taylor's utopia of the worker's body subordinated to the rational intelligence of the engineer, all adopted the metaphor of the human motor, of the working body as a dynamo converting energy into work. By the end of the nineteenth century, the sciences of work had identified certain limits, most importantly fatigue and neurasthenia, each of which seemed to undermine and subvert the productivism that is at the core of the transcendental ideal. Angelo Mosso, whose *La Fatica* (1891) became the standard work for generations of scientists who identified the chief obstacle to work, not in the weakness of moral character, but in the depletion of physical and mental force.[49] Fatigue, unlike subjective tiredness, represented the objective limit or optimal point of exertion of the body, the outermost boundary of the human motor. Liberal and socialist thinkers alike emphasized the importance of reducing fatigue for identifying the limits of productivism and promoting efficiency.[50] Consequently, the "work-centered society" of the nineteenth century was to a large degree a phenomenon of the metaphor of the human motor.

Beyond the Human Motor: Allegory and the Digital

The body no longer occupies the same space in the metaphoric economy of work. The two archetypal models of labor of the nineteenth century—as generation and as conversion—the homology of industry, body, and cosmos no longer obtain. With the eclipse of the metaphor of the human motor, we can ask whether the end of the work-centered model of society can be attributed to the decline of its most compelling metaphor. What metaphors now occupy the space of the mimetic or the transcendental motor? If the body no longer occupies the central metaphor of productivism, what does this mean for the new configuration of labor and the model of labor based on information processing rather than the generation of things or the conversion of force?

By the 1920s, as work in the chemical and electrical industries depended less and less on physical effort, the disabilities of work shifted away from fatigue to new problems of stress, from physiology to psychology. This did not happen only in Europe—as per the previous chapters. Richard Gillespie's brilliantly researched account of the famous Hawthorne experiments at Western Electric in Chicago, documents how Elton Mayo orchestrated a new focus on the quality of management intervention and on the subjective attitudes and perceptions of the workers, supplanting the old dogmas of fatigue and energy.[51] Many observers have pointed out that the new technologies of computerization and new microassembly processes are as taxing on the nerves and sinews of workers in computer barns as was the exhaustion and progressive destruction of bodies in the satanic mills of the nineteenth century.[52] Productivism did not disappear, but the transcendental metaphor of the motor was slowly eclipsed.

With this transformation, the metaphor of the machine ceased to be transcendental and became allegorical in the Benjaminian sense that specific functions of the body have been replaced by the manipulation of signs or symbols. The substitution of images for functions, systems of communication for production, turns the machine metaphor into something that more closely approximates allegorization, the individual sign or image, which signifies not the whole, but the part. Computerization begins with Alan Turing's famous thesis that any mathematical operation can be reproduced mechanically by encoding them symbolically as algorithms, a principle that led not only to the Taylorization of mental activity but to the principle of simulation, since such machines can mimic the operation of any other machine, and vice versa. In the 1940s, this idea was elaborated by John von Neumann in his "The General and Logical Theory of Automata," which proposed that any mathematical process could be replicated and ultimately reproduce itself. This insight led him to the theory of "the universal computer," which von Neumann also extended to "living" mental and physical systems. The threshold of self-generation or reproduction would be crossed when machines can not only replicate themselves physically but also communicate behavior so that any machine can be instructed to conceive and imitate any other machine.[53] Eventually, von Neumann predicted—and current artificial life experts believe—computers will become autonomous in the sense that programs will be generated by self-organization rather than by setting forth logical procedures to be mutely followed.

Computerization has also effected a linguistic turn in industrial organizations, in which the digital text simulates the activity of the plant and the process and monitors the activity of the individual operators at a distance. The digital and the allegorical join hands. As Shoshana Zuboff observes, "the rigid separation of mental and material work characteristic of the industrial division of labor and vital to the preservation of a distinct managerial group . . . becomes not merely outmoded, but perilously dysfunctional."[54]

Whether a bank or paper mill, an insurance company or a robotized auto factory, the organization relies on an electronic text that is a "symbolic surrogate for the vital detail of the organization."[55]

The linguistic turn in the modem workplace has also redefined productivity. What constitutes valuable work is how well the operator can effectively *simulate* a process, anticipate events, and respond to future demands. According to Stanford computer scientist Terry Winograd, one of AI's celebrities, and Fernando Flores, a philosopher and former cabinet minister in Salvador Allende's government, a modern organization can only be viewed through the prism of language as "a network of recurrent conversations."[56] How well one works is defined, not in terms of product or productivity (models-related generation and conversion) but in terms of the integration of the "virtual" micro world of computer representations in the so-called real world.[57]

Consequently, information technology continues to prescribe routine activities for an increasingly obsolete conscious worker, but, it also requires a profound re-skilling and a change in the relations of authority in the workplace. Instead of reducing the "realm of necessity" (labor time) to a few dull hours a week, some work is becoming intellectualized, and "spiritualized." The disciplined rule-bound worker has given way to the ideal of a "flexible, internally motivated, continuously learning workforce," the obsolete bureaucratic structure has been reborn as "a strong internal culture to support information sharing and participation in problem solving," commands have given way to "balancing dialogue and discussion," hierarchy has been redefined as the "delegation or shared responsibility in recognition that dispersed activity requires local action and flexibility."[58]

Shoshana Zuboff argued in *In the Age of the Smart Machine* that the body reduced to an element in the conversion of force may be replaced by the model of work as the computer-driven simulacra of physical and mental labor.[59] With this transformation, we may indeed reach the end of the work-centered society, but not by abolishing labor or reducing it to a socially necessary minimum. Reforms that encourage the reduction of work time, more flexible work situations and arrangements, as well as reductions in unemployment may well demand a rethinking of the relationship between politics and market forces. But these changes, do not address the more profound transformation in the metaphor of the working body that is occurring simultaneously.

A New Panopticon of Work?

If the body has become relatively nonessential for work environments based on an electronic text that codifies formal procedures, registers informal knowledge, and employs feedback mechanisms, the question of discipline has been posed in entirely new terms. Initially, the goal of the computerized workplace, even in manufacturing, was the capacity to simultaneously register, record, and accumulate, monitor and analyze each moment of the process as it occurs. Eventually, and largely by happenstance, data storage systems not only record what is happening but also what had happened—computers functioned as a desktop panopticon to automatically record not only the content of the work but also the behaviors of the men and women who sat at the monitors. Is this Foucault's worst nightmare come true? Does the decentralized digital micromanagement of behaviors—independent of any "presence" of authority—constitute the furthest incision of the "disciplinary society," a visible and transparent world subject only to instrumentally "true" evaluations? Is the "brave new workplace," as Robert Howard argues, simply intensifying and reproducing the logic of scientific management—top-down control, centralization of knowledge, deskilling?[60] Zuboff suggests that this may not be the case. The panoptical dimension is constantly destabilized by the unplanned, unpredictable, autonomous elements of the computerized workplace. She points out the paradox of the new technology: At one level, the automation of industrial and data manipulating industries by computers replicates and "completes" scientific management by establishing basic algorithms, not only to duplicate work processes, but also for what goes on in the "operator's head." Computers consolidate managerial authority and knowledge over an increasingly interdependent environment. "Mutual visibility becomes an additional mechanism for ensuring the viability of that interdependence."[61] Management norms are simply more effectively internalized and shared in the communitarian environment.

On the other hand, Taylorism is undermined by the "textualization" of production: "The worker must be able to grapple with a kind of knowledge that now stands outside the self, which is externalized and public. Intellective skill becomes the means to interact competently with this now-objectified text, to reappropriate it as one's own, and to engage in a kind of learning process that can transform data into meaningful information, and finally into insight."[62] The adversary relationship has not disappeared in the computerized workplace, but the control over the data has expanded, and is generated from the bottom up. Unlike Taylorism, information is generated and exchanged freely and democratically, so that information sharing threatens to destabilize the mechanism of top-down control.[63] "Instead of a single omniscient overseer, this panopticon relies upon shared custodianship of data that reflect mutually enacted behavior."[64]

The chief difficulty in implementing the digital factory is the "inability of managers to wrest themselves from deep-seated images of managerial command."[65] Educated computer workers in the high-tech paper plants Zuboff studied complained that they were not trusted or denied essential information, that they were prevented from learning how to optimize "learning technologies."[66] Fordism and Taylorism reduce adversarialism by imposing discipline, but the simulation of complex processes and the manipulation of vast quantities of data require not only discipline but flexibility, judgment, and accountability. The assertion of authority, characteristic of the Fordist and Taylorist manager inhibited the reciprocity and democracy necessary to optimize the pinpoint production technologies. In the information workplace, where decisions are made constantly based on vast amounts of data, work and responsibility are becoming synonymous. If Taylorism concentrated knowledge in management, information technology demands that knowledge sharing, cooperation, and democracy increase from below. Worker grievances now focus on more pay for more "responsibility," since divorcing knowledge from work is dangerous. Zuboff argues: "The communicative demands of abstract work compel once implicit and largely silent know-how to become psychologically active and individually differentiated. Without the consensual immediacy of a shared action context, individuals must construct interpretations of the information at hand and so reveal what they believe to be significant. In this way, authority is located in the process of creating and articulating meaning, rather than in a particular position or function."[67] Schor's view is that the Japanese model is not especially productive since working hours are too long and Japanese workers suffer serious work-related health problems. Thousands of workers have become victims of "karoshi," death by overtime. In the information workplace, even in the manufacturing sector, the work is invisible, only the data and the simulations of the work processes are visible. With the eclipse of body-centered strategies such as time-motion studies and piece rates, the criteria for measuring "good" and "bad" work is a matter not only of motivation but also of the level of responsiveness and intellectual engagement. Managerial work "about the future happens linguistically," the "basic unit of communication is commitment," and "the basic structure of work is the network."[68] A "networked organization" requires a worker whose watchword is not communication, but "effective collaboration."[69] The ideal workplace is no place at all, especially since the Los Angeles earthquake provided the spectacle of workers unable to reach their job sites and of desperate employers offering home work stations and fax modems for free.

Ironically, the philosopher of choice for the denizens of the new cyber factory in cyberspace is Martin Heidegger. As Heidegger saw the essence of technology as the metaphysics of modernity, he also provided the new technophiles with the argument that the modern language machine (writing in 1957, Heidegger meant the typewriter) "controls the mode and the world of language as such."[70] The idea that technology belongs not merely to the ontic world of presence but defines and structures being itself has been adopted by Heideggerians such as Marshall McLuhan and Walter J. Ong, as well as by Michael Heim. Denying that Heidegger was a "luddite or a technophobe," Heim views computer technology as not merely prosthetic but as the expression of a new epoch of *Seinsgeschichte* (History of Being) in which the limits of standardization are disclosed. The world of cyber text, the infinite network of signs, reveals the limits of the metaphysics of presence, and discloses the superior (beyond the body), alternate world of virtuality.[71]

In the new productivist metaphor of the computer automata as the virtual simulation of life, the strong Cartesian argument that any world that might exist would be an exact duplicate of the rational world as it was created has returned with a vengeance. Descartes, so it is told, once had the temerity to explain to Christina, Queen of Sweden, that animals were a class of automata. The good queen, suddenly pointed to a clock, and commanded the dumbstruck philosopher: "See to it that it produces offspring."[72] This time, however, postmodern philosophers are unfazed by the "problem." Deleuze and Guattari, for example, seized upon the idea of artificial life as confirmation for the thesis that the virtual is the source of the real. Speculating that it might be possible to replicate how "the right conditions for the emergence of life came about in the so-called primeval soup," life is redefined as a sort of primordial "symbol system," not merely governing how codes are communicated across generations, but how the laws of thermodynamics were actually set in motion.[73] However complex, utopian, and futuristic such simulacra are, they differ from the eighteenth-century automata only in their extraordinary complexity, but not in the delusion—which Vaucanson resisted—that everything that quacks is not necessarily a duck.

Conclusion

As I have argued, the "work-centered society" of the nineteenth and early twentieth century was to a large degree a phenomenon that relied heavily on the transcendental metaphor of the human motor. To the extent that this metaphor has begun to wane and become allegorized in the digital reorganization of work, the emphasis on disciplinarity has also begun to disappear. But this does not mean that we are any less subjected to a new kind of regimentation; today's worker may be more disciplined and overworked than his or her predecessors. This suggests that control of the workforce will not diminish; on the contrary, discipline may be far more intense and internalized, coerced by the threat of total insecurity, as the 1999–2001 dot.com collapse made abundantly evident. In fact, the much-touted communicative workplace may have taken a dystopian turn. Not unlike the paleo-industrial textile factories of nineteenth-century Britain, Amazon, according to the *New York Times*, "is conducting a little-known experiment in how far it can push white-collar workers, redrawing the boundaries of what is acceptable." Workers are pressed to compete ferociously and pressured to spy on each other and to stay at their desks long into the night.[74] With the eclipse of the great productivist utopias, work has ceased to be the defining activity of social life and is no longer the center for early twenty-first-century visions of a more just society. The end of the classical utopias of labor is yet one more sign that work has already become just one, and perhaps no longer the most important, dimension of civil society.

1. FROM MIMETIC MACHINES TO DIGITAL ORGANISMS:
THE TRANSFORMATION OF THE HUMAN MOTOR

1. Bruce Mazlish, *The Fourth Discontinuity: The Co-Evolution of Humans and Machines* (New Haven, CT: Yale University Press, 1993), 4.

2. A good example is Tom Siegfried, *The Bit and the Pendulum: From Quantum Physics to M Theory—The New Physics of Information* (New York: John Wiley and Sons, 2000).

3. See the informative preface by David Lasocki at http://instantharmony .net/Music/Vaucanson-1979.pdf. See also Dayton C. Miller, *Catalogue of Books and Literary Materials Relating to the Flute and Other Musical Instruments* (Cleveland, OH: privately printed, 1935); "Beschreibung des mechanischen Flötenspielers," *Hamburgisches Magazin*, Bd. 2 (Hamburg: G. C. Grund, 1747), 1–24; *Beschreibung eines mechanischen Kunststücks, und automatischen Flötenspielers* (Augsburg: J. A. E. Maschenbaur, 1748), 8.

4. Jessica Riskin, *The Restless Clock: A History of the Centuries Long Argument over What Makes Living Things Tick* (Chicago: University of Chicago Press, 2016), 135.

5. See Jessica Riskin, "The Defecating Duck, or, the Ambiguous Origins of Artificial Life," *Critical Inquiry* 24, no. 4 (2003): 599–633; Joan B. Landes, "The Anatomy of Artificial Life: An Eighteenth-Century Perspective," *Genesis Redux: Essays in the History and Philosophy of Artificial Life* (Chicago: University of Chicago Press, 2007), 96–116.

6. On the automata and the application of biomechanics to the animal economy, see A. Doyon and L. Liagre, "Méthodologie comparée du biomécanisme et de la mécanique comparée," *Dialectica* 10, no. 4 (1956): 319. See also Adelheid Voskuhl, *Androids in the Enlightenment: Mechanics, Artisans, and Cultures of the Self* (Chicago: University of Chicago Press, 2015).

7. Walter Benjamin, "On the Mimetic Faculty," in *Reflections: Essays, Aphorisms, Autobiographical Writings*, ed. Peter Demetz, trans. Edmund Jephcott (New York: Harcourt, Brace, Jovanovich, 1979), 336.

8. Here I am reminded of Freud's famous comment that "man has become, as it were, a prosthetic God." Sigmund Freud, *Civilization and its Discontents*, trans. James Strachey (New York: W. W. Norton, 1961), 19. The metaphor of the prosthesis has been aptly applied to a variety of technologies. See, for example, Celia Lurie, *Proesthetic Culture: Photography, Memory and Identity* (New York: Routledge, 1998); and Marquard Smith and Joanne Morra eds., *The Prosthetic Impulse: From a Posthuman Present to a Biocultural Future* (Cambridge, MA: MIT Press, 2006).

9. James Lastra, *Sound Technology and the American Cinema: Perception, Representation, Modernity* (New York: Columbia University Press, 2000), 16–24.

10. On Vaucanson's loom, see Minsoo Kang, *Sublime Dreams of Living Machines: The Automaton in the European Imagination* (Cambridge, MA: Harvard University Press, 2011), 107.

11. Anson Rabinbach, *The Human Motor: Energy, Fatigue, and the Origins of Modernity* (New York: Basic Books, 1990), ch. 2.

12. Hermann von Helmholtz, "Über die Wechselwirkung der Naturkräfte und die darauf Bezüglichen neuesten Ermittelungen der Physik," in *Populäre Wissenschaftliche Vorträge*, Bd. 3 (Braunschweig: F. Vieweg, 1876), 102.

13. Mark Seltzer, *Bodies and Machines* (New York: Routledge, 1992), 29.

14. Michel Serres, *Hermès III: La traduction* (Paris: Minuit, 1974), 258.

15. On Helmholtz, see Lorenz Krüger, ed., *Universalgenie Helmholtz: Rückblick nach 100 Jahren* (Berlin: Akademie Verlag, 1994); Henning Schmidgen, *The Helmholtz Curves: Tracing Lost Time*, trans. Nils F. Schott (New York: Fordham University Press, 2014).

16. Helmholtz, "Über die Wechselwirkung der Naturkräfte," 104. Thomas Kuhn discovered that "Helmholtz used the terms, Arbeitskraft, bewegende Kraft, mechanische Arbeit and Arbeit interchangeably for his fundamental measurable force." Thomas S. Kuhn, "Energy Conservation as an Example of Simultaneous Discovery," in *The Essential Tension: Selected Studies in Scientific Tradition and Change* (Chicago: University of Chicago Press, 1977), 66–104.

17. Helmholtz, "Über die Wechselwirkung der Naturkräfte," 125.

18. Hermann von Helmholtz, *Popular Lectures on Scientific Subjects*, trans. E. Atkinson (New York: D. Appleton, 1885), 182. See also Kang, *Sublime Dreams*, 230.

19. Helmholtz, "Über die Wechselwirkung der Naturkräfte," 125.

20. Helmholtz, *Popular Lectures*, 383.

21. According to Moishe Postone, Marx never adopted the argument from generation. He unpersuasively reduces this decisive shift in Marx's thinking to a matter of correct versus incorrect interpretations. For example, he claims: "The meaning of alienation varies considerably depending upon whether one considers it in the context of a theory based on the notion of 'labor' or in the context of an analysis of the duality of labor in capitalism. In the former case, alienation becomes a concept of a philosophical anthropology; it refers to the externalization of a preexisting human essence. On another level, it refers to a situation in which capitalists possess the power of disposal over the workers' labor and its products. Within the framework of such a critique, alienation is an unequivocally negative process—although it is grounded in circumstances that can be overcome." Moishe Postone, *Time, Labor, and Social Domination: A Reinterpretation of Marx's Critical Theory* (Cambridge: Cambridge University Press, 1993), 161–162. For a careful adjudication of the debate over Marx and thermodynamics, see the thoughtful and comprehensive article by John Bellamy Foster and Paul Burkett, "Classical Marxism and the Second Law of Thermodynamics: Marx/Engels, the Heat Death of the Universe Hypothesis, and the Origins of Ecological Economics," *Organization and Environment* 21, no. 8 (2008): 37.

22. Frederick Engels, "Preface to the First German Edition," *Capital*, vol. 2, in *The Collected Works of Karl Marx and Frederick Engels*, vol. 36 (New York: International Publishers, 1997), 20.

23. In the notebooks to *Das Kapital*, Marx excerpted the work of the French economist Pelligrino Rossi, who, in the late 1830s, used the engineering term *puissance du travail*, propagated by Navier, Coriolis, Poncelet et al. Marx also cites Rossi in connection with his discussion of the physiological aspect of labor power, noting, "To comprehend capacity for labor [*puissance de travail*] at the same time that we make abstraction from the means of subsistence of the labourers during the process of production, is to comprehend a phantom [*être de raison*]." Marx, *Capital*, vol. 1, in *The Collected Works of Karl Marx and Frederick Engels*, vol. 35 (New York: International Publishers, 1997), 183. Marx cites Pelligrino Rossi, *Cours d'Économie Politique* (Brussels: n.p., 1843), 370–371.

24. Marx, *Capital*, 1:54.

25. Ibid., 1:56.

26. Ibid. See also William Robert Grove, *The Correlation of Physical Forces*, 6th ed. (London: Longmans Green, 1874), 203. Grove's text differs slightly from the English translation of *Capital:* "the amount of labor which a man has undergone in the course of twenty-four hours may be approximately arrived at by an examination of the chemical changes which have taken place in his body; changed forms in matter indicating the anterior exercise of dynamical

force." Kuhn notes that "between 1850 and 1875 Grove's book was reprinted at least six times in England, three times in America, twice in France, and once in Germany" ("Energy Conservation," 82). On Grove, see Crosbie Smith, *The Science of Energy: A Cultural History of Energy Physics in Victorian Britain* (Chicago: University of Chicago Press, 1998); see also Elizabeth P. Neswald, *Thermodynamik als kultureller Kampfplatz: zur Faszinationsgeschichte der Entropie, 1850–1915* (Freiburg: Rombach Verlag, 2003) 126, 130.

27. Frederick Engels, *Dialectics of Nature*, in *The Collected Works of Karl Marx and Frederick Engels*, vol. 25 (New York: International Publishers, 1997), 325.

28. Karl Marx, *Grundrisse: Foundations of the Critique of Political Economy* (Rough Draft), trans. Martin Nicolaus (London: Penguin Books, 1973), 410.

29. Marx, *Capital*, 1:179.

30. Albrecht Wellmer, "The Latent Positivism of Marx's Philosophy of History," *Critical Theory of Society* (New York: Seabury Press, 1974), 113.

31. Karl Marx, *Capital*, vol. 3, in *The Collected Works of Karl Marx and Frederick Engels*, vol. 37 (New York: International Publishers, 1997), 807.

32. Helmholtz, "Über die Wechselwirkung der Naturkräfte," 66. See also Neswald, *Thermodynamik*, 181.

33. Neswald, *Thermodynamik*, 180–195.

34. Leszek Kolakowski, *Main Currents of Marxism: The Founders, the Golden Age, the Breakdown* (London: Oxford University Press, 1978), 1136.

35. Neswald, *Thermodynamik*, 36.

36. Juan Martinez-Alier and J. M. Naredo, "A Marxist Precursor of Ecological Economics: Podolinsky," *Journal of Peasant Studies* 9, no. 2 (1982): 207–224.

37. What Engels referred to as the "Podolinski business" has played an important role in a lively discussion of Marx's and Engels's reception of thermodynamics and the ecological implications of Marx's political economy. Especially illuminating is the detailed research on Sergei Podolinsky by John Bellamy Foster and Paul Burkett. They argue that the interpretation of Engels's remarks on Podolinsky's work by Juan Martinez-Alier and J. M. Naredo is excessively dismissive, emphasizing instead "the important but previously underrated role of energy analysis in Marx's *Capital*." They show in considerable detail that Marx and Engels were justified in their criticisms of Podlinski's energetic reductionism. See Paul Burkett and J. B. Foster, "The Podolinsky Myth: An Obituary. Introduction to 'Human Labour and Unity of Force,' by Sergei Podolinsky," *Historical Materialism*, no. 16 (2008): 115–161; "Metabolism, Energy, and Entropy in Marx's Critique of Political Economy: Beyond the Podolinsky Myth," *Theory and Society* 35, no. 1 (2006): 109–156; "Ecological Economics and Classical Marxism: The 'Podolinsky Business' Reconsidered," *Organization and Environment* 17, no. 1 (2004): 32–60; and Martinez-Alier and Naredo, "Marxist Precursor of Ecological Economics."

38. Sergei Podolinsky, "Socialism and the Unity of Physical Forces," *Organization and Environment* 17, no. 1 (2004): 61–75.

39. Frederick Engels in a letter to Karl Marx (December 19, 1882), in Marx and Engels, *Collected Works*, 46:410. Engels writes: "This is how I see the Podolinski business. His real discovery is that human labour is capable of retaining solar energy on the earth's surface and harnessing it for a longer period than would otherwise have been the case. All the economic conclusions he draws from this are wrong."

40. Marx, *Capital*, 2:411.

41. Karl Kautsky, *The Class Struggle*, trans., William E. Bohn (New York: W. W. Norton, 1971), 158.

42. Ibid., 156. The most vociferous opponent of Prometheanism was, ironically, Marx's son-in-law, Paul Lafargue, whose *The Right to be Lazy* appeared in 1880. See Paul Lafargue, *Le droit a la paresse* (Paris: n.p., 1880); and Rabinbach, *Human Motor*, 34, 35.

43. Charles S. Maier, *In Search of Stability: Explorations in Historical Political Economy* (Cambridge, MA: Cambridge University Press, 1987), 26.

44. Angelo Mosso, *Fatigue*, trans. Margaret Drummond and William Blackley Drummond (New York: G. P. Putnam's Sons, 1904). On Mosso, see Rabinbach, *Human Motor*, ch. 5, and Neswald, *Thermodynamik*, 357–359.

45. Jules Amar, *The Human Motor, or, the Scientific Foundations of Labor and Industry* (London: Routledge, 1920), 393.

46. Jules Amar, *The Physiology of Industrial Organisation and the Re-Employment of the Disabled*, trans. Bernard Miall and Albert Frank Stanley Kent (New York: Macmillan, 1919), 129.

47. Amar, *Human Motor*, 421.

48. Amar, *Physiology of Industrial Organisation*, 101.

49. Ibid., 127.

50. On Marey, see Rabinbach, *Human Motor*, ch. 4; and Marta Braun, *Picturing Time: The Work of Etienne-Jules Marey (1830–1904)* (Chicago: University of Chicago Press, 1994).

51. Amar, *Physiology of Industrial Organisation*, 160, 161, 204.

52. Amar, *Human Motor*, 469.

53. Amar, *Physiology of Industrial Organisation*, 127.

54. Amar, *Human Motor*, 393.

55. Jules Amar, "L'organisation scientifique du travail humain," *La technique moderne* 7, no. 4 (1913): 118. Jean-Marie Lahy, *Le système Taylor: analyse et commentaires* (Paris: Masson, 1921), 171.

56. Mia Fineman, "Ecce Homo Prostheticus," *New German Critique*, no. 76 (2000): 85–115. The cultural history of prosthetics is developed in Marquard Smith and Joanne Morra, eds., *The Prosthetic Impulse: From a*

Posthuman Present to a Biocultural Future (Cambridge, MA: MIT Press, 2006); Celia Lury, *Prosthetic Culture: Photography, Memory and Identity* (London: Routledge, 1997). On shell-shock, see Paul Lerner, *Hysterical Men: War, Psychiatry and the Politics of Trauma in Germany 1890–1930* (Ithaca, NY: Cornell University Press, 2003).

57. Walther Moede, "Kraftfahrer-Eignungsprüfungen beim deutschen Heer 1915–1918," *Industrielle Psychotechnik* 3, no. 1 (1926): 79.

58. Fritz Giese, "Psychologie der Arbeitshand," *Handbuch der Biolgischen Arbeitsmethoden*, ed. Emil Abderhalden (Berlin: Urban und Schwarzenberg, 1928), 804.

59. S. Jaeger and I. Stäuble, "Die Psychotechnik und ihre gesellschaftlichen Entwicklungsbedingungen," and François Stoll, "Anwendungen im Berufsleben: Arbeits-, Wirtschafts- und Verkehrspsychologie" in *Psychologie des 20. Jahrhunderts*, Bd. 13 (Zürich: Kindler, 1981), 53–94.

60. Andreas Killen, *Berlin Electropolis Shock, Nerves and German Modernity* (Berkeley: University of California Press, 2006), 209, 210.

61. Ulfried Geuter, *The Professionalization of German Psychology in Nazi Germany* (Cambridge, MA: Cambridge University Press, 1992), 86.

62. Edgar Atzler, *Körper und Arbeit: Handbuch der Arbeitsphysiologie* (Leipzig: G. Thieme, 1927), 419–420.

63. Killen, *Berlin Electropolis*, 197.

64. Ibid., 183–186.

65. I am indebted to Andreas Killen for this insight into Giese. See Fritz Giese, *Handbuch der Arbeitswissenschaft*, Bd. 2., erw. u. veränd. Aufl. d. "Eignungsprüfungen an Erwachsenen" (Halle an der Saar: Marhold, 1925), 209–210.

66. "Philosophen an der Front!" (Philosophers on the frontline!) was the rallying cry in Fritz Giese, *Nietzsche—Die Erfüllung* (Tübingen: Mohr, 1934).

67. Rabinbach, *Human Motor*, 284.

68. Mark R. Beissinger, *Scientific Management, Socialist Discipline and Soviet Power* (Cambridge, MA: Harvard University Press, 1988), 23. See also Zenovia A. Sochor, "Soviet Taylorism Revisited," *Soviet Studies* 33, no 2. (1981): 246–264.

69. Beissinger, *Scientific Management*, 33. See also Peter Beilharz, *Labor's Utopias: Bolshevism, Fabianism, Social Democracy* (London: Routledge, 1992), 30, 31.

70. Beilharz, *Labor's Utopias*, 39.

71. Sheila Fitzpatrick, "War and Society in Soviet Context: Soviet Labor before, during, and after World War II," *International Labor and Working-Class History*, no. 35 (1989): 37–52.

72. Joseph Stalin, *Problems of Leninism* (Moscow: Foreign Languages Press Publishing House, 1940), 369.

73. Stephen K. Kotkin, *Magnetic Mountain: Stalinism as a Civilization* (Berkeley: University of California Press, 1997), 91.

74. Mary Nolan, *Visions of Modernity: American Business and the Modernization of Germany* (New York: Oxford University Press, 1994).

75. Ernst Jünger, *Der Arbeiter: Herrschaft und Gestalt* (1932) (Stuttgart: Klett-Cotta, 1981).

76. Cited in J. Querzola, "Le chef d'orchestre à la main de fer. Leninisme et taylorisme," in *Le soldat du travail: guerre, fascisme et taylorisme*, ed. Lion Murard and Patrick Zylberman (Paris: Recherches, 1978), 69. I am indebted to Werner Hamacher's illuminating study, "Working Through Working," *Modernism/Modernity*, no. 30 (1986): 23–56.

77. Hannah Arendt makes this claim in her Gauss lectures, Princeton University, 1954. I am indebted to Jerome Kohn for making her unpublished manuscript available to me.

78. Hannah Arendt, "Ideology and Terror: A Novel Form of Government," in *The Origins of Totalitarianism* (New York: Harcourt Brace, 1966), 387.

79. Charles F. Heckscher, *The New Unionism: Employee Involvement in the Changing Corporation* (New York: Basic Books, 1988); Peter F. Drucker, "Are Unions Becoming Irrelevant?," *Wall Street Journal*, September 22, 1982.

80. Lee Sproul and Sara Kiesler, *Connections: New Ways of Working in the Networked Organization* (Cambridge, MA: MIT Press, 1992), 175. See also Michael Schrage, *Shared Minds: The New Technologies of Collaboration* (New York: Random House, 1990); and Peter M. Senge, *The Fifth Discipline: The Art and Practice of The Learning Organization* (New York: Currency Books, 1990).

81. Juliet Schor, *The Overworked American: The Unexpected Decline of Leisure* (New York: Basic Books, 1991).

82. Mazlish, *Fourth Discontinuity*, 226.

83. Shoshana Zuboff, *In the Age of the Smart Machine: The Future of Work and Power* (New York: Basic Books, 1988), 393.

84. For an early effort to discuss the relationship between mental and physical labor, see Alfred Sohn-Rethel, *Intellectual and Manual Labour: A Critique of Epistemology* (Atlantic Highlands, NJ: Humanities Press, 1977).

85. D. Davis and D. Milbank, "Employer Ennui," *Wall Street Journal*, February 7, 1992.

86. Kevin Kelly, *Out of Control: The New Biology of Machines* (London: Fourth Estate, 1994), 25.

87. Ibid.

88. Claus Emmeche, *The Garden in the Machine: The Emerging Science of Artificial Life*, trans. Steven Sampson (Princeton, NJ: Princeton University Press, 1994), 146.

89. Ibid.

90. Ibid.

91. John Markoff, "Artificial Intelligence Is Far from Matching Humans, Panel Says," *New York Times*, May 25, 2016. See also Jeffrey Sachs, "The Best of Times, the Worst of Times: The Macroeconomics of Robots," Jeffrey Sachs (blog), June 6, 2016, http://jeffsachs.org/2016/06/the-best-of-times-the -worst-of-times-macroeconomics-of-robots/.

2. SOCIAL ENERGETICISM IN FIN-DE-SIÈCLE EUROPE

1. On "milieu," see Paul Rabinow, *French Modern: Norms and Forms of the Social Environment* (Cambridge, MA: MIT Press, 1989), especially ch. 3.

2. Robert Nye, *Crime, Madness, and Politics in Modern France: The Medical Concept of National Decline* (Princeton, NJ: Princeton University Press, 1984); Daniel Pick, *Faces of Degeneration: A European Disorder, c. 1848–c. 1918* (Cambridge: Cambridge University Press, 1989); and Stephen Jay Gould, *The Mismeasure of Man* (New York: Norton, 1983).

3. Georges Barnich, *Essai de politique positive basée sur l'énergetigue sociale de Solvay* (Brussels: Lebègue, 1919), 373.

4. Ibid., 374.

5. Ibid.

6. Kenneth Bertrams, Nicolas Coupain, and Ernst Homburgm, *Solvay: History of a Multinational Family Firm*, coordinated by Ginette Kurgan-van Hentenryk (New York: Cambridge University Press, 2013).

7. On Solvay's life and work, see Louis Bertrand, *Ernest Solvay: Réformateur social* (Brussels: Agence Dechenne, 1918); Jacques Balle, *Solvay: L'homme, la découverte, L'entreprise industrielle* (Brussels: Sadi, 1968); Armand Detillièux, *La philosophie sociale de M. Ernest Solvay* (Brussels: Lebègue, 1918); *Scientific American Supplement*, "Ernest Solvay, Soda King," December 6, 1913, 364; and Daniel Warnotte, *Ernest Solvay et L'Institut de Sociologie: Contribution à l'histoire de l'énergétique sociale*, 2 vols. (Brussels: Émile Bruylant, 1946).

8. "Ernest Solvay, Soda King," 364.

9. Ibid.

10. Balle, *Solvay*, 139.

11. Ibid., 146.

12. Ibid., 141.

13. Bertrand, *Ernest Solvay*, 30.

14. Ibid., 31.

15. Detillieux, *La philosophie sociale de M. Ernest Solvay*, 14.

16. Bertrand, *Ernest Solvay*, 32.

17. Ernest Solvay, *Science contre religion* (Brussels: Mayolez, 1879), 21.

18. Ernest Solvay, *Principes d'orientation sociale* (Brussels: Misch and Thron, 1904), 33.

19. Ernest Solvay, *Note sur les formules d'introduction à l'énergétique* (Brussels: Lamertin, 1900), 4.

20. Ernest Solvay, *Notes sur le productivisme et le comptabilisme: études sociales* (Brussels: Lamertin, 1900), 1:164

21. Ibid., 2:323.

22. Ibid.

23. Solvay, *Principes d'orientation sociale*, 29.

24. Ibid., 33, 34.

25. Ibid., 38.

26. Warnotte, *Ernest Solvay*, 1:75.

27. Balle, *Solvay*, 96.

28. Ibid., 46

29. Ibid., 51.

30. Ibid., 56.

31. Ibid.

32. Georges Hostelet, "L'action et la conception productivistes de M. E. Solvay," *Revue de l'Institut de Sociologie* (January 1922): 42.

33. Warnotte, *Ernest Solvay*, 2:521; Henry H. Frost, *The Functional Sociology of Émile Waxweiler and the Institut de Sociologie Solvay* (Brussels: Palais des Académies, 1960), 24–26.

34. Balle, *Solvay*, 140.

35. Frost, *Functional Sociology*, 25.

36. Ibid.

37. Warnotte, *Ernest Solvay*, 2:524.

38. Denis, De Greef, and Vandervelde were among the most frequent contributors to the institute's six volumes of the *Annales*. A complete bibliography appears in Warnotte, *Ernest Solvay*, 2:523.

39. Cf. Émile Vandervelde, *Le comptabilisme social* (Brussels: Institut des Sciences Sociales, 1895).

40. Warnotte, *Ernest Solvay*, 2:26.

41. Solvay, *Notes sur le productivisme*, 164, 165 passim; and Detillieux, *La philosophie sociale*, 24, 25.

42. Warnotte, *Ernest Solvay*, 2:530.

43. Georges Barnich, *Essai de politique positive base sur l'energetique sociale de Solvay* (Brussels: Lebègue, 1919), 6.

44. Under this scheme, each individual would register his fortune with the national compatibilist office supervised by the state. All transactions would

then be acquitted by using a "carnet" issued by the office, in which debits and credits were noted. Money, noted Solvay, "would be replaced by the mechanism of writing, pure and simple." This system, which more closely approaches the European postal system money-transfer, rather than American bank-checking, can also be seen as the nineteenth-century forerunner of the credit card (without credit). Ernest Solvay, *Social Comptabilism: Its Principle and Ground of Existence* (Brussels: Institute Solvay, 1897).

45. Frost, *Functional Sociology*, 27.

46. Ibid., 28, 29.

47. Warnotte, *Ernest Solvay*, 2:399.

48. Émile Waxweiler, *Esquisse d'une sociologie* (Brussels: Misch and Thron, 1906) 10.

49. Cf. Louis Wodon, "Quelques observations sur les vues sociologiquies d'Émile Waxweiler," in *Mélanges offerts à Ernest* (Paris: Librairie du Recueil Sirey, 1935), 425.

50. Frost, *Functional Sociology*, 42.

51. Ibid., 63.

52. Ibid., 46.

53. The reader is encouraged to consult the bibliography of his works in Frost and in Warnotte.

54. A. Slosse and E. Waxweiler, *Enquete sur l'alimentation de 1065 ouvriers belges. Notes et memoirs: recherches sur le travail humain dans l'industrie* (Brussels: Misch and Thron, 1910).

55. Frost, *Functional Sociology*, 32, 33

56. Émile Waxweiler, *La Belgique neutre et loyale* (Paris: Payot et Cie., 1915).

57. Friedrich Wilhelm, "Ostwald," in *Complete Dictionary of Scientific Biography*, vol. 15 (Detroit: Charles Scribner's Sons, 2008), 455–469.

58. Among his popular works are *Ostwalds Klassiker der exakten Wissenschaften* (Leipzig: Akademische Verlagsgesellschaft Geest and Portig, 1889); and Wilhelm Ostwald, *Energetische Grundlagen der Kulturwissenschaft* (Leipzig: W. Klinkhardt, 1909).

59. Wilhelm Ostwald, *Lebenslinien: Eine Selbstbiographie*, Bd. 3 (Berlin: Klasing, 1927), 329.

60. Elizabeth P. Neswald, *Thermodynamik als kultureller Kampfplatz: Zur Faszinationsgeschichte der Entropie, 1850–1915* (Freiburg: Rombach Verlag, 2003), 386, 387.

61. Ostwald, *Energetische Grundlagen*, 132.

62. Vladimir I. Lenin, *Materialism and Empirio-criticism: Critical Comments on a Reactionary Philosophy*, in *Lenin Collected Works*, vol. 14 (Moscow: Progress Publishers, 1972), ch. 6. See also Vladimir I. Lenin, letter to Maxim Gorky,

1924, in *Lenin Collected Works*, vol. 13 (Moscow: Progress Publishers, 1972), 448–454.

63. Alfred Kelly, *The Descent of Darwin: The Popularization of Darwinism in Germany 1860–1914* (Chapel Hill: University of North Carolina Press, 1981), 23–29. Daniel Gasman's *The Scientific Origins of National Socialism: Social Darwinism in Ernst Haeckel and the German Monist League* (New York: Macdonald, 1971) is tendentious, and, as Kelly points out, unconvincing in attributing to Haeckel any significant connection to *völkisch* thought. Cf. Kelly, *Descent of Darwin*, 120, 121.

64. The law of the "persistence" or "indestructibility of matter," established by Lavoisier in 1789, may be formulated thus: "the sum of matter which fills infinite space is unchangeable." Cf. Ernst Haeckel, *The Riddle of the Universe*, trans. Joseph McCabe (New York: Harper and Brothers, 1900), 212.

65. Ernst Mach, *Die Principien der Wärmelehre: Historisch-kritisch entwickelt* (Leipzig: Barth, 1896), 333. Cited in J. Thiele, "'Naturphilosophie' und 'Monismus' um 1900 (Briefe von Wilhelm Ostwald, Ernst Mach, Ernst Haeckel, und Hans Driesch)," *Philosophia Naturalis*, Bd. 10, Heft 3 (1968), 298.

66. Ernst Mach, *Erkenntnis und Irrtum: Skizzen zur Psychologie der Forschung* (Leipzig: Barth, 1917), 13. Cited in Thiele, "'Naturphilosophie' und 'Monismus,'" 297.

67. Thiele, "'Naturphilosophie' und 'Monismus,'" 300–302.

68. Friedrich Stadler, *Vom Positivismus zur "Wissenschaftlichen Weltauffassung": Am Beispiel der Wirkungsgeschichte von Ernst Mach in Österreich von 1895 bis 1934* (Vienna: Locker Verlag, 1982).

69. Ostwald, *Energetische Grundlagen*, i. See also Wilhelm Ostwald, *Der energetische Imperativ* (Leipzig: Akademische Verlagsgesellschaft, 1912), 96.

70. Ostwald, *Der energetische Imperativ*, 96.

71. Wilhelm Ostwald, "Studien zur Energetik," *Math, Phys., Ber.* 42, no. 3 (1891): 271–288; *Math, Phys., Ber.* 44 (1892): 211–237, cited in Erwin N. Hiebert, "The Energetics Controversy and the New Thermodynamics," *Perspectives in the History of Science and Technology*, ed. Duane H. D. Roller (Norman: University of Oklahoma Press, 1971), 75.

72. See the interesting discussion of the meeting and its repercussions in Hiebert, "Energetics Controversy," 67–86.

73. Ibid., 68.

74. Ludwig Boltzmann, "Ein Wort der Mathematik an die Energetik," *Annalen der physische Chemie* 57 (1896), 39–71. Cited in Hiebert, "Energetics Controversy," 70.

75. See comments on Hiebert's paper by Lawrence Badash, in *Perspectives*, 92.

76. "Ich schreibe dies von einem Landhaus, das ich mir am Rande des Waldes gekauft und 'Energie' getauft habe." Ostwald to Mach, Sept. 1901, in Thiele, "'Naturphilosophie' und 'Monismus,'" 302.

77. Ostwald, *Energetische Grundlagen*, 2.

78. Ibid., 9.

79. Ostwald, *Der energetische Imperativ*, 83.

80. Ostwald, *Energetische Grundlagen*, 21.

81. Ibid., 79.

82. Ibid., 114.

83. Ibid., 116.

84. Ibid., 120.

85. Ostwald, *Der energetische Imperativ*, 85.

86. Ibid., 85.

87. Details of their meeting are in Wilhelm Ostwald, *Lebenslinien: Eine Selbstbiographie*, Bd. 3 (Berlin: Klasing, 1927), 222.

88. Ibid.

89. Ibid.

90. Kelly, *Descent of Darwin*, 121.

91. Ostwald, *Energetische Grundlagen*, 166.

92. Ibid., 146.

93. Alfred Fouillée, *Esquisse d'une interprétation du monde* (Paris: F. Alcan, 1913), 127.

94. Ibid., 4.

95. Max Weber, "Energetische Kulturtheorien," in *Gesammelte Aufsätze zur Wissenschaftslehre*, ed. Johannes Winckelmann (Tübingen: J. C. B. Mohr, 1968), 400–426.

96. Ibid., 406.

97. Ibid., 425.

98. Max Weber, "Die Grenznutzlehre und das 'psychophysische Grundgesetz,'" in *Gesammelte Aufsätze zur Wissenschaftslehre*, ed. Johannes Winckelmann (Tübingen: J. C. B. Mohr, 1985), 384–399.

99. For a discussion of the structure of scientific models, see Michel Foucault, *The Order of Things: An Archeology of the Human Sciences* (London: Routledge, 1970), 226–232.

100. Wilhelm Ostwald, *Die Überwindung des wisssenschaftlichen Materialismus* (Leipzig: Verlag von Weit, 1895) 28.

101. W. V. Bechterew, *Die Energie des lebenden Organismus und ihre Psycho-Biologische Bedeutung* (Wiesbaden: J. F. Bergmann, 1902) 16.

102. Max Rubner, *Kraft und Stoff im Haushalte der Natur* (Leipzig: Akademische Verlagsgesellschaft, 1909), ch. 6.

103. Ibid., 16.

104. Richard Kremer, "From *Stoffwechsel* to *Kraftwechsel*: Voit, Rubner, and the Study of Nutrition in the 1890s" (unpublished paper, 1983); and Rubner, *Kraft und Stoff*, 27.

105. Rubner, *Kraft und Stoff*, 27.

106. See Max Rubner, *Wandlungen in der Volksernahrung* (Leipzig: Akademische Verlagsgesellschaft, 1913); and Max Rubner, *Über moderne Ernährungsreformen* (Berlin: R. Oldenbourg, 1914).

107. Rubner, *Kraft und Stoff*, 31.

108. ZSTA Merseburg. Rep. 76 VL Sekt. 2. Tit. 23 LITT A. N 115. Kaiser-Wilhelm-Institut für Arbeitsphysiologie, Denkschrift (May 1912), 4.

109. KWI, ZSTA Merseburg, Denkschrift, 4

110. Ibid., 2.

111. Ibid., 5.

112. Félix Le Dantec, *De l'homme à la science* (Paris: E. Flammarion, 1907), 66.

3. SOCIAL KNOWLEDGE AND THE POLITICS OF INDUSTRIAL ACCIDENTS

1. See the suggestive paper by Peter Wagner and Bjorn Wittrock, *Social Sciences and Societal Developments: The Missing Perspective* (Berlin: Wissenschaftszentrum Berlin für Sozialforschung Papers, 1987), 94.

2. Hans-Ulrich Wehler, *The German Empire 1871–1918*, trans. Kim Traynor (Dover: Berg Publishers, 1985), 133.

3. Florian Tennstedt, *Vom Proleten zum Industriearbeiter: Arbeiterbewegung und Sozialpolitik in Deutschland 1800 bis 1914* (Cologne: Bund-Verlag, 1983), 291.

4. Ibid., 335.

5. Dietrich Rueschemeyer and Ronan Van Rossem, "The *Verein für Sozialpolitik* and the Fabian Society: A Study in the Sociology of Policy-Relevant Knowledge," in *States, Knowledge and the Origins of Social Policies*, ed. Dietrich Rueschemeyer and Theda Skocpol (Princeton, NJ: Princeton University Press, 1996) 117–162.

6. Tennstedt, *Vom Proleten*, 370.

7. Theodor M. Porter, *The Rise of Statistical Thinking 1820–1900* (Princeton, NJ: Princeton University Press, 1986), and Ian Hacking, "How Should We Do the History of Statistics," in *Power and Desire: Diagrams of the Social*, ed. Graham Burchell, *I and C*, no. 8 (Spring 1981): 14–26.

8. Judith F. Stone, *The Search for Social Peace: Reform Legislation in France 1890–1914* (Albany: State University of New York, 1985), 38, 39.

9. Raoul Jay, *La protection légale des travailleurs* (Paris: L. LaRose, 1904), 129.

10. François Ewald, *L'état providence* (Paris: Grasset, 1986); and Jacques Donzelot, *L'invention du social: essai sur le déclin des passions politiques* (Paris: Fayard, 1984).

11. The great pioneer of the worker's survey and conservative reformer Louis-René Villermé devoted a pioneering article to the mechanized accident in 1850; see Louis-René Villermé, "Accidents occasionnés par les appareils mécaniques dans les ateliers industriels," in *Annales d'hygiène publique et de médecine légale*, no. 43 (1850): 261–289. Most early nineteenth-century hygienists, however, generally held to the traditionalist view (based on seventeenth-century medical treatises) that the work environment in specific trades—especially the long-term effects of toxic substances in the air, gaseous vapors, poor ventilation, inadequate light, and sundry unsanitary conditions—were ruinous to health and reduced longevity. See Arlette Farge, "Les artisans malades de leur travail," in *Annales: Economies, sociétés, civilisations* 32, no 5. (1977): 993–1007; Bernard-Pierre Lecuyer, "Les maladies professionnels dans les 'Annales d'hygiène publique et de médecine légale' ou une première approche de l'usure au travail," *Le mouvement social*, no. 124 (July–September 1983): 45–60; and Alain Cottereau, "Usure au travail, destins masculins et destins féminins dans les cultures ouvrières en France au XIXe siècle," *Le mouvement social*, no. 124 (July–September 1983): 71–112.

12. Georg Zacher, "Unfallstatistik," in *Handwörterbuch der Staatswissenschaften*, ed. Johannes Conrad, Ludwig Elster, Wilhelm Lexis, and Edgar Loening (Jena: Gustav Fischer, 1911), 56; and H. Mamy, "Aperçu des succès obtenus par les mesures préventatives contre les accidents," in *Bericht über den XIV. Internationalen Kongress für Hygiene und Demographie: Berlin, 23–29 September 1907*, Bd. 4, Tl. 2 (Berlin: August Hirschwald, 1908), 663.

13. Véronique Brumeaux, "La question des accidents du travail a la fin du XIXe siècle," in *Memoire de maitrise* (Paris: Université Paris X-Nanterre, 1979), 73.

14. Labor historians have often overlooked this *terra peligrosa*. An exception is Dieter Groh, "Intensification of Work and Industrial Conflict in Germany 1896–1914," *Politics and Society* 8, no. 4 (1978): 387.

15. Philippe Hesse, "Les accidents du travail et l'idée de responsabilité civile au XIXe siècle," *Histoire des accidents du travail*, no. 6 (1979): 36. The position of German industrialists is discussed in Monika Breger, *Die Haltung der industriellen Unternehmer zur staatlichen Sozialpolitik in den Jahren 1878–1891* (Frankfurt am Main: Haag Herchen, 1982) 87, 88.

16. Paul Kampffmeyer, "Die Gewerkschaften und die Arbeiterschutz- und Arbeiterversicherungsgesetzgebung," *Sozialistische Monatshefte* 1, no. 1 (1904): 35, 36.

17. Brumeaux, "La question des accidents," 109.

18. Anson Rabinbach, *The Human Motor: Energy, Fatigue and the Origins of Modernity* (New York: Basic Books, 1990).

19. Georg Zacher, "Arbeiterversicherung in Deutschland," in Conrad et al., *Handwörterbuch*, 800; H. B. Oppenheim, *Die Hilfskassen und Versicherungskassen der arbeitenden Klassen* (Berlin: n.p., 1875); Max Hirsch, *Die gegenseitigen Hilfskassen und die Gesetzgebung* (Berlin: Duncker, 1875); and Albert Schaffie, *Der korporative Hilfskassenzwang* (Tübingen: n.p., 1884). In France, it was not until the 1830s that the legal status of the *sociétés de secours mutuels* was restored. Before 1848, more than 1,088 such associations were founded. Nicolas Gustave Hubbard, *De l'organisation des sociétés de prévoyance ou de secours mutuels* (Paris: Guillaumin, 1852); and Georg Zacher, "Arbeiterversicherung (Frankreich)," in Conrad et al., *Handwörterbuch*, 820–839.

20. Zacher, "Arbeiterversicherung in Deutschland," 797–801; William Harbutt Dawson. *Social Insurance in Germany 1883–1911, Its History, Operation, Results* (London: T. Fisher Unwin, 1912), 8–11.

21. Dawson, *Social Insurance*, 9.

22. Zacher, "Arbeiterversicherung in Deutschland," 788.

23. For a close analysis of Bismarck's views on the law, see Walter Vogel, *Bismarcks Arbeiterversicherung: Ihre Entstellung im Kräftespiel der Zeit* (Braunschweig: n.p., 1951). On Bismarck's social policy, see Albin Gladen, *Geschichte der Sozialpolitik in Deutschland: Eine Analyse ihrer Bedingungen, Formen, Zielsetzungen und Auswirkungen* (Wiesbaden: Franz Steiner Verlag, 1974); Klaus Witte, *Bismarcks Sozialversicherungen und die Entwicklung eines marxistischen Reformverständnisses in der deutschen Sozialdemokratie* (Cologne: Paul Rugenstein, 1980); Vernon Lidtke, "German Social Democracy and German State Socialism 1876–1884," *International Review of Social History*, no. 9 (1964): 202–225.

24. Zacher, "Unfallversicherung," 49.

25. Though workers were required to contribute to the sickness insurance, they did not directly support accident insurance. However, workers indirectly contributed to the accident system since a substantial portion of the accident insurance fell under sickness insurance, for example, the first thirteen weeks of disability (*Karenzzeit*). In Germany, Austria, and Luxembourg workers contributed two-thirds, employers one-third to the sickness insurance system. In Hungary, Norway, Italy, Finland, the Netherlands, and Luxembourg, workers were also not required to make any contribution to the accident insurance.

26. Zacher, "Arbeiterversicherung in Deutschland," 804.

27. Fanny Imle, "Das schweizerische Kranken- und Unfallversicherungsgesetz und sein Schicksal," *Sozialistische Monatshefte*, no. 4 (1900): 410.

28. See, for example, the debates of the *Congrès International des Accidents du Travail et des Assurances Sociales*, 5th Congress, Paris, 25–30 June 1900, 18–22 (hereafter cited as *CIATAS*, 1900).

29. R. van der Borght, "Arbeiterversicherung (Allgemeines)" in Conrad et al., *Handwörterbuch*, 787; Tonio Bodiker, *Arbeiterversicherung in den europäischen Staaten* (Leipzig: Duncker und Humblot, 1895); Maurice Bellorn, *Les lois d'assurance ouvrière à l'étranger* (Paris: G. Roustan, 1892); and Georg Zacher, *Die Arbeiterversicherung im Ausland*, 5 vols. (Berlin: Verl. d. Arbeiter-Versorgung, 1898–1908).

30. Alfred Manes, "Arbeiterversicherung (Belgien)," in Conrad et al., *Handwörterbuch*, 819; M. Magaldi, "Rapport sur la législation italienne des accidents du travail et son application" (*CIATAS*, 1900), 23.

31. F. L. Finninger, *The Workman's Compensation Act 1906–1909* (London: Stevens, 1910), 14–24.

32. Carl Gersuny, *Work Hazards and Industrial Conflict* (Hanover: University of New Hampshire Press, 1981), 98–99.

33. Borght, "Arbeiterversicherung (Allgemeines)," 790.

34. Ibid., 790.

35. Else Conrad, *Der Verein für Sozialpolitik und seine Wirksamkeit auf dem Gebiet der gewerblichen Arbeiterfrage* (Jena: Gustave Fischer, 1906), 86.

36. Morton J. Horowitz, *The Transformation of American Law 1780–1860* (Cambridge, MA: Harvard University Press, 1977), 228.

37. Jacques Donzelot attributes this shift "from contract to status" to the deskilling of work. See Jacques Donzelot, "Pleasure in Work," in *Ideology and Consciousness*, 9 (Winter 1981/1982): 3–28; and Jacques Donzelot, *L'invention du social: essai sur le déclin des passions politique* (Paris: Seuil, 1994), 121–178.

38. The persistent efforts of the German government to introduce criminal prosecution for breach of contract—a measure directed against strikes—was also predicated on the overriding principle of the state as guardian of the social order. Conrad, *Verein für Sozialpolitik*, 151–157; Alfred Boninger, *Die Bestrafung des Arbeitsvertragsbruchs* (Tübingen: Verlag der Lauppschen Buchhandlung, 1891).

39. Yvon Le Gall, *Histoire des accidents du travail* (Nantes: L'Université de Nantes, 1982), 23.

40. Stone, *Search for Social Peace*, 99–123; and Sanford Elwitt, *The Making of the Third Republic: Class and Politics in France 1868–1884* (Baton Rouge: Louisiana State University Press, 1975).

41. Stone, *Search for Social Peace*, 106.

42. Ibid.

43. Albert Berger, *Modifications introduites dans la législation des accidents du travail, 1902* (Paris: J. B. Baillière et Fils, 1903), 2, 8.

44. Le Gall, *Histoire des accidents*, 35.

45. Ibid., 15, 17.

46. Hesse, "Les accidents du travail," 34.

47. Ibid., 29.

48. Le Gall, *Histoire des accidents*, 36.

49. Berger, *Modifications*, 4.

50. Henri Secretan, *L'assurance contre les accidents: observations chirurgicales et professionnelles* (Geneva: Librairie A. Eggiman et Cie., 1906) 110.

51. Emile Cheysson, "France, les assurances ouvrières," in *CIATAS*, 329.

52. Ibid., 329.

53. Berger, *Modifications*, 7.

54. Cheysson, "France," in *CIATAS*, 329.

55. Hubert Coustan, *De la simulation et de l'évaluation des infirmités dans les accidents du travail* (Montpelier: n.p., 1902), 14.

56. *CIATAS*, 95.

57. Richard F. Kuisel, *Capitalism and the State in Modern France: Renovation and Economic Management in the Twentieth Century* (Cambridge: Cambridge University Press, 1981), 8–26.

58. *CIATAS*, 19.

59. "Le projet de loi sur les accidents du travail au Comité international des accidents," in *Revue pratique de droit industriel* (Paris: A. Rousseau, 1893), 449; Le Gall, *Histoire des accidents*, 11; and Hesse, "Les accidents du travail," 55.

60. Hesse, "Les accidents du travail," 12, 36; and Le Gall, *Histoire des accidents*, 7.

61. Berger, *Modifications*, 5; and Hesse, "Les accidents du travail," 23.

62. Brumeaux, "La question des accidents," 81.

63. Ernst Gruner, *De la responsabilité des accidents du travail d'un point de vue chrétien* (Nimes: n.p., 1891).

64. Le Gall, *Histoire des accidents*, 37.

65. Hesse, "Les accidents du travail," 39.

66. Jules Jamin, "Critique médicale de la loi sur les accidents du travail" (PhD diss., Paris, 1902), 12.

67. Voge, *Bismarcks Arbeiterversicherung*, 68–70; Lujo Brentano, *Die Arbeiter-versicherung gemäss der heutigen Wirtschaftsordnung* (Leipzig: Duncker und Humblot 1879); and *Der Arbeiter-Versicherungszwang, seine Voraussetzungen und seine Folgen* (Berlin: Verlag von C. Habel, 1881).

68. Conrad, *Verein für Sozialpolitik*, 86.

69. Lujo Brentano, *Fortbildung des* Arbeitsvertrags, Schriften *des Vereins für Sozialpolitik*, Bd. 47 (Leipzig: Duncker und Humblot, 1890), 258.

70. Gustav Schmoller, "Haftpflicht und Unfallversicherung," in *Jahrbuch* (1881), 311. See also Dieter Lindenlaub, *Richtungskämpfe im Verein für Sozialpolitik*,

Vierteljahrsschrift für Sozial- und Wirtschaftsgeschichte, Beiheft, no. 52 (Wiesbaden: Franz Steiner Verlag, 1967), 44–52.

71. *Stahl und Eisen: Zeitschrift der nordwestlichen Gruppe des Vereins deutscher Eisenhüttenleute* 7, no. 8 (1887): 585.

72. Hesse, "Les accidents du travail," 5.

73. Le Gall, *Histoire des accidents,* 45.

74. Zacher, "Unfallversicherung," 47.

75. Ibid.

76. "Extraits du procès-verbal officiel de la séance de la chambre des députes, du 28 octobre 1897" in *CIATAS* (1897), 396.

77. Ibid.

78. Coustan, *De la simulation,* 15.

79. Maurice Bellom, "La quatrième session du congrès international des accidents du travail et des assurances sociales," in *CIATAS* (1897), 516.

80. Dietrich Milles, "From Worker's Diseases to Occupational Diseases: The Impact of Experts' Concepts on Workers' Attitudes," in *The Social History of Occupational Health,* ed. Paul Weindling (Dover, NH: Croon Helm, 1985), 55–77.

81. Georg von Mayr, "L'assurance et la fréquence des accidents," in *Congres International des Accidents du Travail et des Assurances Sociales 1–6 October 1894* (Milan: Reggiani, 1894), 344.

82. Reichsunfallgesetz, § 1, Abs. 7.

83. Ludwig Fuld, "Der Begriff des Betriebsunfalles im Sinne der deutschen Gesetzgebung," in *Archiv für soziale Gesetzgebung und Statistik* (1888): 418.

84. The legislative draft of 1881 noted that the purpose of the law was to compensate either victims (or heirs) of accidents caused by "occupational work characterized by the danger of accident." Heinrich Rosin, "Der Begriff des Betriebsunfalls als Grundlage des Entschädigungsanspruchs nach den Reichsgesetzen über die Unfallversicherung," in *Archiv für öffentliches Recht,* no. 3 (1888): 419.

85. Ibid., 320.

86. Reichsversicherungsamt, *Amtliche Nachrichten* III, 355 (hereafter cited as RVA/AN).

87. Rosin, "Der Begriff des Betriebsunfalls," 330.

88. Fuld, "Der Begriff des Betriebsunfalles," 421; and "Betriebsunfall," in *Handwörterbuch des gesamten Versicherungswesens einschließlich der sozialpolitischen Arbeiter-Versicherung,* Hrsg. Eugen Baumgartner (Strasbourg: Verlag Karl J. Trübner, 1899), 721.

89. Georg von Mayr, "L'assurance et la fréquence des accidents," in *CIATAS* (Milan), 1894, 340; also see Georg van Mayr, "Unfallversicherung

und Sozialstatistik," in *Archiv für soziale Gesetzgebung und Statistik* (1888), 203–245.

90. Ernst Gruner, "Résultats de dix années d'assurance obligatoire en Allemagne ct de cinq années en Autriche," *CIATAS* (1897), 338.

91. *CIATAS* (1893), 98.

92. Von Mayr, "L'Assurance," 339.

93. *CIATAS* (Bern, 1891), 340.

94. Ibid., 347.

95. Von Mayr, "L'Assurance," 343.

96. *CIATAS* (1893), 79.

97. Emile Cheysson, "La prévention des accidents," in *CIATAS* (1893), 303, 313. The Italian industrialist association also introduced broad measures of accident prevention; see P. Pontiggia, "Aperçu des succès obtenus en Italic par les mésures préventives contre les accidents du-travail," in *Bericht über den XIV internationalen Kongress für Hygiene und Demographie: Berlin, 23–29 September 1907*, Bd. 4, Tl. 2 (Berlin: Hirschwald, 1908), 668–673; Mamy, "Aperçu des succès obtenus," 661, 662.

98. "Rundschau," in *Sozialistische Monatshefte. Internationale Revue des Sozialismus IX* 2, no. 7 (1903): 534.

99. Klaus Wagenbach, *Franz Kafka: Eine Biographie Seiner Jugend 1883–1912* (Berlin: Francke Verlag, 1958), 144–149.

100. Konrad Hartmann, "Überblick über die Erfolge der Unfallverhütung in Deutschland," in *Bericht über den XIV. Internationalen Kongress für Hygiene und Demographie: Berlin, 23–29 September 1907*, Bd. 4, Tl. 2 (Berlin: Hirschwald, 1908), 648–659.

101. Ibid. Several journals were devoted to accident prevention: *Concordia: Zeitschrift der Zentralstelle für Arbeiterwohlfahrtseinrichtungen*; *Gewerblich-Technische Ratgeber*; *Sozialtechnik*.

102. Henning Rogge, *Fabrikwelt um die Jahrhundertwende am Beispiel der AEG Maschinenfabrik in Berlin-Wedding* (Cologne: DuMont, 1983), 133, 134.

103. Emannuel Roth, *Kompendium der Gewerbekrankheiten und Einführung in die Gewerbehygiene* (Berlin: Schoertz, 1909), 2.

104. "Rapport au Ministre du commerce," *Journal Officiel*, December 22, 1901; and Hubert Coustan, *De la simulation*, 9.

105. "Bericht der am 13. Januar 1887 stattgefundenen General-Versammlung der Nordwestlichen Gruppe des Vereins deutscher Eisen- und Stahlindustrieller," in *Stahl und Eisen*, no. 2 (February 1887): 125; and Gruner, "Résultats statistiques," 68. See also Breger, *Haltung der industriellen Unternehmer*, 87–89.

106. Fritz Stier-Somlo, "Ethik und Psychologie im deutschen Sozialrecht," in *Archiv für Rechts- und Wirtschaftsphilosophie*, Bd. 1 (Berlin: Walther Rothschild, 1907/1908), 232–247.

107. Ibid., 247.

108. Coustan, *De la simulation*, 13.

109. Ibid., 9.

110. Ambroise Tardeiu, *Étude médico-légale sur les blessures* (Paris: J. B. Baillière et Fils, 1879), 449. The standard military medical work is Emile Duponchel, *Traite de médecine légale militaire* (Paris: Félix Alcan, 1890).

111. Tardieu, *Etude médico-légale*, 452.

112. René Sand, *La simulation et l'interprétation des accidents du travail* (Brussels: Maloine, 1907). For some other works of this genre, see R. Giraud, *Etude sur les blessures simulées dans l'industrie* (Lille: Thèse, 1893); Jamin, "Critique médicale"; and P. Chavigny, *Diagnostic des Maladies Simulées dans les Accidents du travail* (Paris: J. B. Baillière et Fils, 1906).

113. Secretan, *L'assurance contre les accidents*, 75.

114. Alfred Bienfait, "La recherche de la simulation chez les victimes des accidents du travail," in *Congres international médicale des accidents du travail à Liège, 29 May 1905, Rapports et Communications* (Brussels, 1905), question vi, 5.

115. Rene Michaud, *J'avais vingt ans* (Paris: Editions Syndicalistes, 1967), cited in Patrick Fridenson, "France-États-Unis: Genèse de l'usine nouvelle," *Recherches*, nos. 32/33 (September 1978): 381.

116. J. Juillard, "Simulation et abus dans les assurances ouvrières au point de vue médical," *CIATAS* (Rome, 1908), 812.

117. Secretan, *L'assurance contre les accidents*, 78.

118. Bienfait, "La recherche de la simulation," 5; S. Baudry, *Étude médico-légale sur les traumatismes de l'œil et de ses annexes* (Paris: J. B. Balliere et Fils, 1904), 54.

119. Juillard, "Simulation," 801.

120. E. Patry, "De l'utilité de l'examen de tous les assurés au point de vue de la hernie," *Revue Suisse des accidents du travail* (1908): 193.

121. Juillard, "Simulation," 809.

122. Brumeaux, "La question des accidents," 116, 117.

123. *CIATAS* (1900), 79.

124. Secretan, *L'assurance contre les accidents*, 7.

125. Juillard, "Simulation," 813.

126. Georges Touchard, "Lenteur judiciaire," *Nouvelle revue* (October 1903): 43.

127. Secretan, *L'assurance contre les accidents*, 109.

128. P. Moller, "Die Simulation in der Unfallversicherung," in *Kompass* (1909): 20, 40.

129. Paul Camille Brouardel, *La responsabilité médicale* (Paris: J. B. Baillière et Fils, 1898), 72–88; and the debate at the Congres International de médecine légale in Brussels, August 4, 1894, reported in *Annales de hygiène et de médecine*

légale, no. 38 (1897): 379; Charles Valentino, "Critique du secret medical," *Revue scientifique* 13, no. 2 (1904): 390–394.

130. Secretan, *L'assurance contre les accidents*, 77.

131. Stier-Somlo, "Ethik und Psychologie," 247.

132. Secretan, *L'assurance contre les accidents*, 78.

133. Alfons Labisch, "Doctors, Workers and the Scientific Cosmology of the Industrial World: The Social Construction of 'Health' and the 'Homo-Hygienicus,'" *Journal of Contemporary History* 20, no. 4 (1985): 599–616; and Ute Frevert, "Professional Medicine and the Working Classes in Imperial Germany," *Journal of Contemporary History* 20, no. 4 (1985): 637–658.

134. Secretan, *L'assurance contre les accidents*, 107.

135. Ibid., 107.

136. Carl Thiem, *Handbuch der Unfallerkrankungen auf Grund Ärzlicher Erfahrungen* (Stuttgart: Verlag Ferdinand Enke, 1898), 38.

137. Ibid., 39.

138. Juillard, "Simulation," 802.

139. Ibid., 805.

140. Paul von Bruns, "Die traumatischen Neurosen-Unfallneurosen," in *Spezielle Pathologie und Therapie*, Bd. 12, Tl. 1 (Vienna: Holder, 1901), 96.

141. Paul Kampffmeyer, "Tendenzwissenschaft gegen Sozialpolitik," in *Sozialistische Monatshefte* 1, no. 1 (1913): 11.

142. Ludwig Bernhard, *Unerwünschte Folgen der deutschen Sozialpolitik* (Berlin: Springer, 1913).

143. Coustan, *De la simulation*, 7.

144. Witte, *Bismarcks Sozialversicherungen*. For the distinction between *Arbeiterschutz* and *Arbeiterversicherung*, see Hertha Wolff, "Die Stellung der Sozialdemokratie zur deutschen Arbeiterversicherunggesetzgebung von ihren Entstehung an bis zur Reichsversicherungsordnung" (PhD diss., Universität Freiburg, 1933).

145. Paul Louis, *L'ouvrier devant l'état* (Paris, 1904), 283; Marc Pierrot, *Le travail et surmenage* (Paris: Temps nouveaux, 1911), 27–29. For a detailed study of the eight-hour-day movement, see Gary Cross, "The Quest for Leisure: Reassessing the Eight-Hour Day in France," *Journal of Social History* 18, no. 2 (1984): 195–206.

146. Victor Griffuelhes and Louis Niels, *Les objectifs de nos luttes de classes* (Paris: La Publication Sociale, 1909), 19.

147. Witte, *Bismarcks Sozialversicherungen*, 114–119. See also Kampff-meyer, "Die Gewerkschaften und die Arbeiterschutz- und Arbeiterversicher-unggesetzgebung," 35, 36.

148. Anonymous, "Bismarcks soziales Programm," *Der Sozialdemokrat*, October 17, 1880, 41–42.

149. Rudolf Wissell, "Täuschung und Übertreibung auf dem Gebiet der Unfallversicherung," *Sozialistische Monatshefte* 1, no. 10 (1909): 635.

150. Julius Frassdorf, "Die Rechtsprechung in der Unfallversicherung," *Sozialistische Monatshefte* 2, no. 9 (1906): 786.

151. Ibid. See also Johannes Heiden, "Die Rechtsprechung in der Arbeiterversicherung," *Sozialistische Monatshefte* 2, no. 9 (1909): 1115–1123.

152. Frassdorf, "Die Rechtsprechung," 787.

153. Robert Schmidt, "Der Streit um die Rente," *Sozialistische Monatshefte* 1, no. 5 (1909): 422; and Frassdorf, "Die Rechtsprechung," 787.

154. Robert Schmidt, "Simulation im Streit um die Unfallrente," *Sozialistische Monatshefte* 2, no. 14 (1908): 878, 879.

155. Sigmund Freud, *Beyond the Pleasure Principle*, trans. James Strachey, in *The Standard Edition of the Complete Psychological Works of Sigmund Freud*, vol. 28 (London: Hogarth Press, 1955), 32. See also Otto Lipmann, *Unfallursachen und Unfallbekämpfung: Veröffentlichungen aus dem Gebiete der Medizinalverwaltung*, Bd. 20, Heft 3, Arbeitswissenschaftliche Monographien aus dem Institut für angewandte Psychologie in Berlin (Berlin: n.p., 1925).

156. P. Leubischer and W. Bibrowicz, "Die Neurasthenie in Arbeiterkreisen," in *Deutsche medizinische Wochenschrift*, no. 21 (1905): 820–824; M. Schonhals, *Über die Ursachen der Neurasthenie und Hysterie bei Arbeiter* (Berlin: University of Berlin, 1906). A survey of the neurasthenia diagnosis among workers indicates that, in contrast to the hysteria diagnosis, neurasthenic symptoms were more equally distributed along age and gender lines.

157. Franz Schröter, "Über die Simulation bei den Versicherungsanstalten," *Ärztliche Zentralanzeiger* (April/May 1909): 13.

158. Schmidt, "Streit um die Rente," 425.

159. Heinrich Sachs, *Die Unfallneurose, ihre Entstehung, Beurteilung und Verhütung* (Breslau: Preuss and Jünger, 1908), 17.

160. Andreas Killen, *Berlin Electropolis: Shock, Nerves, and German Modernity* (Berkeley: University of California Press, 2006), 184, 185.

161. Schmidt, "Streit um die Rente," 422.

162. Wissell, "Täuschung und Übertreibung," 630.

163. Ibid., 633.

164. RVA/AN (1897), 474.

165. Rabinbach, *Human Motor*, chs. 7 and 8; and "The European Science of Work: The Economy of the Body at the End of the Nineteenth Century," in *Work in France*, ed. Steven Kaplan and Cynthia Koepp (Ithaca, NY: Cornell University Press, 1986), 475–513.

166. Armand Imbert and M. Mestre, "Statistique d'accidents du travail," *Revue Scientifique* 13, no. 11 (1904): 386.

167. Armand Imbert, "Les accidents du travail et les compagnies d'assurances," *Revue Scientifique* 1, no. 23 (1904): 711.

168. Ibid., 718.

169. Ibid., 712.

170. Ibid.

171. Armand Imbert, "Le surmenage par suite du travail professionnel," in *Bericht über den XIV. Internationalen Kongress fur Hygiene und Demographie: Berlin, 23–29 September 1907*, Bd. 4, Tl. 1 (Berlin: August Hirschwald, 1908), 644.

172. Imbert and Mestre, "Statistique d'accidents," 385–390.

173. Ibid., 386.

174. Imbert, "Les accidents," 715.

175. Imbert and Mestre, "Statistique d'accidents," 385. Imbert cited statistics from nine additional departments in the area around Toulouse which show strikingly similar general characteristics. Ibid., 387.

176. Emannuel Roth, "Ermüdung durch Berufsarbeit," in *Bericht über den XIV. Internationalen Kongress für Hygiene und Demographie: Berlin, 23–29 September 1907*, Bd. 4, Tl. l (Berlin: August Hirschwald, 1908), 618; H. Bille-Top, "Die Verteilung der Unglücksfalle der Arbeiter auf die Wochentage nach Tagesstunden," in *Zentralblatt für allgemeine Gesundheitspflege*, no. 27 (1908): 197; and Hugo Münsterberg, *Grundzüge der Psychotechnik* (Leipzig: Verlag von Johann Ambrosius Barth, 1914), 394.

177. Roth, *Kompendium*, 14, 15.

178. Ibid., 15.

179. Roth, "Ermüdung durch Berufsarbeit," 606.

180. On the fate of *Blauer Montag*, and *Saint-Lundi* in the late-nineteenth century, see Josef Ehmer, "Rote Fahnen-Blauer Montag: Soziale Bedingungen von Aktions- und Organisationsformen der frühen Wiener Arbeiterbewegung," in Detlev Puls, *Wahrnehmungsformen und Protestverhalten: Studien zur Lage der Unterschichten im 18. und 19. Jahrhundert* (Frankfurt am Main: Suhrkamp, 1979), 143–174; Douglas A. Reid, "Der Kampf gegen den 'Blauen Montag' 1766 bis 1876," in Puls, *Wahrnehmungsformen*, 265–295; Susanna Barrows, "After the Commune: Alcoholism, Temperance and Literature in the Early Third Republic," *Consciousness and Class Experience in Nineteenth Century Europe*, ed. John Merriman (New York: Holmes and Meier Publishers, 1979), 205–218; and Jeffrey Kaplow, "La fin de la Saint-Lundi, étude sur le Paris ouvrier au XIXe siècle," in *Temps libre* (Paris: Temps Libre-Denoel, 1981), 2:107–118.

181. Edmund Fischer, "Trinken und Arbeiten," *Sozialistische Monatshefte* 1, no. 5 (1908): 360–367.

182. Armand Imbert and M. Mestre, "Nouvelles statistiques d'accidents du travail," *Revue scientifique* 4, no. 17 (1905): 525.

183. Frevert, "Professional Medicine," 643.

184. Roth, "Ermüdung durch Berufsarbeit," 619.

185. Roth, *Kompendium*, 13.

186. Fridenson, "France-Etats Unis," 382.

187. Roth, *Kompendium*, 12.

188. Zaccharia Treves, "Le surmenage par suite du travail professionnel," in *Bericht über den XIV Internationalen Kongress für Hygiene und Demographie: Berlin, 23–29 September 1907* Bd. 4, Tl. l (Berlin: August Hirschwald, 1908), 626.

189. Armand Imbert, "Le surmenage par suite du travail professionnel au XIVe congres international d'hygiène et de démographie Berlin, 1907," in *L'année psychologique* (1908), 243.

190. Imbert and Mestre, "Nouvelles statistiques d'accidents du travail," 522.

191. Philippe Delahaye, "La prétendue fatigue des ouvriers envisagée comme cause des accidents du travail," *Revue industrielle*, October 8, 1904, 408.

192. Imbert and Mestre, "Nouvelles statistiques d'accidents du travail," 520, and Armand Imbert and M. Mestre, "A propos de l'influence de la fatigue professionnelle sur la production des accidents du travail," *Revue industrielle*, November 5, 1905, 449.

193. Armand Imbert, "Le surmenage par suite du travail professionnel au XIVe congres international d'hygiène et de démographie" (Berlin: n.p., 1907), 232.

194. Imbert and Mestre, "Nouvelles statistiques d'accidents du travail," 717.

195. Hector Depasse, *Du travail et de ses conditions (Chambres et Conseils du travail).* (Paris: J. B. Bailliere et Fils, 1895), 52, 53.

196. Séance du 22. Fev. 1912, Journal Officiel du 23, fev, 416, cited in Jean Desplanque, *Le problème de la réduction de la durée du travail devant le parlement français* (Paris: Libraire Arthur Rousseau, 1918), 179.

4. NEURASTHENIA AND MODERNITY

1. George Miller Beard, *American Nervousness: Its Causes and Consequences* (New York: Putnam, 1881), 12.

2. Ibid., 35, 99.

3. Robert A. Nye, "Crime, Madness, and Politics," in *Modern France: The Medical Concept of National Decline* (Princeton, NJ: Princeton University Press, 1984), 148–154.

4. Bernard Straus, "Achille-Adrien Proust, M.D.: Doctor to River Basins," in *Bulletin of the New York Academy of Medicine*, no. 50 (1974): 833–836;

Bernard Straus, *The Maladies of Marcel Proust: Doctors and Disease in His Life and Work* (New York: Holmes and Meier, 1980), 81–102.

5. Achille-Adrien Proust and Gilbert Ballet, *L'hygiène du neurasthénique* (Paris: Masson, 1887), translated into English by Peter Campbell Smith as *The Treatment of Neurasthenia* (New York: Edward R. Pelton, 1903), 7.

6. Sigmund Freud, "Hysteria" [1888], in *Standard Edition*, vol. 1, ed. James Strachey (London: Hogarth, 1966), 53.

7. M. Patel, "Neurasthénie," in *La grande encyclopédie* (Paris: Lamirault, 1886), 987.

8. Adrien Proust and Gilbert Ballet, *The Treatment of Neurasthenia* (London: Henry Kimpton, 1902), 33.

9. Otto Binswanger, *Die Pathologie und Therapie der Neurasthenie: Vorlesungen für Studierende und Ärtze* (Jena: Fisher, 1896), 110.

10. Edward Cowles, *The Mental Symptoms* of *Fatigue* (New York: Fless and Ridge Print, 1893), 22.

11. Proust and Ballet, *Treatment of Neurasthenia*, 33.

12. Walter Benjamin, *The Origin of German Tragic Drama*, trans. John Osborne (London: New Left Books, 1977), 183.

13. Proust and Ballet, *Treatment of Neurasthenia*, 96.

14. Ibid., 34.

15. Alfred Binet and Charles Féré, "Recherche expérimentale sur la physiologie des mouvements chez les hystériques," *Archive de physiologie*, no. 10 (1887): 320.

16. Nicole Vaschide and Claude Vurpas, "Contribution à l'étude de la fatigue mentale des neurasthéniques," in *Société de biologie*, March 7, 1903, 296.

17. Albert Deschamps, *Les maladies de l'énérgie, thérapeutique générale* (Paris, 1890), 46, 47.

18. Théodule Ribot, *The Diseases of the Will*, trans. Merwin Marie Snell (Chicago: Open Court, 1896), 2; on Ribot, see M. Reuchlin, "The Historical Background of National Trends in Psychology: France," *Journal of the History of the Behavioral Sciences* 1, no. 2 (1965): 115–122.

19. Jan Goldstein, "The Hysteria Diagnosis in Nineteenth Century France," *Journal of Modern History*, no. 54 (1982): 209–239.

20. Ribot, *Diseases of the Will*, 27–28.

21. Theodor Dunin, *Grundsätze der Behandlung der Neurasthenie und Hysterie* (Berlin: Hirschwald, 1902), 32, 33.

22. Proust and Ballet, *Treatment of Neurasthenia*, 73.

23. The connection between "inhibition to action" (*Handlungshemmung*) in melancholia and in labor was first explored by Wolf Lepenies, *Melancholie und Gesellschaft* (Frankfurt am Main: Suhrkamp, 1972), 207–213.

24. Ribot, *Diseases of the Will*, 10.

25. Angelo Mossa, *La Fatica* (Milan: Fratelli Treves, 1921 [1891]). On Mosso's influence, see Anson Rabinbach, *The Human Motor: Energy, Fatigue and the Origins* of *Modernity* (New York: Basic Books, 1990), chs. 5 and 6.

26. *Congrès international d'Hygiène et de Démographie, tenu à Bruxelles du 3 au 8 Septembre 1903, compte-rendus du congrès,* bk. 5, sec. 4, Hygiène industrielle et professionnelle (Brussels: Congrès international d'Hygiène et de Démographie, 1903), 72.

27. M. G. Ferrero, "Les formes primitives du travail," *Revue scientifique* 45, no. 11 (1896): 331–335.

28. Ferrero, "Les formes primitives du travail," 331–335.

29. Karl Bücher, *Arbeit und Rhythmus* (Leipzig: Teubner, 1899 [1897]), 8–10, 358.

30. Théodule Ribot, "Le Moindre effort en psychologie," *Revue philosophique,* no. 70 (July–December 1910): 364.

31. Pierre Janet, *Les Obsessions et psychasthénie,* vol. 1 (Paris: Alcan, 1911), 335. According to Ribot, the term originated with Cesare Lombroso.

32. Ribot, "Le Moindre effort," 374.

33. Ibid., 376.

5. PSYCHOTECHNICS AND POLITICS IN WEIMAR GERMANY:
THE CASE OF OTTO LIPMANN

1. On the roots of this approach in France, see Georges Ribeill, "Les debuts de l'ergonomie en France à la veille de la Première Guerre mondiale," *Le mouvement sociale,* no. 113 (1980): 3–36. On American developments before 1910, see Alberto Cambrosio, "Quand la psychologie fait son entrée à l'usine: selection et controle des ouvriers aux Etats Unis pendant les années 1910," *Le mouvement social,* no. 113 (1980): 37–66.

2. Ribeill, "Les debuts," 3–36; Anson Rabinbach, *The Human Motor: Energy, Fatigue and the Origins of Modernity* (New York: Basic Books, 1990), 244–253. For a fascinating study of a nearly forgotten figure in this tradition, see Ilana Löwy, "Measures, Instruments, Methods, and Results": Jozefa Joteyko on Social Reforms and Physiological Measures," in *Body Counts: Medical Quantification in Historical and Sociological Perspectives/Perspectives historiques et sociologiques sur la quantification médicale,* ed. Gérard Jorland, Annick Opinel, and George Weisz (Montreal: McGill-Queens University Press, 2005), 145–172.

3. On Britain, see C. B. Frisby, "The Development of Industrial Psychology at the NIIP," *Occupational Psychology,* no. 44 (1970): 35–50; and Bernhard Wilpert, "How European Is Work and Organizational Psychology?" in *European Perspectives in Psychology,* ed. P. J. D. Drenth and R. J. Tobias (Chichester, England: John Wiley and Sons, 1990), 123–140. The Department of

Industrial Research at Harvard University was formed in 1926 with the financial help of the Rockefeller Foundation. See Elton Mayo, "Hawthorne and the Western Electric Company," in *The Social Problems of an Industrial Civilization* (Boston, MA: Division of Research, Graduate School of Business Administration, Harvard University, 1949), 60–76.

4. On the wartime uses of industrial psychotechnics, see Rabinbach, *Human Motor*, ch. 10.

5. Wilpert, "How European Is Work," 125.

6. For the internalist approach, see Friedrich Dorsch, *Geschichte und Probleme der Angewandten Psychologie* (Bern: H. Huber, 1963); Wolfram Burisch, *Industrie und Betriebssoziologie* (Berlin: Walter de Gruyter, 1973); and Ernst Bornemann, "Bestrebungen um die Humanisierung der Arbeitswelt," in *Die Psychologie des 20. Jahrhunderts*, Bd. 13, (Zurich: Kindler, 1981), 53–95. Marxist accounts include: Peter Hinrichs, *Um die Seele des Arbeiters: Arbeitspsychologie. Industrie und Betriebssoziologie in Deutschland, 1871–1945* (Cologne: Paul Rugenstein, 1981); Siegfried Jaeger und Irmingard Staeuble, "Die Psychotechnik und ihre gesellschaftlichen Entwicklungsbedingungen," in *Die Psychologie des 20. Jahrhunderts: Anwendungen im Berufsleben*, ed. F. Stoll, Bd. 13, (Zurich: Kindler, 1981), 53–94; and Angelika Ebbinghaus, *Arbeiter und Arbeitswissenschaft: Zur Entstehung der "Wissenschaftlicher Betriebsführung"* (Opladen: Westdeutscher Verlag, 1984).

7. Biographical information about Lipmann is scant and contradictory. See Dorsch, *Geschichte und Probleme*, 69, 70; Lutz V. Rosenthal, "Otto Lipmann," in *Neue Deutsche Biographie* (Berlin: Duncker und Humblot, 1984), 645–646; William Stern, "Otto Lipmann: 1880–1933," *American Journal of Psychology*, no. 46 (1934): 152–154; William Stern, "Otto Lipmann," *Zeitschrift für Angewandte Psychologie*, no. 45 (1933): 420; and H. O., "Otto Lipmann," in *Encyclopedia Judaica*, vol. 11 (New York: Macmillan, 1971–1972), 283.

8. Stern, "Otto Lipmann," 152–153.

9. Ibid., 420.

10. Otto Lipmann (with Paul Platt), *Die Lüge. In psychologischer, philosophischer, juristischer, pädagogischer, historischer, soziologischer, sprach- und literaturwissenschaftlicher und entwicklungsgeschichtlicher Betrachtung* (Leipzig: Joh. Ambr. Barth, 1927).

11. On Münsterberg, see Rabinbach, *Human Motor*, 191–193, and Orin J. Hale Jr., *Human Sciences and Social Order: Hugo Münsterberg and the Origins of Applied Psychology* (Philadelphia: Temple University Press, 1980).

12. Dorsch, *Geschichte und Probleme*, 59.

13. Hugo Münsterberg, *Psychology and Industrial Efficiency* (Boston, MA: Houghton Mifflin, 1913), 209, 210.

14. Dorsch, *Geschichte und Probleme*, 60.

15. Ibid.

16. Ibid., 64.

17. Jaeger and Staeuble, "Psychotechnik," 63.

18. Dorsch, *Geschichte und Probleme*, 65.

19. Fritz Giese, *Theorie der Psychotechnik* (Braunschweig: F. Vieweg, 1925), 23.

20. Jaeger and Staeuble, "Psychotechnik," 66.

21. Fritz Giese, *Psychologie der Arbeitshand*, in *Handbuch der Biologischen Arbeitsmethoden*, ed. Emil Abderhalden (Stuttgart: n.p., 1928), 804.

22. Walther Moede, "Kraftfahrer-Eignungsprüfungen beim Deutschen Heer 1915–1918," *Industrielle Psychotechnik* 3, no. 1 (1926): 23.

23. Jaeger and Staeuble, "Psychotechnik," 69.

24. Ibid., 68.

25. Volker Trieba and Ulrich Mentrup, *Entwicklung der Arbeitswissenschaft in Deutschland: Rationalisierungspolitik der deutschen Wirtschaft bis zum Faschismus* (Munich: Minerva, 1983), 131; Jaeger and Staeuble, "Psychotechnik," 79.

26. Ludwig Preller, *Sozialpolitik in der Weimarer Republik* (Kronberg: Athenäum-Verlag, 1973) 65.

27. Jaeger and Staeuble, "Psychotechnik," 71.

28. Dietrich Milles, "Krieg und Menschenökonomie: Gewerbehygiene in Deutschland zu beginn der Weimarer Republik." Zentrum für Sozialpolitik, University of Bremen. Paper presented at the University of Liverpool, Liverpool, England, January 1990.

29. Günter Wendel, *Der Kaiser Wilhelm Gesellschaft 1911–1914: Zur Anatomie einer imperialistischen Forschungsgesellschaft* (Berlin: Akademie Verlag, 1975) 214.

30. Gerhard Albrecht, "Arbeitsgebiet und Ziele des KWI Instituts für Arbeitsphysiologie," in *Technik und Wirtschaft* (Berlin: Selbstverlag des Vereines, 1915), 8:284–290, cited in Dietrich Milles, "Prävention und Technikgestaltung. Arbeitsmedizin und angewandte Arbeitswissenschaft in historischer Sicht," in *"Gestalten"—Eine neue gesellschaftliche Praxis*, ed. Felix Rauner (Bonn: Verlag Neue Gesellschaft, 1988), 55.

31. Milles, "Prävention und Technikgestaltung," 54–56.

32. Zentrales Staatsarchiv, Dienststelle Merseburg (ZStA) M. Rep. 76, VL. Sekt. 2., Tit. 23, Litt A. N. 115. KWI, [hereafter, ZSTa M. Rep. 76]. Denkschrift, Carl Stumpf to "Eurer Exzellenz," December 22, 1915. (My appreciation to Prof. Dietrich Milles, for access to his collection of these archival materials.)

33. ZSTa M. Rep. 76, Max Rubner to Kaiser Wilhelm ("Eurer Exzellenz"), May 29, 1917.

34. On Moede, see Paul Devinat, "Scientific Management in Europe," *International Labour Office, Studies and Reports [Series B]* (Geneva, 1927), 81.

Moede was technical advisor to the German State Railways, head of the psychotechnical institute of the Technische Hochschule in Charlottenburg and, after 1924, head of Institut für Wirtschaftspsychologie an der Handelshochschule, Berlin.

35. Jaeger and Staeuble, "Psychotechnik," 81. Between 1918 and 1927, psychotechnical professorships were established at six polytechnic colleges (Technische Hochschulen) throughout Germany, and psychotechnical institutes were established, including several at major universities, especially in Hamburg, Munich, and Berlin. See Ulfried Geuter, *Die Professionalisierung der deutschen Psychologie im Nationalsozialismus* (Frankfurt am Main: Suhrkamp Verlag, 1988), 88–91.

36. H. Ebert and K. Hausen, "Georg Schlesinger und die Rationalisierungsbewegung in Deutschland," in *Wissenschaft und Gesellschaft*, vol. 1, ed. R. Rlirup (Berlin: Springer, 1979), 315–334.

37. Devinat, *Scientific Management in Europe*, 80.

38. ZsTa M. Rep. 151 c. Nr. 903. Institut für Angewandte Psychologie u. Gewerbehygiene u. Arbeitswissenschaft [hereafter ZsTa M. Rep. 151 C]. Der Minister für Handel u. Gewerbe an Preußischen Herrn Finanzminister, January 17, 1922.

39. Richard Seidel, "Die Rationalisierung des Arbeitsverhältnisses," *Die Gesellschaft* 3, no. 7 (1926): 21. On the psychotechnics craze in Weimar Germany, see Andreas Killen, *Berlin Electropolis Shock, Nerves and German Modernity* (Berkeley: University of California Press, 2006), 35–36, 194–205.

40. Geuter, *Professionalisierung*, 218.

41. R. W. Chestnut, "Psychotechnik: Industrial Psychology in the Weimar Republic 1918–1924," *Proceedings of the Annual Convention of the American Psychological Association* 7, no. 2 (1972): 781.

42. Geuter, *Professionalisierung*, 221.

43. Devinat, *Scientific Management in Europe*, 81.

44. Geuter, *Professionalisierung*, 222.

45. Ibid., 223.

46. Ibid., 222.

47. Jaeger and Staeuble, "Psychotechnik," 84, 85.

48. Ibid., 84.

49. Jaeger and Staeuble, "Psychotechnik," 84.

50. Geuter, *Professionalisierung*, 222.

51. Ibid., 222.

52. Jaeger and Staeuble, "Psychotechnik," 85.

53. Walther Moede, "Zur Methodik der Menschenbehandlung," in *Industrielle Psychotechnik* (Berlin: Springer, 1930), 4, and the pamphlet, *Zur Methodik der Menschenbehandlung* (Berlin: Charlottenburg, 1930).

54. *Vorwärts*, no. 7 (July 1930); *Hamburger Echo*, no. 7 (July 1930); and Walter Zadeck, *Weltbühne* (July 1930).

55. Otto Lipmann, "Mehr Psychotechnik in der Psychotechnik," *Zeitschrift für Angewandte Psychologie*, no. 37 (1930): 188.

56. Lipmann, "Mehr Psychotechnik," 191.

57. Otto Lipmann, *Lehrbuch der Arbeitswissenschaft* (Jena: Verlag von Gustav Fischer, 1932), 16.

58. Fritz Giese, *Philosophie der Arbeit* (Halle: Carl Marhold, 1932), 26.

59. Lipmann, *Lehrbuch*, 6.

60. Otto Lipmann, "Angewandte Psychologie Psychotechnik— Arbeitswissenschaft," *Beiheft zur Zeitschrift für Angewandte Psychologie*, no. 59 (1931): 177–184.

61. Otto Lipmann, *Wirtschaftspsychologie und psychologische Berufsberatung: Ein Vortrag von Otto Lipmann* (Leipzig: J. A. Barth, 1918), 8.

62. Lipmann, *Wirtschaftspsychologie*, 22.

63. Otto Lipmann, *Grundriß der Arbeitswissenschaft und Ergebnisse der Arbeitswissenschaftlichen Statistik* (Jena: Gustav Fischer, 1926), 1.

64. Ibid.

65. Ibid., 11.

66. Otto Lipmann, *Das Arbeitszeitproblem* (Berlin: R. Schoetz, 1926), 8.

67. Ibid., 11.

68. Ibid., 14.

69. Ibid., 10.

70. Stern, "Otto Lipmann," 54.

71. Lipmann, *Arbeitszeitproblem*, 7.

72. Ibid., 12–14.

73. Ibid., 16.

74. Ibid., 14.

75. Ibid., 78.

76. Lipmann, *Lehrbuch*, 394.

77. Ibid., 393.

78. Ibid., 395.

79. Ibid.

80. Ibid.

81. ZsTa M. Rep. 76, Communication of Carl Stumpf to Kaiser Wilhelm, December 1916.

82. ZsTa M. Rep. 76, "Arbeitsziele des Kaiser-Wilhelm-Instituts für Arbeitsphysiologie," August 5, 1915.

83. ZsTa M. Rep. 76, Max Rubner, "Eurer Exzellenz," May 29, 1917.

84. ZsTa M. Rep. 76, Protokoll über die Sitzung des Verwaltungsrates des KWI/AP, June 5, 1917.

85. Preußisches Ministerium für Wissenschaft, Kunst und Volksbildung, Rep. 76 v. b, Sekt. 4, Bd. 1, 113–124, cited in Geuter, *Professionalisierung*, 488.

86. "Denkschrift" des Ministeriums für Volkswohlfahrt, May 24, 1922.

87. Ibid.

88. Alfred Beyer, "Arbeit und Seelenkunde: Ein Staatsinstitut für Areitspsychologie," in *Vorwärts*, April 25, 1922, 1.

89. ZsTa M. Rep. 151 c, Preußisches Ministerium für Volkswohlfahrt, May 10, 1922, 1.

90. ZsTa M. Rep. 151 c, Finanzminister, May 29, 1922.

91. ZsTA M. Rep. 151 C Nr. 903. Institut für Angewandte Psychologie u. Gewerbehygiene u. Arbeitswissenschaft. Verhandlungen im preußischen Landtag wegen des Liepmannischen [*sic*] Instituts.

92. ZsTa M. Rep. 151 C Minister für Handel und Gewerbe to Preußischen Herrn Finanzminister, 17 January 1923.

93. ZsTa M. Rep. 151, January 17, 1923.

94. ZsTa M. Rep. 151 c, Niederschrift, June 16, 1922.

95. Stern, "Otto Lipmann 188–1933," 153.

96. Jaeger and Staeuble, "Psychotechnik," 91.

97. Geuter, *Professionalisierung*, 275–276.

98. *Zeitschrift für Angewandte Psychologie* (February 1934): 1.

6. THE AESTHETICS OF PRODUCTION IN THE THIRD REICH

1. Peter Reichel, *Der Schöne Schein des Dritten Reiches: Faszination und Gewalt des Faschismus* (Munich: Carl Hanser Verlag, 1991), 372–375.

2. Anatol von Hübbenet, ed., *Das Taschenbuch Schönheit der Arbeit* (Berlin: Verlag der Deutschen Arbeitsfront, 1938), 17.

3. "Eine der schönsten Aufgaben des neuen Deutschlands; Dr. Ley vor den Mitarbeitern und Referenten des Amtes," *Schönheit der Arbeit* 1, no. 6 (1936): 265.

4. Ibid.

5. Albert Speer, "Schönheit der Arbeit—Fragen der Betriebsgestaltung," in *Schönheit der Arbeit 1934–1936* (Berlin: Verlag der deutschen Arbeitsfront, 1936), 198.

6. Karl Kretschmer, "*Schönheit der Arbeit* ein Weg zum deutschen Sozialismus!" in *Wege zur neuen Sozialpolitik: Arbeitstagung der Deutschen Arbeitsfront vom 16. bis 21. Dezember 1935* (Berlin: n.p., 1936), 180.

7. Hübbenet, *Taschenbuch*, 17.

8. Tim Mason, "Zur Entstehung des Gesetzes zur Ordnung der nationalen Arbeit, vom 20. Januar 1934: Ein Versuch über das Verhältnis 'archaischer' und 'moderner' Momente in der neuesten deutschen Geschichte," in *Industri-*

elles System und politische Entwicklung in der Weimarer Republik, ed. Hans Mommsen et al. (Düsseldorf: Droste Verlag, 1974), 325–327. See also Tim Mason, "Labor in the Third Reich 1933–1939," *Past and Present* 33, no. 1 (1966): 113–116.

9. Arthur Schweitzer, *Big Business in the Third Reich* (Bloomington, IN: Indiana University Press, 1964), 381.

10. Tim Mason, "The Primacy of Politics: Politics and Economics in National Socialist Germany," in *The Nature of Fascism*, ed. S. J. Woolf (London: Routledge, 1968), 171.

11. Jeffrey Herf, *Reactionary Modernism: Technology, Culture, and Politics in Weimar and the Third Reich* (Cambridge: Cambridge University Press, 1984), 200.

12. Albert Speer, *Inside the Third Reich*, trans. Richard and Clara Winston (New York: Macmillan, 1970), 94.

13. Otto Marrenbach, *Fundamente des Sieges: Die Gesamtarbeit der deutschen Arbeitsfront von 1933 bis 1940* (Berlin: Verlag der Deutschen Arbeitsfront, 1940), 325.

14. Kretschmer, *"Schönheit der Arbeit,"* 183.

15. Anatol von Hübbenet, *Die NS-Gemeinschaft Kraft durch Freude: Aufbau und Arbeit* (Berlin: Junker und Dunnhaupt, 1939), 25.

16. Herbert Steinwarz, *Wesen, Aufgaben und Ziele des Amtes Schönheit der Arbeit* (Berlin: Verlag der deutschen Arbeitsfront, NS-Gemeinschaft Kraft durch Freude, 1937).

17. Hübbenet, *Taschenbuch*, 24, 27, 261.

18. Marrenbach, *Fundamente des Sieges*, 325.

19. Die Deutsche Arbeitsfront, *Erlasse, Anordnungen, Aufrufe von Partei, Staat und Wehrmacht über Schönheit der Arbeit* (München: Deutsche Arbeitsfront, 1937), 13.

20. Die Deutsche Arbeitsfront, *Erlasse*, 17.

21. "Amtliches Nachrichtenblatt der Deutschen Arbeitsfront und der Nationalsozialistischen Gemeinschaft," *Kraft durch Freude* 2, no. 1 (1936): 11.

22. For example, "Gute Beleuchtung am Arbeitsplatz" (Berlin: Verlag der Deutschen Arbeitsfront, October 1935); *Schönheit der Arbeit* (Berlin: Verlag der Deutschen Arbeitsfront, July 1936); and *Sport im Betrieb* (Berlin: Verlag der Deutschen Arbeitsfront, December 1936).

23. Hübbenet, *Taschenbuch*, 74.

24. *Amtliches Nachrichtenblatt*, January 12, 1938.

25. Bundesarchiv Koblenz, Deutsche Arbeitsfront, Sozialamt NS51/3–4, Freizeitlager der Hitler-Jugend, June 26, 1936.

26. *Amtliches Nachrichtenblatt*, January 11, 1936.

27. Die Deutsche Arbeitsfront, *Erlasse*, 37.

28. *Wohn- und Tagesunterkünfte für Bauarbeiter nach den Richtlinien und Erfahrungen der Deutschen Arbeitsfront* (Berlin: Verlag der Deutschen Arbeitsfront, 1940); and Marrenbach, *Fundamente des Sieges*, 322.

29. *Schönheit der Arbeit* 1, no. 6 (1936): 267.

30. Hübbenet, *Taschenbuch*, 23.

31. "Bilder aus dem Farbentrickfilm "Musterbetrieb AG," *Schönheit der Arbeit* 1, no. 6 (1936): 299.

32. Hübbenet, *Taschenbuch*, 257.

33. Kretschmer, *"Schönheit der Arbeit,"* 180.

34. Mason, "Labor," 121.

35. "Das Antlitz der Arbeit zwischen gestern und heute," *Schönheit der Arbeit* 1, no. 6 (1936): 290.

36. Hübbenet, *Taschenbuch*, 26.

37. *Schönheit der Arbeit 1934–1936*, 42.

38. Marrenbach, *Fundamente des Sieges*, 325.

39. "Eine Parfümeriefabrik," *Schönheit der Arbeit* 2, no. 6 (1937): 253.

40. Hübbenet, *Taschenbuch*, 185, 187.

41. "A new spirit—a new outward appearance!," *Schönheit der Arbeit* 1, no. 3 (1936): 126. This issue appeared in English, French, and German for international consumption.

42. "Sporthalle im Werk," *Schönheit der Arbeit* 2, no. 9 (1938): 380.

43. Anatol von Hübbenet, *5 Jahre "Kraft durch Freude": Leistungsbericht der NS-Gemeinschaft "Kraft durch Freude"* (Berlin: Verlag der deutschen Arbeitsfront, 1938), 28.

44. *Arbeitertum* 5, no. 23 (Berlin: Verlag der deutschen Arbeitsfront, 1935).

45. Ludwig Heyde, *Die Lage des deutschen Arbeiters* (Berlin: Junker und Dünnhaupt, 1940), 56.

46. Wilhelm Lotz, *Schönheit der Arbeit in Deutschland* (Berlin: Deutscher Verlag, 1940), 61.

47. *Schönheit der Arbeit* 1, no. 3 (1936): 106.

48. Speer, "Schönheit," in *Third Reich*, 198.

49. Charles Fourier, *Design for Utopia*, trans. Julia Franklin (New York: Schocken, 1971), 164.

50. James Silk Buckingham, *National Evils and Practical Remedies, with the Plan of a Model Town* (London: Peter Jackson, late Fisher Son, and Co., 1849). See also Ernst Bloch, *Freiheit und Ordnung: Abriss der Sozialutopien* (Hamburg: Rowohlt, 1969), 168.

51. Lewis Mumford, *The Culture of Cities* (New York: Harcourt, Brace and Co., 1938), 393. A more convincing political interpretation of these attempts to improve the industrial landscape is provided by Leonardo Benevolo, *The Origins of Modern Town Planning* (Cambridge, MA: MIT Press, 1967), 130–147.

See also Enid Gauldie, *Cruel Habitations; A History of Working-Class Housing 1790–1918* (London: Allen and Unwin, 1974), 191–195.

52. A. Heinrichsbauer, *Industrielle Siedlung im Ruhrgebiet* (Essen: Verlag Glückauf, 1936), 67. The publication of this book established the continuity between Nazi industrial policy and the "pioneering" work of Alfred Krupp.

53. Heinrich Tessenow, *Hausbau und dergleichen* (Munich: n.p., 1916), 110.

54. Tessenow, *Hausbau*, 8.

55. Ludwig Heinrich Adolph Geck, *"Schönheit der Arbeit* in England und Schottland," *Soziale Praxis* 44, no. 73 (1935): 75, 76; see also, Ludwig Heinrich Adolph Geck, *Die Sozialen Arbeitsverhältnisse im Wandel der Zeit; Eine geschichtliche Einführung in die Betriebssoziologie* (Berlin: J. Springer, 1931), 141.

56. Hugo Münsterberg, *Grundzüge der Psychotechnik* (Leipzig: Barth, 1914).

57. Geck, *Arbeitsverhältnisse*, 141. See also Janos Czirjak, "Der Sinn der Arbeit" (PhD diss., Universität Bonn, 1934), 40–42; Waldermat Zimmerman, "Das Problem der rationalisierten Industriearbeit in sozialpsychologischer Betrachtung," *Zeitschrift für Wirtschafts- und Sozialwissenschaften*, no. 49 (1925): 107–118.

58. Robert A. Brady, *The Rationalization Movement in German Industry; A Study in the Evolution of Economic Planning* (New York: Fertig, 1974), xix, 3–64.

59. Götz Briefs, "Zur Soziologie des Betriebs," *Soziale Praxis* 40, no. 2 (1931): 33–40; Geck, *Arbeitsverhaltnisse*, 114.

60. Ludwig Heinrich Adolph Geck, *Soziale Betriebsführung* (Munich: n.p., 1938), 94–105; Geck, "England und Schottland," 74–78.

61. Geck, *Betriebsführung*, 94–105.

62. Ibid.

63. Brady, *Rationalization Movement*, 44; Richard H. Lansburgh, *Industrial Management* (New York: John Wiley and Sons, 1928), 337–348.

64. Geck, *Arbeitsverhältnisse*, 130; Geck, *Betriebsführung*, 53.

65. Ludwig Preller, *Sozialpolitik in der Weimarer Republik* (Stuttgart: n.p., 1949), 216.

66. Otto Bauer, *Einführung in die Volkswirtschaftslehre* (Vienna: Verlag der Wiener Volksbuchhandlung, 1956), 350–351.

67. Karl Schmidt, "Kapitalistische Rationalisierung, Krise und Sozialfaschismus," in *Unter dem Banner des Marxismus* 7, no. 4 (1933): 370. For a survey of the problem of the Left and technocracy, see Charles S. Maier, "Between Taylorism and Technocracy," *Journal of Contemporary History* 5, no. 2 (1970): 27–62.

68. Hendrik de Man, *The Psychology of Socialism*, trans. Eden and Cedar Paul (London: Allen and Unwin, 1927), 65.

69. Reinhard Bendix, *Work and Authority in Industry: Ideologies of Management in the Course of Industrialization* (Berkeley: University of California Press, 1956), 339.

70. "Old German Workshops," *Schönheit der Arbeit* 1, no. 3 (1936): 149.

71. *Schönheit der Arbeit 1934–1936.*

72. Immanuel Kant, "Critique of Judgement," in *Kant Selections*, ed. Theodore M. Greene (New York: Charles Scribner's Sons, 1957), 497.

73. F. D. Klingender, *Art and the Industrial Revolution* (New York. A. M. Kelley, 1970), 83–104.

74. *The Collected Works of Marx and Engels*, vol. 3, *Early Works 1835–1844* (New York: International Publishers, 1975), electronic ed., 307.

75. Nikolaus Pevsner, *Pioneers of Modern Design from William Morris to Walter Gropius* (Harmondsworth, UK: Penguin Books, 1960), 35, 37.

76. Pevsner, *Pioneers*, 210. See also, Lewis Mumford, *Technics and Civilization* (New York: Harcourt, Brace and Co., 1934), 350, 351.

77. Maier, "Taylorism," 35, 36.

78. Bloch, *Freiheit und Ordnung*, 132.

79. Franz Kollman, *Schönheit der Technik* (Munich: A. Langen, 1928), 10.

80. Ernst Bloch, *Erbschaft dieser Zeit* (Frankfurt am Main: Suhrkamp, 1962), 217.

81. Speer, letter to the author, July 5, 1975.

82. "*Schönheit der Arbeit* im Büro," *Schönheit der Arbeit* 1, no. 4 (1936): 204; and Hans M. Wingler, *The Bauhaus: Weimar, Dessau, Berlin, Chicago* (Cambridge, MA: MIT Press, 1969), 135.

83. Wiltraut Best, *Die Überwindung nachteiliger Folgen der Rationalisierung durch das Amt* Schönheit der Arbeit (Großenhain: Weigel, 1935), 48.

84. "Fliessende Arbeit—an jedem Arbeitsplatz," *Schönheit der Arbeit* 3, no. 1 (1939): 479.

85. Best, "Überwindung," 48.

86. Ibid., 49.

87. "Warum entwickelte das Amt '*Schönheit der Arbeit*' Mustermodelle?," *Schönheit der Arbeit* 1, no. 9 (1937): 410.

88. *Collected Works of Marx and Engels*, 3:307, http://pm.nlx.com/xtf/view ?docId=marx/marx.00.xml.

89. "Kulturonfilm Licht," *Schönheit der Arbeit* 1, no. 6 (1936): 294.

90. Kretschmer, "*Schönheit der Arbeit*," 161.

91. "Die Arbeit in der Kunst," *Schönheit der Arbeit* 2, no. 7 (1937): 294.

92. Hübbenet, *Taschenbuch*, 49.

93. Paul Mantoux, *The Industrial Revolution in the Eighteenth Century* (New York: Macmillan, 1961), 416.

94. A. R. Sennett, *Garden Cities in Theory and Practice*, 2 vols. (London: Bemrose and Sons, 1905), 578.

95. Tessenow, *Hausbau*, 33.

96. Marrenbach, *Fundamente des Sieges*, 325.

97. George L. Mosse, *The Nationalization of the Masses* (New York: H. Fertig, 1975), 155. See also Lotz, *Deutschland*, 54; and Bruno Malitz, *Die Leibesübungen in der nationalsozialistischen Idee* (Munich: Eher, 1933), 36.

98. Karl Dietrich Bracher, *The German Dictatorship*, trans. Jean Steinberg (New York: Praeger Publishers, 1970), 333.

99. Schweitzer, *Big Business*, 218–219.

100. Bundesarchiv Koblenz, Deutsche Arbeitsfront Zentralbüro, Sozialamt, NS5/l/14, Rundschreiben 245, September 9, 1937.

101. *10. Reichsarbeitstagung Schönheit der Arbeit*, 27–29 April, 1938, Referat des Pg. Baurat Schulte Frohlinde, 13.

102. Speer, *Third Reich*, 200.

103. Hübbenet, *Taschenbuch*, 138–139.

104. Ibid., 137.

105. Speer, *Third Reich*, 202.

106. Best, "Überwindung," 46.

107. Robert R. Taylor, *The Word in Stone: The Role of Architecture in National Socialist Ideology* (Berkeley: University of California Press, 1974), 198. Taylor argues that Nazi modernism was an exception to the general *völkisch* and neoclassical trends, largely employed in Air Force buildings. It was, however, more widespread than his book indicates.

108. "*Schönheit der Arbeit* im Industriebau," *Schönheit der Arbeit* 1, no. 10 (1937): 457.

109. "Der Architekt im Ingenieurbau," *Schönheit der Arbeit* 3, no. 4 (1938): 166.

110. "Industriebau," *Schönheit der Arbeit* 3, no. 4 (1938): 462.

111. Anna Teut, *Architektur im Dritten Reich 1933–1945* (Berlin: de Gruyter, 1967), 247; Barbara Miller Lane, *Architecture and Politics in Germany, 1918–1945* (Cambridge, MA: Harvard University Press, 1968), 204.

112. "*Schönheit der Arbeit* beim Neubau der Deutschen Versuchsanstalt für Luftfahrt Adlershof," *Schönheit der Arbeit* 1, no. 12 (1937): 553.

113. *5 Jahre Kraft durch Freude*, 39.

114. Hermann Hilterscheid, *Industrie und Gemeinde; Die Beziehungen zwischen der Stadt Wolfsburg und dem Volkswagenwerk und ihre Auswirkungen auf die Kommunale Selbstverwaltung* (Berlin: Berlin Verlag, 1970), 61. The primacy of plant over city caused by a permanent housing shortage for workers and families.

115. Ibid., 62.

116. Amt für Technik, Rundschreiben Nr. 7136, 23 März, 1936, Arbeitsordnung des Amtes *Schönheit der Arbeit* (1936), 29; *Die nationalsozialistische Gestaltung der deutschen Technik* (Berlin, 1936), vi.

117. Friedrich von Gottl-Ottlilienfeld, "Müssen wir die Rationalisierung ablehnen?," in *Wirtschaft, Gesammelte Aufsätze* (Jena: G. Fischer, 1937), 48.

118. A. R. L. Gurland, Otto Kirchheimer, Franz Neumann, *The Fate of Small Business in Nazi Germany*, Senate Committee Print No. 14 (1943) (New York: H. Fertig, 1975), 29.

119. "Leistungssteigerung durch nationalsozialistische Betriebsgestaltung im Handwerk," *Schönheit der Arbeit* 3, no. 12 (1939): 521.

120. "Vier Handwerksbetriebe," *Schönheit der Arbeit* 4, no. 2 (1939): 68.

121. "Hand und Machine," *Schönheit der Arbeit* 2, no. 9 (1938): 367.

122. Ibid., 376.

123. Hübbenet, *Taschenbuch*, 46–47.

124. Ibid., 30.

125. "Architekt im Ingenieurbau," 159.

126. Hübbenet, *Taschenbuch*, 74.

127. "Der zweckmassige Arbeitssitz," *Schönheit der Arbeit* 2, no. 8 (1938): 360.

128. "Fliessende Arbeit," 478. See also "Betriebsführer! Dein Beitrag zum Leistungskampf!," *Schönheit der Arbeit* 2, no. 9 (1938): 358.

129. *10. Reichsarbeitstagung, Ansprache des Reichsorganisationsleiters Pg. Dr. Ley*, 11.

130. Schweitzer, *Big Business*, 351.

131. Mason, "Labor," 132–141.

132. Bundesarchiv Koblenz, Deutsche Arbeitsfront Zentralbüro, NS51/3–4, Anordnung 164/37, 27 November, 1937. See also, "*Schönheit der Arbeit*, aber nicht auf Kosten der Gefolgschaft," *Soziale Praxis* 46, no. 43 (1937): 1271–1274.

133. *Sozialordnung: Probleme der deutschen Sozialpolitik*, ed. Propagandaamt des DAF (1939) (unpublished manuscript: Institut für Zeitgeschichte, Munich, L16.RqK17).

134. Best, "Überwindung," 56.

135. *Schönheit der Arbeit* 3, no. 1 (1938): 15.

136. Bundesarchiv Koblenz, Deutsche Arbeitsfront, Sozialamt NS51/3–4, letter, "Herr Betriebsführer," January 1939.

137. Bundesarchiv Koblenz, Deutsche Arbeitsfront, Sozialamt, NS51/42, letter from Dr. (Arnhold), "Stellungnahme zu dem Entwurf 'Nationalsozialistisches Musterbetriebe' und ergänzende Anregungen," October 22, 1936. On DINTA, see Peter C. Bäumer, *Das Deutsche Institut für technische Arbeitsschulung (DINTA)*, in *Probleme der sozialen Werkspolitik*, ed. Götz Briefs (Munich: Duncker und Humblot, 1930), 125–159; and Wolfgang Schlicker,

"Arbeitsdienstbestrebungen des Deutschen Monopolkapitals in der Weimarer Republic," in *Jahrbuch für Wirtschaftsgeschichte*, Bd. 3, Tl. 9 (Berlin: Akademie-Verlag, 1971), 5–122.

138. Karl Arnhold, *Mobilisierung der Leistungsreserven unserer Betriebe* (Berlin: Deutsche Arbeitsfront, 1939), 4, 5.

139. BAK NS51/42; Arnhold, *Mobilisierung*, 34–40.

140. *Was ist ein nationalsozialistischer Musterbetrieb?* (Berlin: Verlag der deutschen Arbeitsfront, 1937), 7–13.

141. Herbert Steinwarz, *"Schönheit der Arbeit" im Kriege und Frieden* (Berlin, 1941); and *Beleuchtung in den Betrieben und ihre Verdunkelung* (Berlin, 1939).

142. Marrenbach, *Fundamente des Sieges*, 325.

143. Ernst Bloch, *Vom Hasard zur Katastrophe: Politische Aufsätze 1934–1939* (Frankfurt am Main: Suhrkamp, 1972), 47.

144. Henry Ashby Turner Jr.'s definition of fascism as "utopian anti-Modernism" does not consider the actualities of fascist modernism in both practice and ideology. See Henry Ashby Turner Jr., "Fascism and Modernization," *World Politics*, no. 24 (1972): 555.

145. "Drei Freundinnen erleben ihren Arbeitstag," *Schönheit der Arbeit* 1, no. 18 (1936): 6.

146. Max Horkheimer and Theodor W. Adorno, *Dialektik der Aufklärung: Philosophische Fragmente* (Amsterdam: Querido Verlag, 1947), 10.

7. METAPHORS OF THE MACHINE IN THE POST-FORDIST ERA

1. D. Davis and D. Milbank, "Employer Ennui," *Wall Street Journal*, February 7, 1992, 1.

2. Lester C. Thurow, *Head to Head: The Coming Economic Battle Among Japan, Europe, and America* (New York: Morrow, 1992).

3. Jeremy Rifkin, *The End of Work: The Decline of the Global Labor Force and the Dawn of the Post-Market Era* (New York: Putnam, 1996).

4. Ralf Dahrendorf, "Entschwinden der Arbeitsgesellschaft: Wandlungen in der sozialen Konstruktion des menschlichen Lebens," *Merkur: Deutsche Zeitschrift für Europaisches Denken* 34, no. 8 (1980): 751. See also Daniel Bell, *The Cultural Contradictions of Capitalism* (New York: Basic Books, 1976), 147–148.

5. Wolf Lepenies, "Weniger kann mehr wert sein," *Die Zeit*, November 12, 1993, 4.

6. "Americans Work Hard, But People in These 15 Countries Work Longer Hours," *Fortune*, http://fortune.com/2015/11/11/chart-work-week -oecd/.

7. Juliet Schor, *The Overworked American: The Unexpected Decline of Leisure* (New York: Basic Books, 1991), 161.

8. André Gorz, *Farewell to the Working Class: An Essay on Post-Industrial Socialism* (London: Pluto Press, 1982), xi.

9. Michael Rose, *Servants of Post-Industrial Power? Sociologie du Travail in Modern France* (New York: M. E. Sharpe, 1979), 45.

10. Gorz, *Farewell*, 45.

11. Gorz, *The Critique of Economic Reason* (New York: Verso, 2011), 14.

12. Hannah Arendt, *The Human Condition* (Chicago: University of Chicago Press, 1958), 125.

13. Gorz, *Critique*, 93–95.

14. Ibid., 117.

15. Ibid., 101.

16. Ibid. 191–219.

17. Schor, *Overworked American*, 157.

18. G. Hofmann, "Verloren zwischen neuen Fronten," *Die Zeit*, February 11, 1994, 3.

19. John Rae, *Contemporary Socialism* (London: Swann Sonnenschein, 1891), 434.

20. Gary Cross, "Time, Money, and Labor's History's Encounter with Consumer Culture," *International Labor and Working-Class History*, no. 43 (1993): 13; also see other responses in the same issue.

21. On Red Vienna, see Helmit Gruber, *Red Vienna: Experiment in Working Class Culture 1919–1934* (New York: Oxford University Press, 1991). On the French Popular Front, see J. Jackson, *The Popular Front in France: Defending Democracy, 1924–1938* (New York: Cambridge University Press, 1988).

22. Cross, "Time, Money."

23. Gorz, *Critique*, 51.

24. *The Marx-Engels Reader*, 2nd ed., ed. Robert Tucker (New York: Norton, 1978), 320–321.

25. Mark Rupert, "Crisis of Fordism," in *Encyclopedia of International Political Economy*, ed. R. J. B. Jones (London: Routledge, 2001), 560.

26. R. Boyer, "Capital-Labor Relations in OECD Countries from the Fordist Golden Age to Contrasted National Trajectories," in *Capital, the State and Labor: A Global Perspective*, ed. Juliet Schor and Jong-il You (New York: Aldershot/Brooksfield, 1995), 18–69.

27. Barabara Ehrenreich, *Fear of Falling: The Inner Life of the Middle Class* (New York: Pantheon Books, 1991).

28. Eric Hobsbawm, *The Age of Extremes: A History of the World 1914–1991* (New York: Random House, 1994), 403.

29. Michel Aglietta, *A Theory of Capitalist Regulation* (London: New Left Books, 1979).

30. K. Bluhm, "Konturen der Fordismusdebatte," *Berliner Debatte: Zeitschrift fur sozialwissenschaftlichen Diskurs*, no. 6 (1996): 3–9.

31. Ash Amin, "Post-Fordism: Models, Fantasies and Phantoms of Transition," in *Post-Fordism: A Reader*, ed. Ash Amin (Oxford: Oxford University Press, 1994), 1–40.

32. Jodi Kantor and David Streitfeld, "Inside Amazon: Wrestling Big Ideas in a Bruising Workplace," *New York Times*, August 15, 2015, 1.

33. Rabinbach, *The Human Motor*.

34. Paul M. Kennedy, *The Rise and Fall of the Great Powers: Economic Change and Military Conflict from 1500 to 2000* (New York: Vintage, 1987).

35. Charles C. Heckscher, *The New Unionism: Employee Involvement in the Changing Corporation* (New York: Basic Books, 1988); P. F. Drucker, "Are Unions Becoming Irrelevant?," *Wall Street Journal*, September 2, 1982.

36. S. Wehowsky, "Der Rohstoff der Phantasie: Eine Neubesinnung auf das Politische," *Neue Züricher Zeitung*, May 4–5, 1996, 49.

37. Lee Sproull and Sara Kiesler, *Connections: New Ways of Working in the Networked Organization* (Cambridge, MA: MIT Press, 1992), 175. See also Michael Schrage, *Shared Minds: The New Technologies of Collaboration* (New York: Random House, 1990); and Peter M. Senge, *The Fifth Discipline: The Art and Practice of the Learning Organization* (New York: Currency Books, 1992).

38. On the eighteenth-century automata and the application of biomechanics to the "animal economy," see A. Doyon and L. Liaigre, "Méthodologie comparée du biomécanisme et de la mécanique comparée," *Dialectica* 10, no. 4 (1956): 292–355.

39. Georges Canguilhem, "Machine and Organism," in *Incorporations*, ed. J. Crary and S. Kwinter (New York: Zone, 1992), 60.

40. Jessica Riskin, *The Restless Clock: A History of the Centuries Long Argument over What Makes Living Things Tick* (Chicago: University of Chicago Press, 2016), 45.

41. Julien Offray de La Mettrie, *Man and Machine and Man a Plant*, trans. Richard A. Watson and Maya Rybalka (Indianapolis: Hackett, 1994), 32.

42. Jean-Claude Beaune, "The Classical Age of Automata: An Impressionistic Survey from the Seventeenth Century to the Nineteenth Century," trans. Ian Patterson, in *Fragments for a History of the Human Body*, vol. 1, ed. Michel Feher with Romona Naddaff and Nadia Tazi (New York: Zone, 1989), 431.

43. Rabinbach, *Human Motor*, chs. 5–8.

44. H. von Helmholtz, "Über die Wechselwirkung der Naturkräfte und die darauf bezüglichen neuesten Ermittlungen der Physik," in *Populäre Wissenschaftliche Vorträge*, Bd. 1 (Braunschweig: F. Vieweg, 1876), 102.

45. Mark Seltzer, *Bodies and Machines* (New York: Routledge, 1992), 29.

46. See the important discussion of this tradition in Peter Beilharz, *Labor's Utopias: Bolshevism, Fabianism, Social Democracy* (Cambridge: Cambridge University Press, 1997), 108.

47. Helmholtz, "Über die Wechselwirkung," 101.

48. Ibid., 103.

49. Angelo Mosso, *La Fatica* (Milan: Treves, 1891); Rabinbach, *Human Motor*, 133–138.

50. Samuel Haber, *Efficiency and Uplift: Scientific Management in the Progressive Era, 1890–1920* (Chicago: University of Chicago Press, 1964); and Cecelia Tichi, *Shifting Gears: Technology, Literature, Culture in Modernist America* (Chapel Hill: University of North Carolina Press, 1987).

51. Richard Gillespie, *Manufacturing Knowledge: A History of the Hawthorn Experiments* (Cambridge: Cambridge University Press, 1991).

52. Jackson Lears, "Man the Machine" (review of *Human Motor*), *New Republic*, July 15 and 22, 1991, 43–45.

53. This criterion was first suggested by Alan Turing in 1937 when he proposed that "it is possible to develop code instruction systems of a computing machine which cause it to behave as if it were another, specified computing machine." Henry M. Gladney, *Preserving Digital Information* (Berlin: Springer, 2007), 228.

54. Shoshana Zuboff, *In the Age of the Smart Machine: The Future of Work and Power* (New York: Basic Books, 1988), 393.

55. Ibid., 393.

56. Terry Winograd and Fernando Flores, *Understanding Computers and Cognition* (Norwood, NJ: Ablex, 1986).

57. Senge, *Fifth Discipline*, 335.

58. Lee Sproull, *Connections*, 175. See also Schrage, *Shared Minds*; and Senge, *Fifth Discipline*.

59. Zuboff, *Smart Machine*, 393.

60. Robert Howard, *Brave New Workplace* (New York: Viking, 1985).

61. Zuboff, *Smart Machine*, 346.

62. Ibid., 304.

63. Ibid., 384.

64. Ibid., 351.

65. Ibid., 278.

66. Ibid., 280.

67. Ibid., 308.

68. Sproull, *Connections.*

69. Schrage, *Shared Minds*, 29.

70. Michael Heim, *The Metaphysics of Virtual Reality* (New York: Oxford University Press, 1993), 60.

71. Ibid., 61, 128–129.

72. Steven Levy, *Artificial Life: A Report from the Frontier Where Computers Meet* (New York: Vintage, 1992), 16.

73. Manuel DeLanda, "Nonorganic Life," in Feher, *Incorporation*, 130.

74. Jodi Kantor and David Streitfeld, "Inside Amazon: Wrestling Big Ideas in a Bruising Workplace," *New York Times*, August 15, 2015, A1.

Lightning Source UK Ltd.
Milton Keynes UK
UKHW040232131218
333563UK00005BB/310/P